9605

GARLAND
PUBLICATIONS
IN
COMPARATIVE
LITERATURE

General Editor
JAMES J. WILHELM
Rutgers University

Associate Editors
DANIEL JAVITCH, New York University
STUART Y. MCDOUGAL, University of Michigan
RICHARD SÁEZ, The College of Staten Island/CUNY
RICHARD SIEBURTH, New York University

A GARLAND SERIES

THEODICY IN BAROQUE LITERATURE

Richard Sáez

Garland Publishing, Inc.
New York & London
1985

Library of Congress Cataloging in Publication Data

Sáez, Richard, 1936-
Theodicy in baroque literature.

(Garland publications in comparative literature)
Based on thesis (Ph.D.)—Yale University, 1967.
Bibliography: p.
1. Baroque literature—History and criticism.
2. Theodicy in literature.
3. Tasso, Torquato, 1544–1595—Religion and ethics.
4. Milton, John, 1608–1674—Religion and ethics.
5. Calderón de la Barca, Pedro, 1600–1681—Religion and ethics.
I. Title. II. Series.
PN56.B3S24 1985 809′.91 84-48375
ISBN 0-8240-6700-2 (alk. paper)

Design by Bonnie Goldsmith

The volumes in this series are printed on
acid-free, 250-year-life paper.

Printed in the United States of America

In
Memory
of
Mariano Sáez Larraz
and for
Nativadad Sáez Kassar

Maturans ad immortalitatem

Irenaeus

Acknowledgments

During the many stages of work on this book over a long period of time, I received grants from the Research Foundation of the City University of New York, Yale University and the National Endowment for the Humanities. And during its various stages many scholars and friends have read and/or discussed the manuscript, and I am happy to name them here: Charles R. Beye, Patrick Cullen, Manuel Durán, Leslie H. Farber, A. Bartlett Giamatti, Richard M. Goldman, Thomas M. Greene, Daniel Javitch, Earl Miner, James V. Mirollo, Lowry Nelson, Jr., and René Wellek. I am grateful to Garland Publishing and to the General Editor of the *Garland Publications in Comparative Literature*, James J. Wilhelm, for the occasion to revise my manuscript for publication. In revising, I was torn between the need to remain loyal to an earlier intuitive reading which still seemed to me to have substantial and unsuperseded validity, and my present feelings as a maturer writer and better informed scholar. I hope to have remained loyal to the former without betraying the latter. The most positive aspect of the arduous task of revision was to inform myself as to how well these baroque authors have fared in recent criticism. To name a few: for Tasso the work of Baldassari, Braghieri and Raimondi; for Milton—Danielson, Low and Radzinowicz; for Calderón—Aubrun, Edwards, Flashe and Ter Horst. These brilliant critics reinspired my interest, and, yet, informed me that my own modest reading in terms of theodicy was still in need of voicing. To Eric G. Bernard I owe a special order of gratitude, and the debt to my dedicatees remains—properly—inexpressible.

Contents

PROLOGUE

Quapropter in his contrariis quae mala et
bona uocantur illa dialecticorum regula
deficit qua dicunt nulli rei duo simul in-
esse contraria.

Saint Augustine

This book began as a Yale Ph.D. thesis in Comparative Literature which studied patterns of "illusion" and "the beneficence of evil" in Tasso, Milton and Calderón. It was called "The Redemptive Circe" because one of the central points of reference was the way in which the heroes' encounters with a malefic enchantress evolved as noetic experiences leading toward regeneration. The thesis had, in turn, begun as a study of uses of myth in late-sixteenth- and seventeenth-century baroque[1] poetry. In studying the authors with whom I am concerned—Tasso, Milton and Calderón—as well as other poets who are considered baroque, I was impressed with a sharp departure from medieval and renaissance allusions to mythology. This seems to be particularly true in regard to the Christian interpretation of pagan myths. While a medieval work such as *L'Ovide Moralisé* or a renaissance poem such as Ronsard's *Hercule Chrestien* merely associates the pagan myth and the Christian interpretation—Hercules' descent into the underworld and Christ's harrowing of hell—through physical analogies or by merely assigning a Christian spiritual interpretation to the pagan myth, the baroque authors tend to transform the myths into concrete symbols. This seems to be done by breaking down the pagan myths into archetypal patterns of natural imagery, and these patterns are discoverable in both the pagan myth and its Christian counterpart. This use of myth is closer to a Jungian conception of archetypes or romantic and modern uses of mythical and archetypal symbols. And for the contemporary reader it may have ecumenical overtones. I identified these differing renaissance and baroque uses of myth with several renaissance-baroque distinctions including Wölfflin's "linear"—"painterly,"[2] i.e., clear outlining of the different mythical planes as opposed to merging. One of the definitions of baroque poetry which most influenced my thought is contained in Frank Warnke's introduction to his *European Metaphysical Poetry*:

> But the Renaissance poets . . . see experience on two levels, the finally real level of the spirit and the provisionally real level of the flesh. They project

> the relationship through a poetic style which leans heavily on simile and its extension, allegory. Neither Metaphysical nor High Baroque poets can rest content with the double vision of reality; they seek neither to reconcile the two worlds nor to resolve their conflict but to reduce them to a unity.[3]

It seemed evident to me that in their use of myth baroque authors—as distinguished from renaissance authors—"seek neither to reconcile the two worlds" of paganism and Christianity or the *Old Testament* and the *New Testament* "nor to resolve their conflict but to reduce them to a unity."

But in the course of my studies, like Western man in general, I was seduced by narcissism and Circe, or, more specifically, the Narcissus and Circe myths. In his study of baroque literature in France, Jean Rousset used the peacock and Circe as symbols for the prevalence of vain ornamentation and metamorphosis.[4] It became increasingly obvious to me that the Narcissus and Circe myths are at the core of much of the literature I was studying and that not only does the use of these myths conform to the general principles I had outlined, but in the baroque period—specifically in Tasso, Milton and Calderón—these myths take on a profoundly new interpretation. It is an interpretation which is related to the Judeo-Christian justification of the ways of God. In these authors narcissism becomes an aspect of the Circe myth, and she is clearly ambivalent, both evil and good. And not only are the Christian and pagan elements totally identified, but the baroque characteristic of unity identified by Mr. Warnke reaches a metaphysical plane in that the ambivalent good and evil in the Circe myth are not merely resolved but, paradoxically, are reduced to a unity. In his essay "The Concept of Baroque in Literary Scholarship" René Wellek argues that the "most promising way of arriving at a more closely fitting description of the baroque is to aim at analyses which would correlate stylistic and ideological criteria."[5] It seemed to me that relating the style of mythological allusion in baroque literature to the theological treatment of evil was a successful way of bringing together "stylistic and ideological criteria."

Having settled on the Circe myth and its relationship to a metaphysical justification of evil, I found it easy to select the works I wished to concentrate on for analysis, and even the steps of my argument followed rather naturally. Tasso, Milton and Calderón have all been considered baroque authors departing from the themes and style of their renaissance predecessors. Furthermore, all three wrote from a consciously Christian viewpoint. The Christian philosophy of Tasso's *Gerusalemme liberata* is specific and obvious; indeed, it is a part of the thematic material of the epic as it is of *Paradise Lost*. In *Gerusalemme liberata* Armida is the Circe figure; she is directly descended from Alcina in *Orlando Furioso*. For reasons I shall discuss in the section of my book devoted to Milton, I found Dalila in *Samson Agonistes* a more satisfactory embodiment of the Circe myth as it interests me than the Lady of *Comus* or the Eve of *Paradise Lost.* While *Samson Agonistes* is not written from a specifically Christian viewpoint, there is no shortage of books and articles which verify and illustrate its Christian orientation.[6] Calderón wrote both a play and an *auto* based on the Circe myth;[7] from these it is relatively easy to discover the Circe archetype in his other works.

But my thesis was not specifically concerned with the Christian philosophy of Tasso, Milton and Calderón or with tracing the evolution of the Circe myth. In recreating this myth, the three authors have created their own myth, the essence of which involves an illusory conflict of good and evil.[8] Behind *Gerusalemme liberata, Samson Agonistes* and the plays of Calderón, there is the shadow of the Circe myth. But in these works the seduction of a virtuous hero by a temptress is linked through the poetic as well as moral language of the poet to man's fall, which is represented in terms of a descent into a world of illusion where change and mutability are the unalterable law. But it is only the involvement with and the full recognition of the world of illusion which, paradoxically, finally orders and stabilizes that mutable world of illusion, defines man's position and unveils the path for his salvation from it. In this process, as we shall see, the hero becomes identified with the enemy—carrying the effect of illusion and reality into the reader's mind as well as into the whole scheme of the universe as it is depicted in these works. If man's estate in a fallen world of illusion is evil and illusion defines that state of evil, it is only by the recognition and use of illusion that he is able to redeem himself. It is in this way that the use of illusion becomes a poetic explanation for the existence of evil in the world or a justification of the ways of God. Illusion and evil are the necessary complements or antecedents to a world in which good triumphs over evil. But in the process evil and good are necessary complements of each other and, in the structure and imagery of the works I shall discuss, often transmutable one into the other. Since the Circe myth and the theme of illusion and reality are in this way linked with the Christian conception of man's fall and redemption, in a very specific way the final concern of my thesis, in fact, returned to one aspect of its genesis, i.e., the Christian interpretation of pagan myth.

What has become increasingly obvious to me is that this baroque manifestation of myth is related to the concept of good and evil which we have come to understand as theodicy. And in revising my thesis into the present book, I have attempted to focus on theodical issues. To speak of theodicy and seventeenth-century baroque literature is both absurd and inevitable: Absurd because use of the term theodicy to discuss the problem of evil was invented by G. W. Leibniz in the eighteenth century;[9] and inevitable because so much of what we have come to associate with the baroque—the prosodic balance of antitheses, Hamlet-like obsessions with ultimate questions, the view of life as an illusory theatrical pageant, paradox, the reduction of multitudinous dichotomies to a unified monadic essence—all of these elements are aspects of the metaphysics of theodicy as well. Theodicy is the paradoxical justification of the existence of evil in a universe created by an omnipotent and beneficent deity. Clearly the ways of this God, as Milton put it, must be justified to man. In most articulations of theodicy, all the flesh-and-blood evil, pain and suffering encountered in the historical world are considered to be essentially testing, tensional elements against which man exercises his free will. Evil is a temporary allusion; it can be an absence, a distortion or a corruption of the good, but it can have no independent *metaphysical* existence. Although this conception of good and evil is—as we shall see— at least as old as the *Old Testament,* and existed in both eastern and western cultures, its theological and philosophical conceptualization began with the fathers of the Catholic Church. Essentially, there have been two branches of theodicy: the Augustinian and the Irenaean (Irenaeus, Bishop of Lyon, A.D. 130–202.[10] In assessing responsibility for the historical existence of evil, Saint Augustine emphasizes above all else will: human failure, original sin, man's fall, and his continued imperfection:

> The cause of evil is the defection of the will of a being who is mutably good from the Good which is immutable. This happened first in the case of angels and, afterwards, that of man.[11]

Augustine also emphasizes the inherent absence of metaphysical existence or being in evil:

> And in the universe, even that which is called evil, when it is regulated and put in its own place, only enhances our admiration of the good; for we enjoy and value the good more when we compare it with the evil. For the Almighty God, who, as even the heathen acknowledge, has supreme power over all things, being Himself supremely good, would never permit the existence of anything evil among His works, if He were not so omnipotent and good that He can bring good even out of evil. For what is that which we call evil but the absence of good? In the bodies of animals, disease and wounds mean nothing but the absence of health; for when a cure is effected, that does not mean that the evils which were present—namely, the diseases and wounds—go away from the body and dwell elsewhere: they altogether cease to exist; for the wound or disease is not a substance, but a defect in the fleshly substance—the flesh itself being a substance, and therefore something good, of which those evils—that is, privations of the good which we call health—are accidents. Just in the same way, what are called vices in the soul are nothing but privations of natural good. And when they are cured,

they are not transferred elsewhere: when they cease to exist in the healthy soul, they cannot exist anywhere else.

And Saint Augustine tends to balance good and evil in structural terms of "aesthetic plenitude" and harmony:

> For God would never have created any, I do not say angel, but even man, whose future wickedness He foreknew, unless He had equally known to what uses in behalf of the good He could turn him, thus embellishing the course of the ages, as it were an exquisite poem set off with antitheses. For what are called antitheses are among the most elegant of the ornaments of speech. They might be called in Latin "oppositions," or, to speak more accurately, "contrapositions"; but this word is not in common use among us, though the Latin, and indeed the languages of all nations, avail themselves of the same ornaments of style. In the *Second Epistle to the Corinthians* the Apostle Paul also makes a graceful use of antithesis, in that place where he says, "By the armor of righteousness on the right hand and on the left, by honor and dishonor, by evil report and good report: as deceivers, and yet true; as unknown, and yet well known; as dying, and, behold, we live; as chastened, and not killed; as sorrowful, yet always rejoicing; as poor, yet making many rich; as having nothing, and yet possessing all things." As, then, these oppositions of contraries lend beauty to the language, so the beauty of the course of this world is achieved by the opposition of contraries, arranged, as it were, by an eloquence not of words, but of things. This is quite plainly stated in the *Book of Ecclesiasticus*, in this way: "Good is set against evil, and life against death: so is the sinner against the godly. So look upon all the works of the Most High, and these are two and two, one against another."

In Irenaean theodicy individual human will, metaphysics and aesthetics are less crucial; the emphasis is on God's own purposes toward universal beneficent ends and his creation of human existence as a vale of soul-making:

> God permitted these things ["The Deceits, Wickedness, and Apostate Power of Antichrist"] . . . for the benefit of that human nature which is saved, ripening for immortality that which is [possessed] of its own free will and its own power, and preparing and rendering it more adapted for eternal subjection to God. And therefore the creation is suited to [the wants of] man; for man was not made for its sake, but creation for the sake of man. [5.29.1]

> For just as the tongue receives experience of sweet and bitter by means of tasting, and the eye discriminates between black and white by means of vision, and the ear recognises the distinctions of sounds by hearing; so also does the mind, receiving through the experience of both the knowledge of what is good, become more tenacious of its preservation, by acting in obedience to God. . . . But if any one do shun the knowledge of both kinds of things, and the twofold perception of knowledge, he unawares divests himself of the character of a human being. [4.34.1][12]

My understanding of theodicy, especially for the purposes of this literary study, is informed not only by the patristic writers but by several other sources which I want to mention here briefly: Recent biblical scholarship has shown that the *Old Testament*'s depiction of a "hidden God" represented not simply an existential absence or a manifestation of anger, but was theodically conceived—at least in the prophetic literature—as a probing and testing of man's faith.[13] And recent comparative religious studies have found remarkably similar theodical analogies in Hindu writings as well as other eastern faiths.[14] Paul Ricoeur's anthropological approach in *The Symbolism of Evil*,[15] which traces the evolution of man's conception of evil from an alien, external force to an increasingly internal and subjective phenomenon, is especially relevant to the literary modes I am concerned with. As brilliant as Ricoeur's study is, a seventeenth-century literary masterpiece focuses a similar view more colloquially for my purposes. Cervantes' *Don Quijote* can be read as the story of a man's evolution from a Manichaean understanding of evil as embodied in external necromancers and other foreign forces to a recognition of evil as endemic to human nature. Don Quijote, however, cannot deal with this vision and is ultimately destroyed by it. (The heroes I've chosen to focus on in this study fare rather better.) What seems to be missing in Don Quijote's understanding—although not in Cervantes' novel—is the metaphysical view of life as "play" or as "a play." In his magisterial *Homo Ludens*,[16] Johan Huizinga has taught us that all games are related to the sense of life as an historical illusion which is nonetheless played in deadly earnest toward either eternal damnation or salvation. And Frank J. Warnke has focused this view of "World as Theatre" and "Art as Play" on baroque literature in particular.[17] Much of what I discuss takes these perspectives for granted.

My understanding of theodicy in baroque literature has also been influenced by a few literary theorists. In his analysis of *Allegory*,[18] Angus Fletcher discusses the tendency in allegorical structures to defeat evil through the total "isomorphic imitation" of evil by virtue. Mr. Fletcher argues "that by paralleling virtue and vice the poet is showing the latter to be magically overcome by its equal antithesis." His analysis is relevant enough to quote at length:

> But allegories tend to stress the equality of the two opposing forces, and the implication is that by paralleling virtue and vice the poet is showing the latter to be magically overcome by its equal antithesis . . . the allegorist assumes that, when virtue imitates vice at the moment of attack, it can, by that very isomorphic imitation, destroy its opposite. Perhaps to avoid a strict Manichaeism, major allegorists may allow a degree of confusion to exist at the very moment when Virtue attacks Vice. This happens in *The Faerie Queene*, where, as Empson points out in his *Seven Types of Ambiguity*, one cannot tell who "he" is when Spenser describes two combatants, using the third singular pronoun.[19]

And in my consideration of literary theodicy, I have found W. K. Wimsatt's discussion in *Hateful Contraries* of this, as he calls it, "tensional element" especially enlightening.[20] Evil as it appears in literature is obviously very different from its manifestation in life. In life there is something about evil, sin and death which remains, whatever happens, has happened or will happen, totally irredeemable. In his analysis of evil in literature, Mr. Wimsatt begins by distinguishing between harmony "in spite of" conflict and harmony "because of or through" conflict.[21] He sees the former balance as a staple of Greco-Roman, medieval and renaissance literature and the latter creative conflict as essential to romantic poetics. (It seems to me that this creative conflict is also present in baroque literature.) Mr. Wimsatt defines the position of the critic:

> He will say that the human condition is intrinsically a material and mixed condition, where faith and love of God and fellow man can scarcely occur except in a milieu that is full of the possibility of their opposites. And this possibility, however it is minimized and pushed to one side by the discipline of the saint, the austerity of the cell, the devotion of the ritual (or the laws of the party), is still a tensional element that is part of the moral quality of experience.[22]

On the other hand, although in the literature I am concerned with theodicy is most characteristically expressed in paradoxically identified antitheses, I should make clear that the views of several modern schools of criticism which insist on the inherent presence in all language of its opposite meaning do not inform my analyses. (These deconstructivist views seem to me to be essentially restatements of Aristotle's doctrine of potentiality as stated in his *Metaphysics* without the "potential" qualification.) It is not that I am uncognizant of these arguments. But in baroque literature antithetically opposed meanings are not an element willy-nilly embedded in language; rather they are created and controlled by the exercise of human choice and understanding. Even an approach such as Rosalie Colie's in her brilliant *Paradoxia Epidemica*,[23] which understands paradox as a way of evading meaning, must be rejected as opposite to the interpretations I propose. The Judeo-Christian tradition of theodicy as manifested in literature embraces paradox; but its essence is meaning.

Through the medieval period, theodicy remained pretty much on center stage, so that Dante's *Commedia* presents the ridges of the *Inferno* as an inverse mirror reflection of the ledges of the *Purgatorio* (literally the hollowed out absence of the other). In the Renaissance and succeeding centuries theodicy is no less an important thematic element in literature, but it relies on increasingly distanced literary modalities: for example, in an aesthetic Augustinian mode of harmoniously balanced opposites—

prosody with perfectly balanced chiasma;[24] or, in an Irenaean mode—a hero's recognition and self-discovery within his own negative shadows, paradoxically, providing the impetus for heroic achievement. Indeed, it is doubtful whether literary phenomena, such as, the *culteranismo* and *conceptismo*[25] of Spanish baroque poetry with their tendency to suggest the occult relationship of all things in the universe, or our view of sixteenth and seventeenth century tragic characters—complex, multifaceted, paradoxical and, yet, unique—could exist without theodical doctrine. At least there is no question as to which came first. Baroque literature seems to have informed itself with both the Augustinian and Irenaean traditions. The Augustinian contributed more to structural and formal elements, while the Irenaean found expression in an essentially tragic view of the trajectory of man's existence. Typical of baroque literature and, perhaps, unique to it is a tendency to join these two traditions in a vision of isometrically balanced natural, social and prosodic structures which metamorphose one into the other according to the moral evolution of the hero. But it is not my intention to trace the precise transmission of theodical ideas or to make exact correlations between the ideology and literary modes—although this can be done as has recently been demonstrated by D. R. Danielson's study of theodicy in Milton's epics.[26] In such an approach the unified vision which I am interested in delineating would quickly become lost in, for example, measuring the degree to which an Augustinian sense of predestination in Calderón seems to result in an evident Manicheism regardless of disclaimers (as it does in Saint Augustine himself) as compared to the degree to which an Irenaean sense of good evolving out of the historical process in Tasso seems to deny any visceral reality to evil. Furthermore, such an approach of point-by-point comparisons of doctrine and literary modes would not suit the baroque authors I am specifically concerned with. Centuries of mythic, allegoric and hermeneutic traditions helped to transform these theological elements into a literary myth which is surprising in its consistency as it appears in several national literatures of both Catholic and Protestant countries. (My tripartite division is a necessary minimum "control" in that it includes both denominations and two different authors in at least one.)

I allow the baroque theodical myth to speak for itself because as responsive as it is to many basic principles of Augustinian and Irenaean theodicy, it nonetheless has its own dimensions and definitions. (Renaissance mythographers were no more precise in reading Christian doctrine and narrative into pagan myths than the baroque poets were in creating myths from theology.[27]) It would be difficult to find in Saint Augustine something directly responsive to the precise effect of the total isomorphic imitation of antithetical worlds in Calderón which—when accomplished—seems to transfer all power to the will of the hero. In such a weightless balance, he has only to choose. But as we shall see Calderón's myth and structure is about the non-metaphysical reality of evil and the freedom of choice. And to interpret in theodical terms Calderón's description in his mythological plays of pagan gods as learning from their errors (even though Calderón uses a theologically charged word—*escarmentar*: to purge through punishment, to learn through suffering) would quickly lead to a type of nonsense. Nonetheless, *escarmentar* in Calderón is always about the divinely ordained beneficence of suffering. A final barrier to precise doctrinal definition is that, not unexpectedly of the baroque, there is a tendency not only to combine an Augustinian sense of "aesthetic plenitude" with an Irenaean sense of ennobling suffering, but to reduce them to a unity, so that the mirroring of antithetical dichotomies is equated with the fully human awareness of the baroque hero.

I describe the myth in the following stages: First there is the background of a world of illusion, mutability, deception and evil in the various works I discuss. This is the mutable world, the confused labyrinth, the dark forest, the shipwreck of the fallen world, the Pandora's box which must be justified. There is a general tendency to depict this world as binary with good and evil halves. Some of the imagery here involves simple dichotomies of war and love, enemy and friend, pagan and Christian, night and day, darkness and light, *engaño* and *desengaño*. Some of the imagery is more subtle and involves disguises and hidden identities. And there is a type of metaphysical bisexuality with the female beloved disguised as an enemy warrior: a ray of beauty which emanates from the horror and destruction of war machines. The most radical form of this dichotomy is the bed trick of baroque drama through which adultery and its simulation are both the occasion of a fall and the restitution. And in the baroque world of inverted mirror reflections, imagery of narcissism and monosexuality carries implications not of monism but of Manicheism—betraying as it does an incomplete faith in the oneness of apparent dualism. As this world comes into focus, its specific configurations into familiar archetypes begins to articulate the myth: a theater with antithetical scenes of prison and palace, a battlefield and pastoral landscape divided by an enchanted forest, and places of concealment—the prison and the cave—metamorphosed into transcendent revelations of freedom and fulfillment. Along with these patterns and *topoi* there are several indications of a paradoxical beneficence in illusion and evil. These range all the way from the white lie to instructive example through another's misfortune: the several instances developing into a major theme. Gradually deception or illusion becomes identified with a sense of beneficent evil, and the only possibility of revelation or disillusionment is awareness by the hero of the ambiguity inherent in illusion. The central expression of this paradox in Tasso is the Tancredi-Clorinda battle: the enemy turns out to be a beloved and his/her death is her/his salvation. In Milton, Samson becomes gradually aware that the very feminine wiles of Dalila which betrayed him and which he so despises must become the instruments of his heroic fulfillment. In Calderón the same paradox is expressed through the elaborate dance he develops in the majority of his plays between *engaño* and *desengaño*: *desengaño* is the reflection in the mirror which is achieved when *engaño* is embraced. In more mythic terms, Circe is the mirror in which Ulysses discovers himself.

These paradoxes have a remarkable mirror reflection in the prosody of the three authors. A few of the more constant features are generalized expressions, such as "l'un e l'altro" and unspecific pronouns which tend to merge opposite identities; the joining of two antithetical elements in a verb or a repeated word or through rhyme; the symmetry of divided hendecasyllabic verse; and, more dramatically and more specifically baroque, the triadic merging of a verse's bilateral symmetry through enjambement into a single unity—verb, noun or generalized phrase—of the next verse. Indeed, prosody is so integral a part of the meaning that I have decided to include brief trots within my text rather than risk misleading translations. Any reader with some knowlege of romance languages will be better off.

To return to the narrative level: in the baroque myth the paradox of the *nemica amante* is increasingly internalized in the consciousness of the hero. In *Gerusalemme liberata* this occurs in stages. The early Tancredi-Clorinda battle—overt in its theatricality—seems to be continued within the mind of pagan Erminia who is in love with the Christian Tancredi but is forced to witness silently the battles between him and her fellow pagan Argante. This internalized division is later developed further in Rinaldo's awareness of his own identity with Armida. In *Samson Agonistes* the external dichotomy between Manoa and Harapha is joined in the figure of Dalila, but it is increasingly reflected within Samson's consciousness. Calderón likes to select a monadic symbol—lyre, mirror, stage—which seems to reflect the divided loyalties of his hero, but eventually becomes the focus of their resolution. This mental resolution of opposites is important enough that awareness of the paradox becomes in itself an heroic quality. (We are very close here to a conception of the hero as saint, and yet it remains unique to baroque literature.) Consciousness on the part of the hero is so central to the myth because in precisely such an Augustinian sense of harmonious balance is registered the perspective of the hero's awareness of good and evil and the crisis of faith which it effects. The *loci* of these dynamic tensions and resolutions moves quickly from the binary dichotomies of battlefield horror and pastoral tranquility to the hidden cave or the prison and finally to the mind of the hero, which is revealed to be the threshold of a transcendent fulfillment and liberation. It is that single internalized locus which allows for the ultimate power of metamorphosis and its source as free will, and denies any possibility of a Manichaean division. In these baroque works traditionally separate and antithetical roles—lover and enemy, revenger and revenged, protagonist and antagonist, savior and nemesis—reside in a single character,[28] and Manicheism is the temptation to hide from an adverse fate rather than to embrace it in the full confidence of conquest. Paradoxically, the cave or the prison is not a safeguard from adversity, but rather the meditative center of encounter.

Ultimately the baroque theodical myth develops with surprising similarity in Tasso, Milton and Calderón toward a symbiosis of the Circe and Narcissus myths. The heroes discover themselves in their Circean enchantresses who are identified with the world of illusion and evil. But it is this very awareness of evil in themselves which frees them toward their noblest achievements. The elaborate parallelism between the ambivalent worlds delineates the Narcissus myth because the binary pattern is developed to such an extent that it creates a mirror reflection or total isomorphic imitation: friend and enemy, Christian and pagan, good and evil, etc. From this develops a tendency toward allegory, accounting for a great deal of the antithetical imagery and obsession with illusion: the phenomenal world is seen as a reflection of the heroes' moral landscapes and metamorphoses according to their moral choices. With the shift of focus from illusion and evil to the power of metamorphosis, illusion is far from absent. But it no longer resides in the perceptions of heroes or readers; illusion has rather become the phenomenal world itself. This is epitomized in Calderón's totally allegoric *autos*: each *auto* presents a still point in which all the antithetical aspects of the fallen and unfallen (or redeemed) world are "reduced to a unity." But this tendency is also recognizable in the solitary and meditative figures of Solimano *(Gerusalemme liberata)* and Samson as they seem to destroy but in fact metamorphose themselves and their circumspect worlds.

Finally I discuss the many subtle hints in these baroque works through imagery, such as softly heard, distant music, the shadows and *sfumatura* of twilight hours, and thoughts which are felt or intuited but remain unspoken—I discuss these hints of a mystery which is greater than the paradoxes illuminated by the work and which, however strongly felt, must by its very nature evade final understanding. The mystery is read both as the poet's imaginative intuition and the Christian *mysterium*.

TASSO

Non so se il molto amaro
che provato ha costui servendo, amando,
piangendo e disperando,
raddolcito esser puote pienamente
d'alcun dolce presente.
Ma se più caro viene
e più gusta dopo'l male il bene,
io nonti chieggio, Amore,
questa beatitudine maggiore.

Aminta, Tasso

LA GIERVSALEMME
LIBERATA
DI TORQVATO TASSO
Con le Figure di Bernardo
CASTELLO;

E le Annotationi di Scipio
GENTILI, e di Giulio
GVASTAVINI.

IN GENOVA. M.D.LXXXX.

Title page illustrated by Annibale Carracci from the Genoa, 1590 edition. Courtesy of the Rare Book Division, New York Public Library.

Although no critic has undertaken a study of the relationship between the play of illusion and reality and ideas of good and evil in Tasso's poetry, in *Gerusalemme liberata* it is a central thematic element. Perhaps one reason for this lack of critical study is that illusion, enchantment, deceit, etc., are an endemic part of the epic tradition out of which *Gerusalemme liberata* grew. However, in *Morgante, Orlando Innamorato* and *Orlando Furioso* illusion is not rooted in a metaphysics of good and evil as it is in Tasso, and it does not serve the same function.[1] Except for the purposes of contrast, it is best to consider Tasso's theodicy independently of his precursors in the epic tradition. A meaningful and informative comparison will be found in Milton, Calderón and other baroque authors.

My discussion is in twelve sections which are divided with key titles and correspond to the steps delineating the theodical myth in my introduction. I hope my titles will serve as a mnemonic device for the reader in holding together the steps of an unavoidably complex argument—not only within this essay but throughout the book. In the first section *(Docere delectando)* I introduce the theme of illusion and suggest a connection between Tasso's use of romantic legends to teach sacred history and an Irenaean sense of the way illusion and evil in the world work toward beneficent ends. In the second section *(Volto Ascoso al volto)* I show how the major themes of the poem are present in the initial Olindo-Sofronia episode. In the third section *(Mondo mutabile)* I discuss the world of multiplicity, change and reversal—seemingly resolved in the "aesthetic plenitude" of Augustinian binary opposites—which forms the background for the action of the poem. In the fourth section *(Adorno inganno)* I point out the innumerable instances in which deception is used or works out toward a good purpose, which pattern, thereby, develops into an Irenaean leitmotif of soul-making. In the fifth section *(L'un l'altro guarda)* I explicate the Clorinda-Tancredi battle in terms of hidden and discovered identity: a Christian disguised as a pagan, a beloved hidden beneath the armor of an enemy . . . good in the illusory emanation of evil. In the sixth section *(Sotto mentito aspetto)* I concentrate on Erminia and her warrior disguise as a theodical symbol for the poem. In the seventh section *(Securi fra l'arme)* I relate the joy which Erminia finds paradoxically amid the war machines to the rest of the poem. The eighth section *(Movon concordi)* describes the parallelism between the opposing camps—again, to my mind, in an Augustinian mode of "aesthetic plenitude." In the ninth section *(Narciso)* I discuss the Armida and Rinaldo relationship in which illusion and disguise appear as unconscious desires (another unknown identity). In the tenth section *(Colpe umane)*—the most Irenaean—the parallel identity between the antithetical opposing forces of the poem is discovered in a common humanity, one aspect of which is the understanding of a monistic relationship between good and evil. The recognition of this common humanity is the goal of the heroes' quest. In the eleventh section *(Un sol punto)* I describe the poem's tendency away from narrative toward allegory, accounting for a great deal of the presence of illusion and theodical imagery. The final section *(Segni ignoti)* points toward the ultimate surrender to mystery in *Gerusalemme liberata*.

I.   Docere delectando

The first canto of *Gerusalemme liberata* provides a gradual but revealing introduction to the theodical theme of illusion and beneficent evil and Tasso's use of it. In his Proem Tasso asks pardon of his Muse for mixing the truth of his story, i.e., the historical crusade for the liberation of Jerusalem, with elements of fiction, i.e., ornamentation and profane fables patterned after the legends of Romance. He uses the well-worn simile of a child taking sugar-coated medicine. In this first antithesis (a mode of expression so essential to *Gerusalemme liberata*) between the sacred truth and profane ornamentation, sweet and sour, a child thinking he is eating candy when he, in fact, is being deluded into taking medicine, there is no question as to the relative merits between the two: sacred history and frivolous legend, medicine and candy. Tasso is here excusing the Romance element of his epic, the stories of love which will follow, as a necessary evil. But this evil has a redeeming quality. It is only at first that the relative merits of the two parts of the antithesis are clear. From illusion and deception, even in this simple simile about the child, comes life:

> e da l'inganno suo vita riceve.   (1, 3*)

It is significant in the theodical context of the poem that Tasso says it is from the "inganno," and not the medicine, that the child receives life.

---

*Throughout my book I quote from the standard edition of *Gerusalemme liberata* by Lanfranco Caretti (Milan, 1957). Instead of page numbers, I always include within my text the canto and stanza so that the passage may be easily referred to in most editions. When it is clear that I am discussing a specific episode within a canto I have already mentioned, I give only the stanza number. *All the italics are my own for the purpose of emphasis.*

The "inganno" is more than a means to an end. It is the source of life, a vital part of existence.

Here the theme of illusion and beneficent evil as Tasso uses it in the poem is established as well as the special character of his antitheses. Illusion is associated with evil (profane ornamentation in sacred history), but it is the necessary means toward a good end. Sacred history and profane ornamentation, medicine and candy, are opposed as the two elements of an antithesis, but they are also inextricably related to one another. And at crucial moments they move toward unity. Tasso did not invent the use of paradoxical antithetical conceits. His most important literary model is Petrarch. But his particular use of antitheses in *Gerusalemme liberata,* his obsession with them so that they appear not only interminably in individual stanzas of the poem but reveal themselves as reflections of the larger patterns of the poem in an atmosphere of hovering shadows' and darkness, the confusing light of dawn or sunset in which the identity of the two members of the antithesis merge, is one of the outstanding characteristics of Tasso's epic.

II.   *Volto ascoso al volto*

The major episode of the second canto of *Gerusalemme liberata* presents Olindo and Sofronia. From the very first publication of *Gerusalemme liberata,* some of Tasso's readers criticized the episode as an example of both a lack of unity in the poem and its profane nature.[2] What these readers were objecting to is that in its relation to the poem, the episode lacks a type of unity: the mechanical unity of the *Orlando Furioso,* perhaps, in which episode leads into episode and there is a causal relationship between them. For these critics the episode is profane because it is not necessary to or even linked to the central episode of the poem, the conquest of Jerusalem, and it seems to be no more than a love story like those which filled the pages of the profane romances. But the episode is very much obsessed with the love and death, peace and war and reality and illusion patterns of the poem. Indeed, this type of internal or organic unity can be seen as baroque or "painterly" as opposed to the more external and causal relationships within *Orlando Furioso,* and it can be linked to some critical attempts to study these different types of internal structures in literature in terms of Wölfflin's renaissance and baroque categories.[3] Far beyond the hints of the first canto of *Gerusalemme liberata,* this second canto introduces us to the key themes and even resolutions of the poem.

The Olindo-Sofronia episode begins with the disappearance of an image of the Virgin which had been placed in a mosque by the pagan king of Jerusalem.[4] Aladino, not able to discover the person who removed it, decides to punish the whole Christian population. Sofronia, who is described in terms of the greatest modesty, is motivated, in order to save the Christian population, to pretend that she stole the image. This forces Olindo, who loved her silently, to declare his love by insisting that it was he who stole the image and, therefore, should die instead of her. Aladino decides to have both of them burned. It is in this *Old Testament* theodical play of concealment and revelation—of using deception toward the virtuous end of saving the Christian population—that Olindo's love for Sofronia is revealed. They are to be united in death. Finally, they are saved by Clorinda, married and exiled from Jerusalem. Each of these stages has several parallels within the poem as well as a parallel in the general pattern of the poem. Even the language of the Olindo and Sofronia episode introduces the reader to the world of illusion as it is represented in *Gerusalemme liberata*.

Sofronia herself is described in terms of pointed contrasts and paradoxes. The modest virgin neither conceals nor reveals her beauty ("non coprí sue bellezze, e non l'espose," II, 18), and in regard to her beauty, it is difficult to tell whether it consists of adornment or neglect, chance or art. Characteristically, Tasso resolves these conflicts—a triadic resolution of opposites into a third paradoxical element—by stating that in this case neglect *is* artifice:

> Non sai ben dir s'adorna o se negletta,
> se caso od arte il bel volto compose.
> Di natura, d'Amor, de' cieli amici
> le negligenze sue sono artifici.   (II, 18)

Contrast is mounted upon contrast and paradox upon paradox until they become the very fabric of the episode. Sofronia's story is a "Magnanima menzogna," 22; she is stared at but does not look back ("Mirata da ciascun passa, e non mira," 19); the softness of her flesh is contrasted with the hardness of her bonds ("stringon le molli braccia aspre ritorte," 26). Sofronia is even able not merely to transform shame into audacity but to make shame *itself* audacious:

> vince fortezza, anzi s'accorda e face
> se vergognosa e la vergogna audace.   (II, 17)

Behind the whole episode is, of course, the fact that Sofronia is being punished for a noble deed. While she calls herself guilty ("Il reo si trova al tuo cospetto," 21), she refers almost immediately afterward—without any transition—to her deed as "la mia Gloria," 23. No less important is the contrast between Sofronia and Olindo, which Clorinda notices:

> Mira che l'una tace e l'altro geme,
> e piú vigor mostra il men forte sesso.   (II, 42)

Clorinda feels greater sympathy for the less afflicted of the two:

> Pur maggior sente il duol per chi non duolse,
> piú la move il silenzio e meno il pianto.   (II, 43)

Significantly, it is Clorinda who registers this because she is the presence joining this episode to the theodical concerns of the poem—a relationship which is no less real for not being causal. When Sofronia and Olindo are each attempting to persuade Aladino of her/his sole responsibility for the theft, one of the poem's most stark and radical paradoxes is introduced:

> Oh spettacolo grande, ove a tenzone
> sono Amore e magnanima virtute!
> ove la morte al vincitor si pone
> in premio, e 'l mal del vinto è la salute!   (II, 31)

Death to the victor and life to the vanquished. Here we have a mirror reflection of the Tancredi and Clorinda battle. Clorinda (the vanquished) receives salvation and eternal happiness, whereas Tancredi (the victor) is left with the death-in-life knowledge that he has killed his beloved. Indeed, when Clorinda looks at the plaintive Olindo and the stoic Sofronia, she is previewing her later situation, when, at death and after death, she will have to support the weaker Tancredi. And this reflection of major episodes in minor ones and larger patterns in smaller ones (a baroque painterly unity) recurs significantly—as in this case—again and again in the poem.

The contrast and identity between Clorinda and Sofronia is very revealing. Sofronia is modest and feminine:

> Vergine era fra lor di già matura
> verginità, d'alti pensieri e regi,
> d'alta beltà, ma sua beltà non cura,
> o tanto sol quant'onestà se 'n fregi.
> E il suo pregio maggior che tra le mura
> d'angusta casa asconde i suoi gran pregi,
> e de' vagheggiatori ella s'invola
> a le lodi, a gli sguardi, inculta e sola.   (II, 14)

Clorinda is arrogant and aggressive:

> Costei gl'ingegni feminili e gli usi
> tutti sprezzò sin da l'età piú acerba:
> a i lavori d'Aracne, a l'ago, a i fusi
> inchinar non degnò la man superba.
> Fuggí gli abiti molli e i lochi chiusi,
> ché ni' campi onestate anco si serba;
> armò d'orgoglio il volto, e si compiacque
> rigido farlo, e pur rigido piacque.   (II, 39)

But these descriptions do not remain isolated portraits. As we have seen, Sofronia, in order to achieve her purpose, turns herself into a Clorinda and renders "la vergogna audace." I think it would have to be said that Tasso's central theme in *Gerusalemme liberata* is the theodical justification of evil, hostilities, war—everything the external person of Clorinda represents. It is toward that end, in this Olindo-Sofronia episode where illusion and deception (later identified with war) are used to the good end of saving the Christian populace, that Clorinda, the enemy warrior, appears—armor, tiger-crest and all—as the savior of the two Christians. As if to underline her inverted role, Clorinda requests Aladino to reverse the usual order of presenting her with a reward after her service ("che preceda a i servigi il guiderdone," 49). She requests that the two Christians be saved now.

These themes become clearer later in the poem. The episode itself is almost emblematic.[5] Olindo reveals his love for Sofronia at the point of death. He realizes on their funeral pyre that the flames and bed of love and death are related:

> Altre fiamme, altri nodi Amor promise
> altri ce n'apparecchia iniqua sorte.
> Troppo, ahi! ben troppo, ella già noi divise,
> ma duramente or ne congiunge in morte.
> Piacemi almen, poich'in sí strane guise
> morir pur déi, del rogo esser consorte,
> se del letto non fui; duolmi il tuo fato,
> il mio non già, poich'io ti moro a lato.   (II, 34)

(One should observe the triadic chiastic-rhyme: "sorte," "morte" and "consorte." I discuss Tasso's prosody later in my essay.) Death will similarly be related to the loves of Tancredi and Clorinda and Erminia. If the episode as a whole is emblematic, their position on the pyre is more specifically so:

> Sono ambo stretti al palo stesso; e vòlto
> è il tergo al tergo, e 'l volto ascoso al volto   (II, 32)

They are tied back to back as one ("tergo al tergo"); however, the antithetical forces which ultimately fulfill them as lovers (love and death, savior-warrior, illusion) remain like their hidden faces shrouded in mystery ("volto ascoso al volto"). Note the play on "turned" and "face": "*vòlto*" and "*volto*." The two faces look in opposite directions as if they were antithetical forces joined by the third element, "*vòlto*."

Although it could seem as if Tasso has Aladino banish the pair from Jerusalem after the wedding because their role as characters in the poem is over, their banishment can also be seen as symbolic of the vast psychological abyss which, we shall see, separates the other heroes of the poem, once their goals have been accomplished, from their former simple and dualistic dreams of conquest and victory.

III. *Mondo mutabile*

At the beginning of Canto V Goffredo, attempting to dissuade some of his soldiers from following Armida, advises them to change their minds because in a mutable world constancy often consists of change:

> ché nel mondo mutabile e leggiero
> costanza è spesso il variar pensiero.   (V, 3)

There are several such key statements in *Gerusalemme liberata*. All of them specifically define the world as illusory, deceptive and inconstant. They usually involve Goffredo, who, as the central (if not most important) character in the poem, often plays the role of judge or interpreter. When in a dream Ugone transports Goffredo to the temple where God rewards his creatures, Ugone reveals the insignificance, vanity and baseness of the world which to humanity seems so vast:

> Lei come isola il mare intorno chiude,
> e lui, ch'or ocean chiamat'è or vasto,
> nulla eguale a tai nomi ha in sé di magno,
> ma è bassa palude a breve stagno.   (XIV, 10)

Goffredo remains amazed at the folly of human concerns: "che pur a l'ombre, a i fume,/ la nostra folle umanità s'affise," 11. Finally he asks to be shown the least false road on the earth, since there is none totally free from error:

> prego che del camin, ch'è men fallace
> fra gli errori del mondo, or tu m'informe.   (XIV, 12)

In describing the fierce fighting during Solimano's night attack on the Christians in Canto IX, the narrator gives up trying to distinguish truth and falsehood: "e piú direi, ma il ver di falso ha faccia," 23. It would be needlessly repetitive to list all such statements in *Gerusalemme liberata*. They serve as a "backdrop" for the more important uses of illusion in the poem.

Similar to these "backdrop" statements are episodes such as in Canto XX, 15 where Goffredo admonishes his men not to be frightened by the size and apparent strength of the Egyptian army because it is, in fact, poorly organized. Illusion also comes in the form of dreams. In Canto VIII Aletto inspires a dream in Argillano in which he sees Rinaldo (whom Goffredo banned from the Christian armies and whose abandoned armor has been found) holding his own severed head and inciting Argillano to revolt against Goffredo whom he accuses of having slain him for personal glory. Argillano is successful in arousing the Christians to his falsely inspired cause. It is again Goffredo who, in his prayer after having heard about the revolt, describes the illusion which burdens the Christians. He prays to God for reversal:

> tu squarcia a questi de la mente il velo,
> e reprimi il furor che sí trascorre.   (VIII, 76)

It is perhaps worth stating that the various and many descriptions of the illusion and deception suffered by the Christians are enormous as compared to the few references to the pagans. This does not signify a difference between the two, since the deception of the pagans is taken for granted, but rather that illusion is an intrinsic part of existence in the world of Tasso's poem.

But with these statements about the illusion of the world and their parallel episodes in dream and enchantment we still have an aspect of illusion which could almost come out of *Orlando Furioso*. It is rather in the type of illusion patterned after the use of deception by Sofronia to save the Christians and the verbal paradoxes, such as "victor-vanquished" from the Olindo-Sofronia episode, that the more profound obsessions of the poem are revealed and worked out. I shall discuss the former first.

IV.   *Adorno inganno*

There are several minor and major episodes in which deception is used for beneficent ends, and these episodes are pervasive enough to develop into a leitmotif and to become a part of the major themes of the poem which they, in fact, help to interpret. Goffredo is developed extremely carefully by Tasso so as never to share the weaknesses and fallacies of the other heroes of the poem. The latter are frequently victims of deception; but it is Goffredo who, although he never falls victim to illusion, as Rinaldo does to Armida, for example, nevertheless uses deception in a way similar to Olindo and Sofronia. Significantly, Goffredo's use of illusion is characterized as considerably more conscious than Sofronia's and Olindo's. In their case the reader is more aware of a condition as victims and martyrs.

At the end of Canto V when Goffredo simultaneously has become aware of the large number of his men who have deserted to Armida and has been informed about the rapid approach of the Egyptian armies and the shortage of food, we are informed that he consoles the Christians with an external appearance of serenity while he is internally anxious:

> Con questi detti le smarrite menti
> consola e con sereno e lieto aspetto,
> ma preme mille cure egre e dolenti
> altamente riposte in mezzo al petto.   (V, 92)

During Goffredo's dream in Canto XIV, he asks Ugone for the least false path in a world which is full of errors. Ugone's answer, his definition of "la via verace," requires of Goffredo another constructive deception. The expelled Rinaldo must be called back in order to free the enchanted forest which, as we shall see, is, along with Armida, one of the most important symbols for illusion in the poem. But since Rinaldo is an offender, Goffredo, as the leader of the Christians, cannot call him back. Tasso's resolution is that God will inspire another to request Rinaldo's return. When Goffredo, after awakening from his sleep, receives this request from Guelfo, Goffredo responds to the request as if he had never heard anything about it:

> Onde Goffredo allor, quasi egli pieghi
> la mente a cosa non pensata in pria.   (XIV, 25)

Goffredo's diplomacy is almost an amusing or comic displacement of the poem's theme of illusion and deception.[6] While these episodes remain very much a part of that theme, I do not think their comic nature is intentional but is rather due to the artificiality of Goffredo as a character. It is implied that Goffredo uses a similar tactic against the enemy by postponing battle: "Forse ne'suoi nemici anco la folle/ credenza di se stessi ei nudrir volle," XX, 4. The other heroes share these diplomatic deceptions. Rinaldo, for example, in Canto V, when Eustachio elects him as leader in order to put him out of competition with Armida, pretends not to be aware of Eustachio's motivations ("i mal celati suoi pensier ardenti," 12) because he is more interested in avenging the death of Dudone than in Armida.

These are all an important part of the elaborate pattern of illusion and reality which Tasso has created in *Gerusalemme liberata.* Closer to the central theme of beneficent evil are the deceptions of Eustachio and the other members of Goffredo's army who desert him in order to follow Armida. She, with the true intention of subverting the Christian army, invents her maiden-in-distress story:

> e celò sí sotto mentito aspetto
> il suo pensier ch'altrui non diè sospetto.   (IV, 85)

Both Eustachio and the others feign motives of honor for their amorous desire and persist in their decision:

> Cosí conclude, e con sí adorno inganno
> cerca di ricoprir la mente accesa
> sotto altro zelo; e gli altri anco d'onore
> fingon desio quel ch'è desio d'amore.   (V, 7)

The next we hear of these soldiers is in Canto IX, 91 when they appear suddenly to *aid* the Christian army in a crucial battle against the pagans. When the battle is over and the pagan armies have fled, Goffredo, who recognizes them as the defectors to Armida and sees Tancredi in their

number, asks them how they happened to be present at a time of such
need:

> "e come poscia vi trovaste pronti
> in si grand'uopo a dar sí gran soccorso."   (X, 59)

We learn that Rinaldo has freed them and that Tancredi had also ended
up as a victim of Armida when he was following Erminia disguised as
Clorinda. (Here, Tancredi, following a disguised beloved [Erminia]
whom he believes to be an enemy [Clorinda] with whom he is nonetheless
in love, is an inversion of the symbolic patterns we will see in the
Tancredi-Clorinda battle.) The fall into illusion of Tancredi and the
defectors and the defectors' own deceptiveness have led to this fortuitous
circumstance in which Rinaldo's feared death is revealed to be an illusion. It is as if the disgrace of the soldiers who followed Armida were, in
view of the outcome, no longer real or, at least, no longer something
negative. These accumulated incidents unavoidably make the reader
allow that adversity is something more or something else than it seems. It
is Goffredo who, after hearing the story, expresses this feeling:

> "Vive" dice "Rinaldo, e l'altre sono
> arti e bugie di femminile inganno.
> Vive, e la vita giovanetta acerba
> a piú mature glorie il Ciel riserba.   (X, 74)

Clorinda is perhaps the figure who most closely links this pattern of
either beneficent deception or, as with the defectors, a fall into illusion
with the poem's revelations and intimations about the theodical relationship between good and evil, love and death. When in Canto XII Clorinda
volunteers to go into the Christian camp in order to burn the tower they
have been using to assail the walls of Jerusalem, her lifelong eunuch
servant, Arsete, uses the occasion to inform Clorinda of her true origins.
She was born a Christian of the negro wife of Senapo, King of Ethiopia.
Although she is a legitimate child, her mother decides, because she was
bórn so light of skin, to safeguard her against the possible mad jealousy
of her husband and exchanges her for a black child, entrusting Clorinda
to Arsete with instructions that she be raised as a Christian. With this first
deception Clorinda's life is saved.[7] Arsete never fulfills his promise. The
episode which follows is filled with illusion, all toward disguising Clorinda's identity with the reward of salvation in each case.

The final salvation is the true Christian one, and by making this
connection Tasso's poem suggests that the use of disguise in each case is
necessarily related to the salvation the Christian heroes are seeking for
themselves as well as for Jerusalem. Clorinda's life began by hiding her
identity among the pagans in order to avoid death at the hands of her

father. When she is locked outside Jerusalem (as are the Christians) because of the confusion of battle, she pretends to be one of the Christians in order to escape: "Di lor gente s'infinge," XII 50. Tancredi mistakes her identity for one of the pagan soldiers and does not recognize her until it is too late. At one point he asks her to identify herself, but Clorinda refuses. This willful and final hiding of her identity on the part of Clorinda leads to her death. Before she dies she is baptised by Tancredi. Thus deception has led not only to Clorinda's Christian salvation but to the dissolution of Tancredi's destructive love obsession with one of the enemy ("tanto un suo vano armor l'ange e martira" I, 9). Piero reprimands Tancredi's anguish over having slain his beloved by reminding him of its benefi-cence:

> "A gli atti del primiero ufficio degno
> di cavalier di Cristo ei ti rappella,
> che lasciasti per farti (ahi cambio indegno!)
> drudo d'una fanciulla a Dio rubella.
> Seconda aversità, pietoso sdegno
> con leve sferza di la su flagella
> tua folle colpa, e fa di tua salute
> te medesmo ministro; e tu 'l rifiute?"   (XII, 87)

As for Clorinda herself, she appears to Tancredi in a dream and describes how fortunate the outcome has been for her:

> "Tale i' son, tua mercé: tu me da i vivi
> del mortal mondo, per error, togliesti;
> tu in grembo a Dio fra gli immortali e divi,
> per pietà, di salir degna mi fèsti."   (XII, 92)

It is difficult not to see in this episode the significance of three phenom-ena which shall become increasingly important in my discussion of *Gerusalemme liberata*: 1) complex questions of identity, 2) the beneficent effects of illusion whenever Clorinda hides or feigns her identity and 3) the balance in beneficent effects whether Clorinda hides her identity among the pagans or among the Christians.

V. *L'un l'altro guarda*

The Clorinda and Tancredi battle is the major episode in which Tasso elaborates a paradoxical conceit between love and war. The episode is full of confused identities (which gradually reveal themselves not so much confused as paradoxical) and the balancing and paralleling of the poem's antitheses. Clorinda is really a born (unbaptized) Christian in disguise to herself as well as to the world as a pagan. Ironically in the middle of fighting she is forced to revert the disguise to a Christian in order to save herself. Tancredi approaches Clorinda as her enemy, but he is, in fact, her

lover. The language and rhetoric of the episode supports these contrasts
and paradoxes. Tasso places his narrative in a theatrical setting:

> Degne d'un chiaro sol, degne d'un pieno
> teatro, opre sarian si memorande.
> Notte, che nel profondo oscuro seno
> chiudesti e ne l'oblio fatto sí grande,
> piacciati ch'io ne'l tragga e 'n bel sereno
> a le future età lo spieghi e mande.
> Viva la fama loro; e tra lor gloria
> splenda del fosco tuo l'alta memoria.   (XII, 54)

Here the dark and bitter mysteries of love and war and salvation and
death are going to be brought to light even though they can never
completely emerge from their shadows and mysteries.

As the battle progresses the confused identities and contrasts within
Clorinda as pagan and Christian and Tancredi as enemy and lover
become indistinguishable in the darkness and, symbolically, the battle
draws closer together: "D'or in or piú si mesce e piú ristretta/ si fa la
pugna," 56. (It is no wonder composers and choreographers have gravitated to this episode as a vehicle for the harmonious resolution of the
dissonances and consonances and the duple and triadic rhythms of music
and the contraction and release, the centripetal and centrifugal dynamics
of dance.[8]) In rhythmical opposition (mirroring the three metamorphoses
of her identity as Christian and pagan) Clorinda is bound and then
loosened from Tancredi's embraces:

> Tre volte il cavalier la donna stringe
> con le robuste braccia, ed altrettante
> da que' nodi tenaci ella si scinge,
> nodi di fer nemico e non d'amante.   (XII, 57)

When the passage is read on an allegorical level, Tancredi represents
Christianity for Clorinda and his embraces are her salvation in Christianity. He is lover but also enemy, and his final embrace is Clorinda's death.
The rhetorical expression of binary antitheses, "di . . . e non di," con-
tributes to the paradox and is used repetitively by Tasso. In one beautiful
verse, so typical of Tasso (a type of verse to which I shall pay increased
attention), he joins Tancredi's symbolic function for Clorinda as enemy
and savior. After the battle Tancredi gives life to the slain Clorinda:

> vita con l'acqua a chi co 'l ferro uccise.   (XII, 68)

Death and life are balanced in the centrally located, single pronoun
"chi."

The battle is filled with many rhetorical expressions, such as, "l'uno e
l'altro" and "questi e quegli," the uniting of the two warriors in the

action of a verb, such as *"e questi e quegli* al fin pur si ritira,"* and, then, the narcissistic mirror image in "L'un l'altro guarda, e del suo corpo essangue/ su 'l pomo de la spada appoggia il peso." In these two verses "l'uno e l'altro" have been drawn even closer together. Although "L'un l'altro guarda" remains a subject-object relation, the impersonality of the repeated pronouns has effected a deeper unity. It's as if Tasso had already provided for the composer and choreographer the greater degree of abstraction which their arts require.

This triadic structure in which two antithetical elements are identified in what becomes a third element is present even in simple verses such as one describing the stability of the foot and the motion of the hand in battle: *"sempre* è il piè fermo e la man *sempre* 'n moto,"* 55. The verse seems to join the polarized elements in "sempre." The contrasts and antitheses are infused into the texture of the episode. When Clorinda refuses to reveal her identity and thus unconsciously affirms for the last time the mystery of hidden and ambiguous identities which has so many times saved her life, a paradoxical motivation from her enemy-lover brings on her death blow which, ironically, is at the same time her salvation:

> "il tuo dir e 'l tacer di par m'*alletta.*"   (XII, 61)

Again the antithesis ("dir/tacer") is joined in the action of a singular finite verb ("alletta"). In reference to Clorinda, "rubella" and "ancella," the paradoxical aspects of her nature, are joined in chiastic rhyme (65). After the battle Tancredi still sees his condition as paradoxical ("e da me stesso/ sempre fuggendo, avrò me sempre appresso," 77), though with a difference I shall consider later in my essay.

All of the rhetorical expressions I have referred to in the Tancredi-Clorinda battle—generalized expressions such as "l'uno e l'altro," the joining of the two antithetical elements in a verb or a repeated word or through rhyme, and the symmetry of a divided endecasyllabic verse—these rhetorical elements are repeated many times, not only in this central episode but throughout the whole poem. The function of this episode is largely interpretative. Through it we see the battle between pagans and Christians on a microscopic level, and by describing it Tasso is not only bringing the light of the sun to the dark and mysterious fortune of these two lovers; his whole poem is meant to enlighten the equally mysterious and more obviously theodical meaning of the larger battle between the Christian and pagan armies. That *Gerusalemme liberata* can be interpreted through the paradoxes and resolutions of this episode is understood when we discover the same language and poetic devices throughout the poem. The larger war is cloaked in similar mysteries. Indeed, in the middle of the Clorinda-Tancredi battle, when Tancredi takes pride in his marks against the unknown enemy, Tasso reminds us of the backdrop of a world of illusion, deception and paradox which he draws for this particular episode as well as for the whole poem:

Ne gode e superbisce. Oh nostra folle
mente ch'ogn'aura di fortuna estolle!

Misero, di che godi? Oh quanto mesti
fiano i trionfi ed infelice il vanto!   (XII, 58–59)

VI.   *Sotto mentito aspetto*

In his *Allegory* of *Gerusalemme liberata* Tasso informs the reader that he thought of himself as following Homer's *Iliad* in dividing the nature of his epic hero among several characters.[9] What Tasso adds to this Homeric technique and seems to be a characteristic of baroque literature is that he also develops within his characters various degrees of awareness of the function of illusion and evil within their lives and the world as well as degrees of awareness of the theodical relationship between love and war, Christians and pagans and good and evil. We have already seen Goffredo using illusion consciously. Tancredi, in his battle with Clorinda, becomes increasingly aware of a paradox within himself and life in general. At first, in the line already quoted, he seems to be angered by the darkness in which he is kept and the paradox which assails him and, formulating this paradox, blurts it out enraged at Clorinda: "il tuo dir e 'l tacer di par m'alletta." The dramatic effect of this statement within the context of the poem is magnificent. Tancredi's anger exceeds its cause in Clorinda's silence, and the formulation of that anger, in that it prefigures the outcome of their tragic battle, seems to indicate that Tancredi is here beginning to sense the mystery and horror of the battle in which he is engaged. After the battle and its terrifying revelation (that Tancredi's role as lover and enemy, savior and destroyer, are one), he seems to accept the imponderable mystery of his own nature: "e da me stesso/ sempre fuggendo avrò me sempre appresso." However, the very image of these lines, involving flight, indicates the limitations with which Tancredi has understood and accepted his nature, his fate and his identity.

Erminia, in both her own awareness and that which she affords the reader of the function of illusion and paradox in *Gerusalemme liberata*, represents a further development over Tancredi. In the Tancredi-Clorinda battle the reader enjoys a degree of knowledge over Tancredi. He realizes that Tancredi's enemy is Clorinda. Tancredi's angry and agonized statements during and after the battle indicate what his reaction would have been if he had been conscious of his dual identity as lover and enemy. In many respects Erminia may be considered an emanation of the Tancredi-Clorinda conflict on a higher level of cognizance. The moment in which Erminia most clearly expresses a paradoxical relation between life and death is her discovery of Tancredi's almost lifeless body while returning to the Christian camp: simultaneous and timeless gain and loss.

e trovando ti perdo eternamente.   (XIX, 105)

Tancredi is still prostrate from his battle with Argante, who, although he was in this case the real enemy and not the beloved, nevertheless engaged Tancredi in a battle as ambiguous as the one with Clorinda. Erminia, like Clorinda in the Tancredi-Clorinda battle, is about to take her final refuge in the Christian camp. These parallels are not fortuitous, as is demonstrated by Erminia's statement which could almost serve as an epigram for the Tancredi-Clorinda battle and Tasso's tragic view of life.

Erminia's story begins with the first conflict between Argante and Tancredi in Canto VI, and it ends here after the final defeat of Argante. After that we hear nothing else of her, but there is no need to. Like the Fool in Shakespeare's *King Lear,* she disappears once her function in the narrative is over. The battle between Tancredi and Argante, between Christians and pagans, has been going on within Erminia. Her movements between the Christian and pagan camps are symbolic of this internal struggle, and with the final victory of Tancredi and the defeat of Argante her story is over.

In this first battle between Tancredi and Argante in Canto VI the techniques which are used later in the Tancredi-Clorinda battle to draw parallels between lover and enemy, Christian and pagan, as well as to identify and confuse their identities, are already present:

quinci Tancredi e *q̈uindi* Argante *venne.*   (VI, 40)

L'uno e l'altro cavallo in guisa urtosse
che non fur poi cadendo a sorger pronti.   (VI, 41)

Cautamente *ciascuno* a i colpi *move*
la destra, a i guardi l'occhio, a i passi il piede.   (VI, 42)

giunta or piaga a la piaga, ed onta a l'onta.   (VI, 45)

In this battle between Argante and Tancredi, however, Tasso extends the parallel structure between individual Christian and pagan to the whole two camps. Just as in "il tuo *dir* e il tuo *tacer* m'*alletta*" the two opposites are joined in the grammatically inconsistent singular verb, so does Tasso join both camps in a parallel structure and, again, a grammatically inconsistent singular verb.[10] (In both cases, by using "alletta" instead of "allettano" and "pende" instead of "pendono," the effect is to emphasize the parallel and identification between the two opposites.):

Questo popolo e quello incerto pende
da sí nuovo spettacolo ed atroce,
e fra tema e speranza il fin n'attende,
mirando or ciò che giova, or ciò che noce.   (VI, 49)

Here not only are the two sides paralleled and joined, but the singular subject is continued and we see *one* side oscillating between two points (fear and hope) according to the developments of the battle. In fact, of course, the two different camps oscillate separately between opposite ends. The introduction of Erminia at this point, when the battle is interrupted because of the approaching night, is one of the most obvious moments in *Gerusalemme liberata* suggesting that the whole battle between pagans and Christians can be read allegorically as the progress toward the personal salvation of an individual or individuals and that the pagans represent the tensional evil encountered during the individual's pilgrimage. Tasso states as much in his *Allegory*. Here is one of the places in the poem where it is poetically realized. We have seen the two opposite camps described as if they were one, oscillating with the fortunes of the battle. As Erminia looks down on the battle, she seems to become that one: a personification of the stylistic technique:

Ma piú di ciascun altro a cui ne cale,
la bella Erminia n'ha cura e tormento,
che da i giudizi de l'incerto Marte
vede pender di sé la miglior parte.   (VI, 55)

Even the same verb, "pende," with which Tasso had unified the two camps, is repeated. The effect is extraordinarily subtle. What Tasso could not do fully even by unifying the two camps through prosody is accomplished in Erminia. The internalization of conflict is carried even further in that Canto VI progresses toward an elaborate description (70–78) of the debate which takes place within Erminia between honor and love when she is struck with the idea of joining the enemy: "entro al suo core/ duo potenti nemici, Onore e Amore," 70. This is, of course, just one of the many antithetical conflicts in the poem. But it can also be seen, more specifically, as an internalization of the conflict involved in the seduction by Armida of Goffredo's soldiers in Canto IV. They are seduced from the honor of their holy war. In both cases, profane love wins toward an eventually fortuitous outcome.

Beginning with the Olindo and Sofronia episode a major aspect of the symbolic content of *Gerusalemme liberata* is that of a mask or one person disguised behind the appearance of another. Behind the mild-mannered Sofronia known to all the inhabitants of Jerusalem is the vigorous defender of the faith. Behind the figure of Clorinda-as-enemy, who burned down the Christian tower, is Clorinda as Christian and as beloved. Tancredi himself has dual identity as enemy-lover or savior-destroyer. But these figures are in general unconsciously disguised. It is fate which reveals their binary identities and uses illusion to work out their destinies. Erminia objectifies this. She assumes the disguise of Clorinda in order to escape the pagan city and join the Christians, not on a mission of war, as her disguise would suggest, but on a mission of love. Erminia-the-lover disguised as Clorinda-the-warrior is a powerful symbol for *Gerusalemme liberata*. Its full significance is revealed very slowly: not only does Erminia use deception to fulfill a desire which will finally unite her with the Christians after the Tancredi-Argante battle, but the illusion or disguise she uses—that of a pagan warrior—enables us to see the whole pagan camp and the war itself as an if not indistinguishable at least essential aspect of the Christians and their final victory.

VII.   *Securi fra l'arme*

Episodes involving Erminia seem more than others to lend themselves to allegorical interpretations. We have seen that the conflict between Argante and Tancredi is internalized within Erminia. This internal conflict mirrors the fight between Tancredi and Clorinda with a higher degree of awareness. Lover and enemy are one. The enemy must die in order to free the lover. Clorinda the warrior dies as Tancredi the enemy dies, and Tancredi the lover and Clorinda the saved Christian soul are born at once. But the enemy-lover in the battle Erminia is watching is not hidden behind another appearance (at least not in the conventional and obvious sense), but is actually a member of the enemy Christian camp. Significantly, therefore, Tancredi is never really freed to become Erminia's lover. But if Erminia internalizes in the light of consciousness the struggle which Tancredi was fighting as lover and enemy, she also—after assuming her disguise and escaping to the enemy camp—projects the paradox of her own situation as a lover disguised as a warrior onto the battle between Christian and pagans. This is most powerfully expressed when, having arrived at the enemy camp, the disguised Erminia finds beauty, new breath, comfort, peace in the middle of the enemy's tents and arms:

> Poi rimirando il campo ella dicea:
> "O belle a gli occhi miei tende latine!
> Aura spira da voi che mi ricrea
> e mi conforta pur che m'avicine;
> così a mia vita combattuta e rea
> qualche onesto riposo il Ciel destine,
> come in voi solo il cerco, e solo parmi
> che trovar pace io possa in mezzo a l'armi.   (VI, 104)

Echoing Olinda at the stake, Erminia goes on to reflect that here in war she finds the "pietà" which seemed to have been promised to her in love.

And so the camp, the arms, the war become a part of Erminia's love, or, more exactly, are identified with the disguise which Erminia has assumed. Much later in the poem, XIX, 83, Erminia re-invokes the paradox of her prison-happiness and war-freedom. Even in the very first canto of the poem, the instruments of war had been identified with happiness:

> Il dí seguente, allor ch'aperte sono
> del lucido oriente al sol le porte,
> di trombe udissi e di tamburi un suono,
> ond'al camino ogni guerrier s'essorte.
> Non è sí grato a i caldi giorni il tuono
> che speranza di pioggia al mondo apporte,
> come fu caro a le feroci genti
> l'altero suon de' bellici instrumenti.   (I, 71)

When Erminia is first introduced, her motif of hiding under a cloak of hatred is presented immediately. She purposefully confuses the wounds of war and of love. When Erminia identifies Tancredi for Aladino, she has to hide her obvious emotion:

> Poi gli dice infingevole, e nasconde
> sotto il manto de l'odio altro desio:
> "Oimè! bene il conosco, ed ho ben donde
> fra mille riconoscerlo deggia io,
> ché spesso il vidi i campi e le profonde
> fosse del sangue empir del popol mio.
> Ahi quanto è crudo nel ferire! a piaga
> ch'ei faccia, erba non giova od arte maga.   (III, 19)

Demonstrating how closely linked, in regard to theoretical content, all the pairs of the poem are, it is immediately after Erminia has hidden her love for Tancredi under feigned hatred and a sigh escapes her ("e fuor n'uscí con le sue voci estreme/ misto un sospir che 'ndarno ella già preme" 20) that Tancredi first (within the poem) encounters Clorinda in the field. Accidentally her helmet falls off and, not unlike Erminia's sigh and "pace fra l'arme," his beloved appears to Tancredi in the middle of battle:

> e le chiome dorate al vento sparse,
> giovane donna in mezzo 'l campo apparse.   (III, 21)

Erminia has only love for Tancredi and her hatred (like Clorinda's cloak) is a disguise, an expedient, a means. Clorinda will die as the saved (in the Christian sense) beloved of Tancredi, and her role as pagan warrior in comparison with the vision of beauty on the war field is metaphorically parallel to Erminia's disguise and pretense of hatred in comparison with the love her sigh reveals. It is precisely here that Tancredi asks Clorinda to go off with him to fight, and, when they are alone, declares his love.

But they are caught up by the battle. Once they are separated, Clorinda engages in battle with the confusion in roles that we have already noted in the Argante-Tancredi battle:

> or si volge or rivolge, or fugge or fuga,
> né si può dir la sua caccia né fuga.   (III, 31)

The hidden identities of the pairs of lovers are diffused into the battle between Christians and pagans. This scene, in which Tancredi's proclamation of love is suddenly interrupted when they are caught up in the sea of battle (Clorinda disappears almost as suddenly as she appeared), demonstrates the identity between the microcosmic and macrocosmic battles.

The closer one reads *Gerusalemme liberata*, the more obvious becomes the metaphorical connection between Erminia's hostile disguise in comparison with what her sigh of love for Tancredi reveals and Clorinda's role as pagan warrior in comparison with Tancredi's vision of her. The same metaphor may be extended to the battle between Christians and pagans as a whole. Of course, the pagans are not Christians in disguise in any simple or complicated sense. But they are identified with illusion, deception and evil, and, as I shall demonstrate in my discussion of the Armida and Rinaldo relationship, the enemy's mirroring of these evils for the individual heroes and the Christians as a whole permits the Christians finally to recognize and overcome their own weaknesses. Some of the aspects of the poem which I have already discussed have a significant parallel in the general war between Christians and pagans, and it will be helpful to point them out before discussing Armida and the enchanted forest: two major manifestations of illusion in the poem. Dynamics which may be only a *liebestod* metaphor for the lovers become a full-blown myth—the theodical baroque myth—in the general context of the poem.

VIII. *Movon concordi*

Nowhere in *Gerusalemme liberata* is there a stronger sense of an Augustinian "aesthetic plenitude" than in the elaborately choreographed larger battles between pagan and Christian armies. And, making the bridge to another essential aspect of Augustinian theodicy (the non-metaphysical or illusory aspect of evil), war is frequently compared in one sense or another to illusion: At the beginning of the poem Goffredo addresses himself to the Christians saying that God will guide them:

> e securi fra l'*arme* e fra gl'*inganni*.   (I, 21)

In Canto IV, the evil counselors of hell plan to use both the force of arms and deception, alternately, against the Christians:

fra loro entrate, e in ultimo lor danno
or la *forza* s'adopri ed or l'*inganno*.   (IV, 16)

The effects of "forza" and "inganno" are frequently similar. We have
seen in the initial Olindo-Sofronia episode that "inganno" brought them
together in a sort of love-death duet. In an almost symmetrical parallel
toward the end of *Gerusalemme liberata* another pair is brought together
in a love-death duet which is not without symbolic significance in the
poem. This time it is war and not deception which brings the two lovers
together. Gildippe and Odoardo, unlike Olindo and Sofronia, are married. They fight together against the enemy, and their story is infused
with images not unrelated to those in the earlier Olindo-Sofronia episode
as well as other episodes of the poem. Coming to the aid of Christians
being destroyed by Solimano, Gildippe herself receives a fatal blow. This
blow is described as having entered a region proper only to the arrows of
love:

> percossa temeraria e fera
> ch'osò, rompendo, ogn'arme, entrar nel seno
> che de' colpi d'Amor segno sol era.   (XX, 96)

There are significant resonances in the description of Odoardo coming to
Gildippe's aid. What had distinguished Tancredi was an almost schizo-
phrenic split between his roles as lover and warrior. The *contraposto*
position Odoardo takes when he is torn between attending to Gildippe
and avenging her on Solimano is almost emblematic of Tancredi's
schism:

> Ira e pietade
> a varie parti in un tempo l'affretta:
> questa a l'appoggio del suo ben che cade,
> quella a pigliar del percussor vendetta.
> Amore indifferente il persuade
> che non sia l'ira o la pietà negletta.
> Con la sinistra man corre al sostegno,
> l'altra ministra ei fa del suo disdegno.   (XX, 97)

It is this dualism in both Tancredi and Rinaldo which renders them
ineffective in the war (Rinaldo only temporarily), and the same division
is attributed to Odoardo in the following stanza:

> Ma voler e poter che si divida
> bastar non può contra il pagan sí forte
> tal che non sostien lei, né l'omicida
> de la dolce alma sua conduce a morte.
> Anzi avien che 'l Soldano a lui recida
> il braccio, appoggio a la fedel consorte,
> onde cader lasciolla, ed egli presse
> le membra a lei con le sue membra stesse.   (XX, 98)

However, all the lovers in the poem achieve at least a paradoxical unity or victory, and Gildippe and Odoardo are no exceptions; but their exile is more tragic than that suffered by their predecessors:

l'un mira l'altro, e l'un pur come sòle
si stringe a l'altro, mentre ancor ciò lece:
e si cela in un punto ad ambi il die,
e congiunte se 'n van l'anime pie.   (XX, 100)

It is clear from even these few examples how war and illusion are related in Tasso's poem. But what is the symbolic end toward which he uses the war between pagans and Christians? In considering the war between Christians and pagans and the language which is used to describe it, I have taken most of my examples from Cantos XIX and XX, which, unlike the other cantos of the poem, are almost totally devoted to the battle. In these canti the battle reaches a climax and conclusion. A few of my examples are from Canto IX, a large part of which is devoted to the battle, and from other sections of the poem.

The juxtaposition of episodes and characters is not accidental in *Gerusalemme liberata*, as we saw when the initial conflict between Argante and Tancredi was transposed to a conflict within Erminia. As Tasso is about to devote his full attention to the battle between Christians and pagans and to its climax in the last two cantos, he returns to the long-delayed continuation of the Argante-Tancredi battle which had been delayed by Erminia, Clorinda and Armida, as well as by the enchanted forest. Significantly, just as the first encounter between Argante and Tancredi had been transposed to a conflict within Erminia, Erminia is present at their next and final conflict, and the ultimate confusion between the Christian and pagan warrior is mirrored within her mind.

Both disguises and the darkness of night are essential accompaniments to the fulfillment of something essential in Erminia, Tancredi and Clorinda. A warlike disguise and the night allow Erminia to find peace among the enemy tents and war machines, and it is only the hiding of identity through the dark of night that allows Tancredi to assume his dual role as enemy and lover, destroyer and savior, in regard to Clorinda, who has herself been constantly saved through disguises. As Tancredi and Argante meet and go off to battle, the parallelism of their initial encounter—a balance so important to Tasso's description of the pagan and Christian forces—is repeated:

movon concordi a la gran lite il passo.   (XIX, 6)

As Tancredi draws Argante away from the Christians in order to keep him for private battle, we are reminded of Clorinda's safety amid the enemy, if not Erminia's peace among the war machines:

sí che salvo il nimico infra gli amici
tragge da l'arme irate e vincitrici.   (XIX, 7)

The darkness (suggested in "ombrosa") and hidden identities—here described as "secreti avolgimenti"—of the Tancredi-Clorinda duel are also present:

Escon de la cittade e dan le spalle
a i padiglion de le accampate genti,
e se ne van dove un girevol calle
li porta per secreti avolgimenti;
e ritovano ombrosa angusta valle.   (XIX, 8)

Within the battle the familiar rhetorical balances and paradoxes prevail (the resolution of two binary elements—"due legni ineguali"—in a third element—"egual si mira"):

fra due legni ineguali egual si mira,   (XIX, 13)

and depersonalizing words, such as "l'un 'laltro," are also present:

l'un calcò l'altro e l'un l'altro recinse.   (XIX, 17)

The entire poem's obsession with pressing opposites into "un tempo" or "un sol punto," which I shall consider later, is also present here:

Tai fur gli avolgimenti e tai le scosse
ch'ambi in *un tempo* il suol presser co 'l fianco.   (XIX, 18)

Ma come a l'Euro la frondosa cima
piega e in un tempo la solleva il pino,   (XIX, 19)

The episode's repetition of the word "avolgimenti" reminds the reader of the Tancredi-Clorinda battle and the poem's theme of confused identities joined in some mysterious purpose. Life and death, if they are not paradoxically joined, as in Clorinda's death, are at least compared:

Moriva Argante, e tal moria qual visse.   (XIX, 26)

Finally, at the conclusion of the battle, the identity of the two is left confused:

Al fin isviene; e 'l vincitor dal vinto
non ben saria nel rimirar distinto.   (XIX, 28)

This confusion is further emphasized when later in the canto Erminia stumbles onto the battle scene and onto Tancredi—imagining him to be dead:

Dopo gran tempo i' ti ritrovo a pena,
Tancredi, e ti riveggio e non son vista:
vista non son de te benché presente,
e trovando ti perdo eternamente.   (XIX, 105)

The allegoric content in Tancredi's paradoxical role as enemy and lover and Erminia's disguise is present in the Tancredi and Argante battle and in the larger Christian and pagan conflict which follows. I have, in discussing the former episodes, been mostly concerned with this allegoric content. Tasso depends upon these episodes to carry the meaning of his poem, and it is mostly the similarities in language I have just indicated which link them with the general war.

It has been observed that the most natural division of the hendecasyllabic verse (not only in Italian but in romance languages in general) is into almost symmetrical halves of balanced content and prosody.[11] Although *Gerusalemme liberata* contains many such symmetrical verses (for example, the description of Goffredo responding to Gabriel, "d'occhi abbagliato, attonito di core," I, 17), they are far from typical of the poem's poetry. In most cases, the two parts of the verse contain contrasts which are linked only by the prosody. For example, Solimano says to the pagans that the Christian's arms are now a pagan prize rather than a Christian defense:

"preda fian vostra, e non difesa loro."   (IX, 17)

These binary contrasts in the verse of *Gerusalemme liberata* are related to the paradoxical identities of lover and enemy, Christian and pagan in the poem. Even in the last-quoted line, however simple, the echoes of the microcosmic Clorinda-Tancredi battle are clear. Her arms, in an obvious sense, become Tancredi's spoils. But if their identification in the verse says something further, it is that Clorinda's arms—which performed the service of hiding her identity from Tancredi and thus enabled him to kill her—are the spoils of a greater salvation for her.

Critics have observed that more typical of Tasso's verse (especially in *Gerusalemme liberata*) and of baroque verse in general than the symmetrical division so prevalent in Petrarch is enjambement.[12] In a verse such as the one just quoted, "Ma come a l'Euro la frondosa cima/ piega e in un tempo la solleva il pino," XIX, 19, the enjambement serves to further unify the two contrary actions of bending and lifting ("piega" and "solleva"). When Rinaldo is about to initiate the action that will finally end the war, Goffredo tells him to defeat the enchanted forest and monsters in harm of the enemy but for the Christian's advantage:

e 'n *danno* de' nemici e 'n *pro* de nostri
vincer convienti de la selva i mostri.   (XVIII, 2)

The symmetrical division of the "pro" and "danno" of the first verse are joined in the "vincer" of the second. Enjambement is not the only or the most prevalent means by which Tasso joins binary antinomies in *Gerusalemme liberata*. Frequently, as I have pointed out in discussing the initial Argante-Tancredi battle, the two (opposites already depersonalized by words such as "questi" or "l'un l'altro") are joined in a singular verb ("e questi e quegli al fin pur si *ritira*"). Occasionally, a verb is placed in the middle of a verse, thereby disrupting its symmetry, and is allowed to serve for two separate clauses. For example, Armida describes herself as enemy and lover, equally conquered and despised in both roles. In my discussion of Armida I shall elaborate a parallel between these two roles which resembles Tancredi's dual role as enemy-lover:

> e *inerme* io *vinta sono*, e *vinta armata:*
> nemica, amante, egualmente sprezzata.   (XX, 66)

These characteristics of the poem's prosody, as well as others, all serve to underline the paradox which is more clearly seen in Tancredi's dual role. In the action of the poem, in Tancredi's act of killing Clorinda, his roles are inextricably and mysteriously linked.

Earlier I observed how Clorinda and Tancredi, during their first encounter within the poem, were suddenly dissolved into the texture of the general battle. At the conclusion of the Tancredi and Argante battle in Canto XIX which initiates the final battle between Christians and pagans, there is a subtle link between the individual and general battles. At the end of the former it had been difficult to distinguish victor from vanquished: "Al fin isviene; e 'l vincitor dal vinto/ non ben saria nel rimirar distinto," 28. These lines are followed by an initial description of the general battle ("Mentre qui segue la solinga guerra," 29), which, almost immediately, confuses victor and vanquished in a life-death emblem:

> là i feriti su i morti, e qui giacieno
> sotto morti insepolti egri sepolti.   (XIX, 30)

The parallelism between the individual and larger battle is clear. The general battle is consistently (even at the beginning of the poem) described in verse forms and language similar to what I have been describing in the individual battles:

> Né la gente fedel piú che l'infida,
> né piú questa che quella il campo tinge,
> ma gli uni e gli altri, e vincitori e vinti,
> egualmente dan morte e sono estinti.   (IX, 51)

Through repetition, the depersonalization of the opposing camps ("questa" and "quella" still refer specifically but it is difficult to tell to what "gli uni" and "gli altri" refer) becomes a close identification of the two, further strengthened by the singular verbs ("il campo tinge") and anonymous comparisons ("*egualmente* dan morte e son estinte"). The next stanza totally and very beautifully depersonalizes and identifies the opposing forces through naturalistic imagery and pure mirror or echo reflections (i.e., "scudo a scudo," etc.):

Come pari d'ardir, con forza parte
quinci Austro in guerra vien, quindi Aquilone,
non ei fra lor, non cede il cielo o 'l mare,
ma nube a nube e flutto a flutto oppone;
così né ceder qua, né là piegare
si vede l'ostinata aspra tenzone:
s'affronta insieme orribilmente urtando
scudo a scudo, elmo a elmo e brando a brando.   (IX, 52)

In the final battle of Canto XX, the image of Argante and Tancredi is repeated, and depersonalization is achieved by calling both sides "nemico" (as, of course, they are to each other):

giace il nemico appo il nemico, e spesso
su 'l morto il vivo, il vincitor su 'l vinto.   (XX, 51)

These repeated mirror images become very much a part of the fabric of the poem. Their full meaning is revealed, as we shall see, in what we could consider the allegoric epiphany of the Rinaldo-Armida episode.

There is also a certain symmetry in the action of the pagan and Christian camps. Canto IX begins with a description of the Christians fleeing. It ends with the pagans fleeing. The reader is reminded in this enlarged reflection of the description of Clorinda's flight in Canto III: "or si volge o rivolge, or fugge o fuga, ne si può dir la sua caccia ne fuga," 31. In Canto XI a rather elaborate description of both sides praying and preparing for war could be worked out, and in Canto XII Christians and pagans are both described repairing their war machines and caring for the wounded. Even Armida, during the course of the poem, is seen seeking aid in both camps.

It should be pointed out that the beauty and peace which Erminia finds on the battlefield and which could be compared with the sudden revelation in the middle of battle to Tancredi of Clorinda's beauty (III, 21) or with Erminia's sigh of love has a parallel in the general war. There are several instances in which the armies, war camps and war machines appear as scenes of great beauty. There is a very simple instance in the first canto of the poem where Tasso compares the happiness of the Christian soldiers at the sound of war trumpets and their promise of battle to the happiness of warm days at the sound of thunder and its promise of rain.

Non è sí grato a i caldi giorni il tuono
che speranza di pioggia al mondo apporte,
come fu caro a le feroci genti
l'altero suon de' bellici instrumenti.   (I, 71)

Canto XX, Tasso's major description of the general war, contains perhaps the most significant of these aesthetic beautifications of war. After a description of the armies lined up, in the usual depersonalized language ("*quando quel* campo e *questo* a fronte venne," XX, 28) which is further transformed into naturalistic language ("Sembra d'alberi densi alta foresta *l'un* campo e *l'altro*," 29), Tasso evokes the beauty of the scene in a stanza which is typical and significant because of its antithetical language:

> Bello in sí bella vista anco è l'orrore,
> e di mezzo la tema esce il diletto.
> Né men le trombe orribili e canore
> sono a gli orecchi lieto e fero oggetto.
> Pur il campo fedel, benché minore,
> par di suon piú mirabile e d'aspetto,
> e canta in piú guerriero e chiaro carme
> ogni sua tromba, e maggior luce han l'arme.   (XX, 30)

This paradoxical beauty in horror is like the joy Erminia experiences amid the enemy tents. Here it is evoked along with the paradox that the smaller army makes the better show. And it is difficult to find in the cultural traditions available to Tasso a source—not to say justification—for this vision of beauty in horror other than the "aesthetic plentitude" of Augustine's theodicy.

At the beginning of this essay, I discussed the backdrop of a world of mutability in which the action of the poem takes place. At the point in Canto II, and in the whole poem, where the two opposing camps are most indistinguishably joined,

> giace il compagno appo il compagno estinto,
> giace il nemico appo il nemico, e spesso
> su 'l morto il vivo, il vincitor su 'l vinto,   (XX, 51)

at this point, the most startling and carefully described mutation in the poem takes place. With words like "apparia" and "sembianza" and sudden leaps between the past and present tense, Tasso describes the metamorphosis of the beauty of the war scene into a vision of horror:

> L'arme, che già sí liete in vista foro,
> faceano or mostra paventosa e mesta:
> perduti ha i lampi il ferro, i raggi l'oro,
> nulla vaghezza a i bei color piú resta.
> Quanto apparia d'adorno e di decoro
> ne' cimieri e ne' fregi, or si calpesta;
> la polve ingombra ciò ch'al sangue avanza,
> tanto i campi mutata avean sembianza.   (XX, 52)

Tancredi's individual quest in the poem also involves the identification of lover and enemy as one and horror at the realization of this identity. The essentially tragic nature of *Gerusalemme liberata* is revealed in the fact that the point of fullest identity or realization by its heroes, individual and collective, is with their opposite element and this identity is the nadir of their experience. It is Rinaldo's experience with Armida which most clearly illustrates this aspect of Tasso's poem.

IX.   *Narciso*

Gerusalemme liberata mixes episodes which are obviously meant to be allegorical with episodes, or parts of episodes, which are strictly narrative and have no function other than to keep the story moving or to expand it for the sake of aesthetic perfection. The episodes involving Rinaldo and Armida are particularly mixed in this sense. As their story is told by Tasso, it shows considerable psychological insight into the nature of romantic passion.[13] However, elements such as the fact that Rinaldo still feels sentimental involvement with Armida after he has learned that she is a "maga" who has seduced him deceptively or Armida's transformation from what is at times little more than a magical device into a woman in love are less satisfactory or convincing as story. In considering the Armida and Rinaldo episodes in regard to the use of illusion and beneficent evil, I am, as with the other episodes I have discussed, mostly concerned with allegory. Since the use of illusion is so central to the poem as a whole, those aspects of each episode which I have chosen to discuss are filled with echoes and references to the rest of the poem and are, I believe, closest to the heart of the matter. Therefore, even though I do not discuss the Armida and Rinaldo relationship in every detail, I do not feel that I distort it.

As soon as Armida is introduced in Canto IV, she is associated very strongly with the illusion, antitheses and paradoxes which are so central to the poem. Armida is the sorceress, the enchantress, the archetypal Circe figure of Tasso's epic, descended from Alcina in *Orlando Furioso*. However, she is a siren who bears a very particular relationship to the hero which involves a theodical metaphysics of narcissism, passion and redemption.

Armida is presented as the niece of Idroate, King of Damascus and a magician. Initially, her central motivation is to deceive Goffredo and the Christians into thinking that she is a young princess in distress whose life and kingdom are threatened by a cruel and ruthless uncle. She does this in order to enlist their aid and, thereby, divert their forces from the war in Jerusalem. Almost immediately this simple deception is given another dimension by the antinomies with which Armida tells her story and by which she is surrounded. She tells Goffredo that he should uplift ("sollevar") as well as overthrow ("atterrar," 41) peoples and that if he has taken kingdoms away from many, there would be equal glory in restoring hers ("e s'hai potuto a molti il regno tòrre/ fia gloria egual nel regno or mi riporre," 41). She was born on the same day her mother died ("giorno ch'a lei die *morte*, a me *natale*," 43), and her story contains reflections of the deceptive act in which she herself is engaged. She talks about the concealments of her uncle: "che 'l maligno suo pensiero interno/ celasse allor sotto contrario manto," 45, which is precisely what Armida herself is doing:

> e celò sí sotto mentito aspetto
> il suo pensier ch'altrui non diè sospetto.   (IV, 85)

Her uncle succeeded in deceiving the populace against her:

> Ch'avara fame d'oro e sete insieme
> del mio sangue innocente il crudo avesse,
> grave m'è sí; ma via piú il cor mi preme
> che 'l mio candido onor macchiar volesse.   (IV, 58)

And to recall our discussion of *Adorno inganno*, the beneficent effects of illusion (the ultimate effect of Armida herself) are hinted at in this introduction to Armida in that her false ("finto") tale brings true ("vere") tears: "Questo finto dolor da molti elice/ lagrime vere," 77. Armida herself is seen as the embodiment of change ("ma cangia a tempo atti e semblante," 87). The passion which she inspires in the Christians and which will inspire them to feign ("sotto manto"), in their turn, honor for lust is depicted in the final stanzas of Canto IV in the most antithetical terms possible: "le medicine e i mali," "in ghiaccio e in foco," "in riso e in pianto," and "fra paura e spene."

Gerusalemme liberata is almost exclusively devoted to Armida and Rinaldo from the end of Canto XIV, where Il Mago d'Ascalona narrates their love story, to the end of Canto XVIII, where, as a result of the strength earned by his purgation through Armida, Rinaldo disenchants the forest and initiates the assault on the walls of Jerusalem. By the beginning of Canto XIV Clorinda is dead, Erminia has disappeared from the action of the poem, except for her brief codalike appearance at the end, and Tancredi and Argante have only their final duel to perform. Rinaldo and Armida take on most of the narrative and allegorical meaning of these lovers and warriors. The introduction to their story is especially significant in both its form and content. At the beginning of Canto XIV Goffredo has a dream. During this dream he is advised to recall Rinaldo in order that he may free the enchanted forest. But the central vision of Goffredo's dream (already quoted) is of the illusion, vanity and folly of human aspirations:

> ed ammirò che pur a l'ombre, a i fumi,
> la nostra folle umanità s'affise,
> servo imperio cercando e muta fame,
> né miri il ciel ch'a sé n'invita e chiama.   (XIV, 11)

Dream, or the visions of the subconscious, is an important part of the Rinaldo and Armida story, and the content of Goffredo's dream, even the language in which it is expressed, is also repeated in the story of the two lovers.

All of the major characters of *Gerusalemme liberata* have dual characters or roles. And it is illusion which—despite its association with deception, evil, war—has allowed them to fulfill both roles and, thus, achieve their fullest identity and freedom: Erminia's peace among the war machines, Clorinda's salvation in Christianity, and Tancredi's dual role as lover and enemy. Rinaldo also has a dual character and role. On the surface he is the overly zealous leader of the Christian soldiers who allows some of his colleagues to follow Armida so that he himself will have a more central role in the battle. Beneath this surface (like Erminia beneath the armor of Clorinda) he is also the effeminate and lustful paramour of the enemy's sorceress. Certainly this latter role is subconscious, but it is only when it comes to the level of consciousness that Rinaldo is free to aid the Christians.

The darkness which surrounded Erminia's joy among the enemy and instruments of destruction and the loss of identity which surrounded Tancredi's fulfillment of himself as enemy as well as lover are seen in Rinaldo in something more like modes of the subconscious. The psychology is at once subtle in its meaning and associations and yet rather coarse, as is frequently the case with allegory in its surface representation. The concept and the image of something hidden ("ascosto")—like a repressed desire—dominates the episode. My association of the hidden, the repressed and the disguised with Clorinda's death is not gratuitous. Rinaldo is involved in both disguise and death. In his narrative at the end of Canto XIV, Il Mago d'Ascalona informs us that Rinaldo, in order to escape detection, had hidden his person with pagan armor, just as Clorinda had hidden herself among the Christians:

> Quivi egli avendo l'arme sue deposto,
> indosso quelle d'un pagan si pose;
> forse perché bramava irsene *ascosto*
> sotto insegne men note e men famose.   (XIV, 53)

The illusion of Rinaldo's death, which results from Armida's exposure of his own abandoned armor, is almost like a ritual death. It comes close to evoking civil war among the Christians, just as Clorinda's real death had awakened a war within Tancredi:

>   e di sospetto
> sparse quel seme in lor ch'indi nutrito
> fruttò risse e discordie, e quasi al fine
> sediziose guerre e cittadine.   (XIV, 55)

Indeed, in seducing Rinaldo, Armida puts him to sleep before the journey to her island—a sleep compared to death:

> né i tuoni omai destar, non ch'altri, il ponno
> da quella queta imagine di morte.   (XIV, 65)

And when Rinaldo's involvement with Armida is over, he comes out of it like someone emerging from sleep:

> Qual uom da cupo e grave sonno oppresso
> dopo vaneggiar lungo in sé riviene,
> tal ei tornò nel rimirar se stesso,
> ma se stesso mirar già non sostiene;
> giú cade il guardo, e timido e dimesso,
> guardando a terra, la vergogna il tiene.   (XVI, 31)

The concept of ritual death is important not only here but also in other parts of the poem where we have encountered the *appearance* of death, i.e., Tancredi as a mirror reflection of the dead Argante and the mirror images of "vincitori e vinti." An aspect of themselves has died giving life to something else. Recently the concept of ritual death in Tasso has received attention in the work of Paolo Braghieri,[14] but my own interest is to subordinate those elements to theodical concerns. Behind the whole poem lies the Christian concept of rebirth which Tasso states in Canto III:

> che se mori nel mondo, in Ciel rinasci.   (III, 68)

He also applied it to the war in Canto IX:

> ove se stesso il mondo strugge e pasce
> e ne le guerre sue more e rinasce.   (IX, 61)

Of course, what is happening to Rinaldo is an ironic version of this. His sleep and awakening are more in tune with Freudian conceptions. As his conscience is put to sleep, his character dies and he becomes the slave of his desires. In the extraordinary symbolic economy of the poem this is an inverse mirror reflection of Erminia's experience of liberation when she joins the enemy camp.

Indeed, the imagery of something hidden dominates the Armida-Rinaldo episode. We have seen that Rinaldo puts on the pagan armor "perche bramava irsene *ascosto*." When Armida falls in love with Rinaldo, he is sleeping, but even his closed eyes ("d'occhi *nascosi*," XIV, 67) conquer her. As the subconscious desires come to fruition through Armida, the consciousness must, as it were, remain asleep. Armida's island is described as an "*ascosa*/prigion," XIV, 71). On the island the girl who taunts Carlo and Ubaldo (come to rescue Rinaldo) is partially hidden by her hair and the water ("Cosí da l'acque e da' capelli *ascosa*," XV, 61), and a bird sings of the half-hidden beauty of the rose:

che mezzo aperta ancora e mezzo ascosa,
quanto si mostra men, tanto è piú bella. (XVI, 14)

Even Carlo and Ubaldo, who will bring Rinaldo back to consciousness, must remain hidden:

Ascosi
mirano i due guerrier gli atti amorosi. (XVI, 19)

Given the general theodical concerns of Tasso's epic, it is difficult not to read these references to the "ascoso" as related to the *Old Testament* concept of a hidden God which I discuss in my Prologue. There is some ambiguity in the imagery in *Gerusalemme liberata* because consciousness and subconsciousness frequently shift roles. But that is expected.

In fact, Rinaldo and Armida are related in the way that we have seen "vincitori e vinti," Argante and Tancredi and Clorinda and Erminia are related. There is an element of reflection or self-projection in their relationship. Narcissistic mirror imagery also dominates their episode. When Armida has stealthily captured Rinaldo and, looking at him asleep, first falls in love with him, the Narcissus myth is invoked:

e' n su la vaga fronte
pende omasi sí che par Narciso al fonte. (XIV, 66)

The myth and mirror imagery is evoked more strongly in Armida's garden:

Dal fianco de l'amante (estranio arnese)
un cristallo pendea lucido e netto.
Sorse, e quel fra le mani a lui sospese
a i misteri d'Amor ministro eletto.
Con luci ella ridenti, ei con accese,
mirano un vari oggetti un solo oggetto:
ella del vetro a sé fa specchio, ed egli
gli occhi di lei sereni a sé fa spegli. (XVI, 20)

I have several times referred to the triadic resolutions of the poem. In one of the most stunning such resolutions, Rinaldo and Armida see themselves in "un solo oggetto": she by looking at the glass and he by looking into her eyes. Significantly, there is some ambiguity in the "un solo oggetto." Although Rinaldo is looking at Armida and she is looking at herself in the glass, he also sees himself reflected in her eyes. Armida is a reflection of Rinaldo; he sees himself when he looks into her eyes. And in a sense it is only through Rinaldo that Armida exists at all; he holds the glass and contains the subconscious of which she is a reflection.

The dualism which modern criticism has found inherent in allegory,[15] and which I have elaborated in Tancredi, Clorinda and Erminia, is capable of more logical explanation in Rinaldo than in the other characters. If Erminia, in observing the Tancredi-Argante battle, carried the Tancredi dualism as lover and enemy to a higher degree of awareness, Rinaldo carries it even further. In the very first canto, Rinaldo is characterized as excessively desirous of honor ("spirti di riposo impazienti," "d'onor brame immoderate," 10). I have pointed out that he is totally unmoved by Armida's initial appeal to the Christian camp, whereas most of the other soldiers are deeply agitated by her. Even Goffredo sees the strength of her pleas. Such strong resistance, a psychological reading of Rinaldo's character would say, must be based on opposition, resistance to repressed inclinations. The subconscious and conscious elements of the character are, therefore, closely related and dependent on each other. Whether or not Rinaldo will bear this psychological reading, the relation between the two aspects of his character in their alternating movement is at least clear. After Rinaldo has been freed from Armida the identification is carried further. In language which evokes mirrorlike imagery, Armida says that she, once the scorner of Rinaldo, is now the scorned ("la tua schernitrice abbia schernito," XVI, 48); just as the words are unified in their root, so is Rinaldo related to Armida.

The poetic and linguistic expressions I have observed in the battle between Christians and pagans, Argante and Tancredi, are also present in the episodes involving Armida and Rinaldo. It would be redundant to rehearse them. They all serve to unite the two opposing elements or antitheses and to show them as aspects of each other, existing simultaneously in one person. The conscious and subconscious Rinaldo are also pictured iconographically. One of the emblems on the entrance to Armida's garden represents the fleeing/pursuing Antony:

> E fugge Antonio, e lasciar può la speme
> de l'imperio del mondo ov'egli aspira.
> Non fugge no, non teme il fier, non teme,
> ma segue lei che fugge e seco il tira.
> Vedresti lui, simil ad uom che freme
> d'amore a un tempo e di vergogna e d'ira,
> mirar alternamente or la crudele
> pugna ch'è in dubbio, or le fuggenti vele.   (XVI, 6)

This reminds the reader of the stance taken by Odoardo and the dying Gildippe and the weakening division of Tancredi's forces, as well as Odoardo's, between love and war.

X. *Colpe umane*

The lowest point in the heroes' quest in *Gerusalemme liberata* is identification with their opposite element, and it is illusion which brings them to this climax: the dark night which joins enemy and lover in Tancredi and in which Erminia flees disguised as Clorinda, the confusion of battle which joins Christian and enemy, and Rinaldo's subconscious or hidden desires. But we have come to expect that this confusion of identities works toward some purpose. This nadir is, paradoxically, the fullest identity which the heroes attain.

Rinaldo's experience with Armida enables him to free the enchanted forest, which initiates the victory and the end of the war for the Christians. It is, in part, what Rinaldo learns about evil that enables him. Tancredi had a parallel experience with Clorinda but did not achieve total regeneration. In considering the Tancredi-Clorinda battle, I discussed the phrase "L'un l'altro guarda" as central not only to that episode but to the whole poem. It is also—in its context—profoundly ironic. At that moment, although Tancredi and Clorinda look at each other they do not see each other completely. When Tancredi finally does see more clearly he exclaims: "Ahi vista! ahi conoscenza!" XII, 67. But even this recognition remains incomplete. The Tancredi-Clorinda battle contains manifestations in Tancredi's speech that he is becoming aware of a paradoxical reality:

"il tuo dir e 'l tacer di par m'alletta,"   (XII, 61)

"da me stesso
sempre fuggendo, avrò me sempre appresso."   (XII, 77)

However, despite the fact that Pietro l'Eremita (the Christian prophet of the poem) spells out for Tancredi the beneficent aspects of illusion and the fact that in killing Clorinda he not only effected her Christian salvation but his own ("e fa di tua salute/ te medesmo ministro," 87), Tancredi remains negative and doubtful. The incompleteness of Tancredi's regeneration is revealed several ways. He remains oriented toward death:

ciò che 'l viver non ebbe, abbia la morte."   (XII, 99)

He says this anticipating an eventual reunion with Clorinda. But it is his attempt to free the enchanted forest (especially as compared to Rinaldo's) which most clearly reveals the incompleteness of Tancredi's regeneration.

No single phenomenon or character (with the possible exception of Armida) is described more in terms of illusion and deception than the enchanted forest—the poem's radical theater. The words used throughout the poem to describe illusion—"simulacro," "apparenze," "sogno," "chimera," "le cagioni ascose," "falseggiando," "trasformando," "sembran," "fantasmi ingannevoli e bugiardi," "error," "i finti aspetti"—appear with exceptional density in the episodes involving the forest. When several of the foremost Christian warriors have failed in their attempt at the forest, Tancredi decides to confront it. But it is not a very resolute

Tancredi ("benché in volto sia languido e smorto," XIII, 32). In confronting the wall of flames which has turned back the others, Tancredi shows that he has learned something from his battle in the darkness of illusion:

> forse l'incendio che qui sorto i' vedo
> fia d'effetto minor che di sembianza.   (XIII, 35)

He gets through the illusory wall. Yet, when with his sword he confronts the tree which protests that it is Clorinda's spirit, Tancredi turns back. Undoubtedly, he betrays an incomplete faith in accepting this illusory post-mortem existence. However much Tasso borrowed the episode from Dante, it does not represent the Christian hell. What the episode seems to concentrate on is that although Tancredi has learned to be skeptical of appearance ("a pien non crede"), he has not fully absorbed the lesson ("e pur ne teme e cede"):

> Qual l'infermo talor ch'in sogno scorge
> drago o cinta di fiamme alta Chimera,
> se ben sospetta o in parte anco s'accorge
> che 'l simulacro sia non forma vera,
> pur desia di fuggir, tanto gli porge
> spavento la sembianza orrida e fera
> tal il timido amante a pien non crede
> a i falsi inganni, e pur ne teme e cede.   (XIII, 44)

Rinaldo seemingly goes through two purgations before he is able to conquer the enchanted forest: his experience with Armida and, when he returns to Jerusalem from Armida's island, his confession with Pietro l'Eremita and prayers and meditations on Mount Olive. After the latter there is the appropriate imagery of a new appearance in himself ("mutata vesta," XVIII, 17) which is to be complemented in the forest ("e sovra e intorno a lui la selva annose/ tutte parea ringiovenir le foglie," 23). However, the religious aspects of Rinaldo's purgation seem to be rather formal. They are not as intimately related to the rest of the poem as the concept and expression of Armida are.

Ironically, it is Armida herself who points out to Rinaldo the vanity of his overly zealous drive for fame:

> La fama che invaghisce a un dolce suono
> voi superbi mortali, e par sí bella,
> è un'ecco, un sogno, anzi del sogno un'ombra,
> ch'ad ogni vento si dilegua e sgombra.   (XIV, 63)

The irony is appropriate since it is Armida who, contrary to her purpose (but not the purpose for which she is used by fate), so completely frees Rinaldo from illusion that far from his initial arrogance he comes to recognize his own involvement in human sins and folly. In parting from Armida, he says:

Errasti, è vero, e trapassati i modi,
ora gli amori essercitando, or gli odi;

ma che? son colpe umane e colpe usate;
scuso la natia legge, il sesso e gli anni.
Ancho'io parte fallii; s'a me pietate
negar non vuo', non fia ch'io te condanni.   (XVI, 53, 54)

The narcissistic identification between Rinaldo and Armida is not lost here but finds expression in the recognition of evil as an endemic aspect of the human condition. And the tenderness of the recognition seems to ameliorate considerably the degree of suffering. If the rhetorical structures of Tasso's verse in binary descriptions of warriors and battles remind us most forcibly of an Augustinian sense of "aesthetic plenitude," here the theodical echo is more nearly an Irenaean sense of the forging of mature souls through suffering.

When Rinaldo approaches the forest, after the metamorphoses of himself and nature, he also encounters an appearance of Armida, and she suggests a return to their former mirroring situation:

"Togli questo elmo omai, scopri la fronte
e gli occhi a gli occhi miei, s'arrivi amico;
giungi i labri a le labra, il seno al seno,
porgi la destra a la mia destra almeno."   (XVIII, 32)

But Rinaldo's enlightenment has been complete. He attacks the "sembianza," which metamorphoses into a monster. Finally, the entire wood returns to its natural state, and Rinaldo closes the episode with:

                    "Oh vane
sembianze! e folle chi per vio rimane!"   (XVIII, 38)

Carrying the knowledge of sin and his own involvement in it, Rinaldo sees the enchanted forest not as "i campi stigi" but as a pastoral landscape. This is the most important of the landscapes or battlefields with dual identities, horrible or beautiful. At the end of the poem, when the Christians are victorious and Armida contemplates suicide, Rinaldo diverts her from this, thus bringing her life at the point of death. In yet another way, this links Rinaldo and Armida with the Tancredi and Clorinda, the Olindo and Sofronia, and the Gildippe and Odoardo episodes.

Knowledge of good and evil within the human condition seems, therefore, to be the unconscious goal of the heroes' quest in *Gerusalemme liberata*. We have seen this in Tancredi and Rinaldo. Just as Christian and pagan are paralleled in battle, there is a final mirror reflection in this aspect of the poem. The pagans share Rinaldo's vision. Perhaps the most eloquent expression of the human tragedy comes through Solimano

rather than one of the Christian soldiers.[16] In the middle of the final
battle, he climbs one of Jerusalem's towers and looks down on the battle
which he generalizes as the human condition:

> Or mentre in guisa tal fera tenzone
> è tra 'l fedel essercito e 'l pagano,
> salse in cima a la torre ad un balcone
> e mirò, benché lunge, il fer Soldano;
> mirò, quasi in teatro od in agone,
> l'aspra tragedia de lo stato umano:
> i vari assalti e 'l fero orror di morte,
> e i gran giochi del caso e de la sorte.   (XX, 73)

If the vision at which Rinaldo arrived seems to be mirrored here, the
deaths of Argante and Solimano are also significant in this regard. It is
emphasized that Argante falls, finally, by his own weight:

> Tu, dal tuo peso tratto, in giú co 'l mento
> n'andasti, Argante, e non potesti aitarte:
> per te cadesti, aventuroso in tanto
> ch'altri non ha di tua caduta il vanto.   (XIX, 24)

Solimano, rather than being defeated by the superior force of Rinaldo, is
conquered by his own resolutions; a sort of paralysis comes over him:

> Quante scintille in lui sorgon d'ardire,
> tante un secreto suo terror n'ammorza.   (XX, 106)

The balancing and paralleling of forces is present here, but they are both
within Solimano.

Perhaps one aspect of the significance of these self-inflicted defeats is
made clearer in the consideration of similar images used for Armida.
When Armida again sees Rinaldo in Canto XX during the final battle,
she is filled with ambivalent feeling ("con occhi d'ira e di desio tre-
manti," "ella si fa di gel, divien poi foco," 61). Even as she directs her
arrow at Rinaldo, she immediately repents. She would prefer to destroy
herself:

> Lo stral volò, ma con lo strale un voto
> súbito uscí, che vada il colpo a vòto.
>
> Torria ben ella che il quadrel pungente
> tornasse indietro, e le tornasse al core.   (XX, 63-64)

What we have here is the dualism permeating the entire poem. One thing
recalled in particular is the debate between love and honor which goes on
within Erminia in Canto VI. But Rinaldo has already conquered those of
his weaknesses represented in Armida, and he did it himself. To say that
Armida in the lines just quoted is a reflection of Rinaldo attacking

Armida in the enchanted forest or overcoming his own weaknesses is perhaps to overstrain Tasso's allegory. However, the poem offers little explanation for the force which paralyzes Solimano in his final fight with Rinaldo and which conquers Armida, and to understand it as a reflection of Rinaldo's self-conquest is in harmony with the major themes of the poem.

XI. Un sol punto

The poem's allegorical nature which makes the various characters reflections of one central figure is eloquently expressed in Solimano's vision of history as taking place within a theater or arena ("agone"). The one agon is ritualistically (in the sense that it not only embodies but effects) symbolic of the whole flux of history. This aspect of the poem, apart from the manifestations I have already considered in the major episodes, is specifically revealed in several ways.

The shepherd and his flock, the archetypal Christian metaphor for a ritualistically symbolic relationship between a leader and his followers, is a favorite with Tasso, and he uses it not only with the Christians but with the pagans as well (XIX, 47). Both Solimano (XIX, 56) and Goffredo (IX, 40-50) are described affecting their soldiers by their own example. In Canto XII the Christians' repair of the war damage occurs simultaneously with and seems to be related to the healing of Goffredo's wounds. Rinaldo, who initially stands apart from the weakness the Christian soldiers reveal toward Armida and the deceptions they practice for her, is gradually associated with this weakness and these deceptions. It is also typical and significant that Godfredo does not accept Tancredi's relativistic argument, when he suggests that Rinaldo, who has killed Gernando, be given special treatment (V, 37). In Canto I all of the crusaders are joined in a single will ("E questi, che son tutti insieme uniti/ con saldissimi lacci in un volere," 80). When the tyrant Aladino sees the direction in which the war is moving in Canto XIX, he associates his own death with the death of the kingdom in a verse form we have seen to be so typical of the poem (the two are linked in singular verb—"cade"):

> "e la mia vita e 'l nostro imperio cade.
> Vissi, e regnai; non vivo piú, né regno.
> Ben si può dir: 'Noi fummo.' A tutti è giunto
> l'ultimo dí, l'inevitabil punto."   (XIX, 40)

The "inevitabil punto" which Aladino evokes has many reverberations throughout the poem. I have quoted verses with the phrase "un sol punto" several times. It represents an even further concentration of both the tendency to join the various leaders and their followers and the paradoxical identity between the antitheses of the poem. All of the impersonalizing words, such as "l'un l'altro" and the poetic techniques associated with them, are pushing towards "un sol punto." Rinaldo and Goffredo come together to fight at this point ("chè da duo lati opposti in un sol punto/ il sopran duce e 'l gran guerriero è giunto," XIX, 46). From what I have said about the identity between leaders and followers, it could be guessed that both armies also come together. Goffredo tells the Christians before the final battle:

> ogni vostro nimico ha qui congiunto
> per fornir molte guerre in un sol punto.   (XX, 14)

Goffredo and Emireno come together with the impersonalizing "l'un verso l'altro": "in un medesmo punto/ l'un verso l'altro per ferir si lancia," XX, 139. After Tancredi has mortally wounded Clorinda and then recognized her (and his dual role), the moment in which he baptizes her is described as "quel punto" amid antitheses which are joined as usual:

> Non morì già, ché sue virtuti accolse
> tutte in quel punto e in guardia al cor le mise,
> e premendo il suo affanno a dar si volse
> vita con l'acqua a chi co 'l ferro uccise.   (XII, 68)

The ebb and flow of battle is described as taking place "in un momento," so that it is not specifically space which Tasso intends with the often repeated phrase:

> Cede chi rincalzò; chi cesse, or preme:
> così varian le cose in un momento.   (XX, 88)

Even Gildippe and Odoardo, whose dualistic final posture I described as almost emblematic of certain aspects of the poem, expire together "in un punto," XX, 100. In Goffredo's dream vision of the world as illusion, he sees it as "un punto sol":

> ché vide un punto sol, mar, terre e fiumi,
> che qui paion distinti in tante guise,   (XIV, 11)

as, indeed, does God at the very beginning of the poem:

> e in un sol punto e in una
> vista mirò ciò ch'in sé il mondo aduna.   (I, 7)

While in a work less allegorical than *Gerusalemme liberata*, such as Milton's *Samson Agonistes*, the tendency to identify the hero with both Hebrews and pagans is present, it is realized in a much less specific and physical way. They merely share moral attributes, and the conflicts and character of the hero are illustrated through their reflection in the world outside of him. In totally allegorical works, such as Calderón's *autos*, the whole action of the play is understood to take place within the mind of the hero.[17] All of nature is merely a reflection of his moral status, and nature totally metamorphoses at the slightest change in the hero. In Tasso's poem we have also seen the further impersonalization of "l'un l'altro" into nature imagery and the metamorphoses of nature to reflect, for example, Rinaldo's rebirth. Although in *Gerusalemme liberata* the Christian and pagan armies, forests, etc., do exist to some degree independently of the hero, it is undoubtedly in the direction of the *autos* that the endless repetition of "un sol punto" and everything it implies moves. Ultimately, the antinomies of good and evil and the paradoxes of a beneficent evil which are at the thematic core of *Gerusalemme liberata* are resolved in God, and Tasso's symbol of *un sol punto* is to the point. From the time of Plotinus it has been used to image God as a sphere of which the center is everywhere and the circumference nowhere. Indeed, Dante used the phrase *un sol punto* as a symbol for God internally possessed in a human moment, which as precisely as language can put it is the metaphysical goal of Tasso's poem.

XII. *Segni ignoti*

Much of the use of illusion in *Gerusalemme liberata* can be accounted for by the allegorical nature of the poem. Armida, the enemy, the enchanted forest, etc., are to some extent external manifestations of something within the heroes. As the hero changes so does this external reality. Reality will metamorphose with the internal changes of the hero. A hellish landscape of war machines will suddenly appear as a pastoral scene, and beneath the fearful war armor of Clorinda there is the gentle and beautiful Erminia. We will see this particular aspect of allegory greatly magnified in Calderón's *autos*. But there is another reason for the presence of so much illusion, paradox and antithesis in *Gerusalemme liberata*: Tasso's deference to the ultimately mysterious ways of fate and a step beyond the semi-logical explanations of theodicy. Like "un sol punto," this hidden or unknown element, this mystery, has many manifestations in Tasso's poem. Frequently, it is specifically referred to as in the "segni ignoti" (XIII, 39) or "le cagione ascose" (XIII, 47) of the enchanted forest. At these moments the distinction between the two parts of the antitheses—even if they are conflicting elements of the same character or fate—break down and they are identified in some mysterious purpose. Of course, when this happens, Tasso's poetry also ceases to be allegory or simply narrative and becomes, as modern criticism would have it, mythic.

Mario Fubini has pointed out Tasso's obsession with the "ignoto."[18] As Fubini demonstrates, a favorite moment in the day for Tasso is either dawn or sunset, when it is impossible to distinguish day from night as

they melt into each other. Rinaldo directs himself toward "l'Oliveto" in
this setting.

> quinci notturne e quindi mattutine
> bellezze incorrottibili e divine.   (XVIII, 12)

The enchanted forest creates the same effect:

> Qui, ne l'ora che 'l sol piú chiaro splende,
> è luce incerta e scolorita e mesta,
> quale in nubilo ciel dubbia si vede
> se 'l dí a la notte o s'ella a liu succede.   (XIII, 2)

The mysteriousness of this moment is frequently taken up by night itself,
which confuses the identity of other objects ("Sorgea la notte intanto, e de
le cose/ confondea i vari aspetti *un solo aspetto,*" XVII, 56). Most significantly, perhaps, it is the night which engulfs Tancredi and Clorinda
(XII, 54) and makes the escape of the disguised Erminia possible (VI, 89).
As *un sol punto* exists both in space and time, the mystery embodied in
this indistinguishability of sight seems to be captured in sound also. The
sounds of the forest are significant in this respect ("tanti e sí fatti suoni
un suono esprime," XVIII, 18), but the most haunting description is of
the "mormorio" heard when the Christians first see Jerusalem. It is a
sound which echoes both their joy and sadness ("in un s'allegra e
duole"), and in so doing seems to prophesy the rest of the poem and the
indefinable mysteries which will haunt it:

> Sommessi accenti e tacite parole,
> rotti singulti e flebili sospiri
> de la gente ch'in un s'allegra e duole,
> fan che per l'aria un mormorio s'aggiri
> qual ne le folte selve udir se suole
> s'avien che tra le frondi il vento spiri,
> o quale infra gli scogli o presso a i lidi
> sibila il mar percosso in rauchi stridi.   (III, 6)

In summary: Tasso's development of the theme of illusion and beneficent evil is manifold. While illusion is always associated with deception
and evil, Tasso's attitude toward it is ambivalent. This ambivalence is
explained by the fact that Tasso in his own baroque theodicy sees God
working mysteriously—using evil, deception, cruelty, suffering, war and
death toward beneficent ends. Even with this metaphysics, it is difficult
for the poet to embrace totally the powers of darkness. Therefore, he
shrouds his poem—thereby imitating the "hidden" God—in mystery
and confused and hidden identities. The allegorical tendency of the poem

further evolves the poet's attitude in that the evils of deception and war as they exist in the poem are not so much absolute realities in themselves as they are reflections of the moral experience of the central characters. Tasso is questioning the very nature of reality which he sees as the ultimate illusion.

MILTON

I am not of that seared impudence that I dare defend women, or pronounce them good; yet we see physicians allow some virtue in every poison.

Paradoxes and Problems, Donne

SAMSON
AGONISTES,

A
DRAMATIC POEM.

The Author
JOHN MILTON.

Arifot. Poet. Cap. 6.

Τραγωδια μίμησις πραξεως σπυδαίας, &c.

Tragœdia eſt imitatio actionis feriæ, &c. Per miſericordiam &
metum perficiens talium affectuum luſtrationem.

LONDON,

Printed by *J. M.* for *John Starkey* at the
Mitre in *Fleetſtreet*, near *Temple-Bar.*
MDCLXXI.

i

Title page from the London, 1671 edition. Courtesy of the Rare Book Division,
New York Public Library.

In discussing illusion and beneficent evil in Milton, I concentrate on *Samson Agonistes*. Based on an *Old Testament* myth, Milton's drama is more analogous with the romance and mythological modes of Tasso and Calderón than either of his epics. In general I follow the pattern in my Prologue and essay on *Gerusalemme liberata*, again using mnemonic keyword headings. After an introductory section in which I argue that the gradual recognition and acceptance of the use of illusion and deception by the hero in *Samson Agonistes (Changest thy count'nance)* parallels its use in *Gerusalemme liberata (Docere delectando)*, I go on to demonstrate how the backdrop of a world of mutability and illusion which we found in Tasso's poem *(Mondo mutabile)* also exists in Milton's drama *(Shipwreck't)*. The tendency of the imagery to divide itself into antithetical elements in *Gerusalemme liberata (Sotto mentito aspetto)*—of which Erminia the lover disguised as an enemy warrior was a focal example—is also present in *Samson Agonistes (Race of glory/race of shame)*. And just as there were patterns of beneficent evil in Tasso's poem *(Adorno inganno)*, so there are several such patterns in Milton *(Thir Superstition yields)*. In both works the division of imagery into the antithetical dichotomies of an Augustinian "aesthetic plenitude" eventually leads to a complex identity between good and evil. This paradox was shrouded in the darkness of the Tancredi-Clorinda battle *(L'un l'altro guarda)*, and there are various indications of it in Milton's drama *(A rougher tongue)*. But there were also direct and forceful statements in central episodes in Tasso—the joy and beauty Erminia discovers among the enemy war machines *(Securi fra l'arme)*—as there are by Milton's central character *(House of liberty)*. Just as the deceptive seductress Armida helped Rinaldo to discover himself *(Narciso)*, Dalila reveals hidden identities to Samson *(Th' example)*. One of the ways the imagery helped to prepare for a theodical understanding of evil in Tasso's poem was the elaborate identification of the opposing Christian and pagan warriors *(Movon concordi)*. In *Samson Agonistes* the Israelites and Philistines are identified through Samson *(These two proportion'd)*. The turning point in *Gerusalemme liberata* which allowed Rinaldo to conquer the enchanted forest was an Irenaean recognition of evil as an endemic part of the

human condition *(Colpe umane)*. In *Samson Agonistes*, I understand
Samson to come to the same recognition in his sudden reverse decision
consciously and purposefully to immerse himself in the use of deception
(Sole Author, I). But before describing this process, I make a comparison
between the Christ of *Paradise Regained*, on the one hand, and Adam and
Samson, on the other, in order to illustrate *Samson Agonistes'* conception
of mutability and evil *(Unmov'd)*. Finally, just as the allegorical imagery
of Tasso's poem indicated that the world therein was a reflection of the
moral experience of the central characters *(Un sol punto)*, in many
respects the conflicting realities of *Samson Agonistes*—the antagonism
between Israelites and Philistines—reflect the moral struggles of its hero
(Inmost mind). Ultimately, both Tasso *(Segni ignoti)* and Milton *(Intimate impulse)* are questioning reality and probing it for the hidden
beneficent purposes of God.

I.   Changest thy count'nance

In *Gerusalemme liberata* illusion, deception and evil are shown working
toward beneficent ends. In theodical terms, Tasso is justifying the existence of evil in the world, a world which he, like Milton, believed to be
monistic and good. However, even in Tasso's essentially allegorical epic,
there is the sense that the heroes' greatest fulfillment comes at their lowest
ebb and that their fullest identification is with their opposite element.
The tragic element in *Samson Agonistes* is much stronger. There is less
sense of an Augustinian predestined "aesthetic plenitude" and a greater
Irenaean awareness of the noetic and purgatorial offices of suffering.
Illusion and deception, death and evil, are an intrinsic part of human
existence in Milton's drama: the enchanted forest is life itself, the enchantress is the hero's wife, the devious roads of battle which eventually lead to
victory are the hero's death. This is not to deny that *Samson Agonistes*
has allegorical dimensions. It seems a question of degree. *Samson Agonistes* is more tragic than *Gerusalemme liberata*, but it is certainly less
tragic than *Hamlet*. Much of the best criticism of *Samson Agonistes*, such
as the essays of A. S. P. Woodhouse,[1] Una Ellis-Fermor[2] and, of course,
the recent magisterial *Toward Samon Agonistes* by Mary Ann Radzinowicz,[3] attempts to distinguish it as a specifically Christian or religious
drama.

   One of my central concerns will be to illustrate *Samson Agonistes'*
allegorical dimensions. In this the analogy with Tasso will be helpful.
Samson experiences not only a reversal of fortune and recognition of his
own guilt. That happens before the drama begins. What Samson finally
realizes is what he himself illustrates; he comes to embody the truth that
illusion and deception and reversals are a meaningful and purposeful
dimension of the ways of God, who, as the Chorus puts it, also changes

his own countenance (684).* This is but one of the many references in the drama to the mutability of fortune. They could all be taken as no more than that familiar classical idea. But as we shall see, Milton develops an Augustinian ethic of mutability and immutability which gives these seemingly simple references to reversal of fortune broader metaphysical implications.

II. Shipwreck't

Mutability, illusion, deception and fraud and their inevitable association with evil form one of the central themes of *Samson Agonistes*. From a certain perspective Samson's regeneration may be said to be the major theme of the drama.[4] But Samson's regeneration is *from* deception and is accomplished *through* deception. From a certain archetypal perspective we are dealing with a displaced version of the fall of the two *Old* and *New Testament* Adams here which has literary modalities considerably more distanced than *Samson Agonistes*. One of the most distanced—also involving deception—is the bed trick of renaissance drama. In Shakespeare's *Measure for Measure* as well as many Spanish Golden Age dramas it is a "bed trick" which both precipitates and resolves the crisis. But a rather detailed analysis of the imagery in *Samson Agonistes* is necessary before I can begin to justify this theodical reading.

The five major episodes of the drama: 1) Samson's opening soliloquy and his dialogue with the Chorus, the visits of 2) Manoa, 3) Dalila and 4) Harapha, and 5) Samson's exit and death offstage as reported by the Messenger,[5] are all concerned specifically in various ways with illusion. The differences in the faces of deception in each of these episodes eventually help to define Milton's specific attitude which is arrived at, or possibly intuited, by Samson. Before a discussion of Samson's final relation to illusion and beneficient evil it is necessary to look at the various attitudes (which are all constituents of the final one) individually.

As the drama begins with Samon's soliloquy, the major chord is struck. Samson describes himself as "Betray'd" and speaks of his "dark in light" exposure to "fraud." The soliloquy concentrates on Samson's blindness as the worst aspect of his present condition, and his primary fear of blindness seems to be that it will expose him even more to the deception he has already suffered:

> Of man or worm; the vilest here excel me,
> They creep, yet see; I dark in light expos'd
> To daily fraud, contempt, abuse and wrong,

*All my quotations and line references are from the text of Merritt Y. Hughes, ed., *John Milton: Complete Poems and Major Prose* (New York, 1957). I do not retain the italicizing of names; all the italicizing is my own for the purpose of emphasis.

> Within doors, or without, still as a fool,
> In power of others, never in my own.   (74-78)

Samson echoes this theme when he later confronts Dalila:

> How wouldst thou use me now, blind, and thereby
> Deceivable, in most things as a child
> Helpless, thence easily contemn'd, and scorn'd,
> And last neglected?   (941-944)

Prefiguring an irony which is to become more important as the play progresses, Samson sees fraud and deception even where it is less likely to appear: "How counterfeit a coin they are who friends/ Bear in their Superscription" 189-190).

In the opening soliloquy and even more in the colloquy with the Chorus which follows, the imagery of illusion seems to build toward or become a background for the observation that life itself is deceptive in that it is subject to dramatic and sudden change. Samson's thoughts rush upon him "and present/ Times past, what once I was, and what am now." He contrasts his former great promise with the decline into which fate has brought it:

> Promise was that I
> Should Israel from Philistian yoke deliver;
> Ask for this great Deliverer now, and find him
> Eyeless in Gaza at the Mill with slaves,
> Himself in bonds under Philistian yoke.   (38-42)

The Chorus paints the picture more vividly:

> O change beyond report, thought, or belief!
> See how he lies at random, carelessly diffus'd,
> With languish't head unpropt,
> As one past hope, abandon'd,
> And by himself given over;
> In slavish habit, ill-fitted weeds
> O'erworn and soil'd;
> Or do my eyes misrepresent? Can this be hee,
> That Heroic, that Renown'd,
> Irresistible Samson? whom unarm'd
> No strength of man, or fiercest wild beast could withstand;
> Who tore the Lion, as the Lion tears the Kid,
> Ran on embattled Armies clad in Iron,
> And weaponless himself,
> Made Arms ridiculous, useless the forgery
> Of brazen shield and spear, the hammer'd Cuirass,
> Chalybean temper'd steel, and frock of mail
> Adamantean Proof;
> But safest he who stood aloof,
> When insupportably his foot advanc't,
> In scorn of thir proud arms and warlike tools,
> Spurn'd them to death by Troops.   (117-138)

This metamorphosis—and its bipartite articulation—becomes the major theme of the Chorus: "the glory late of Israel, now the grief" (179). While Samson seems to take deception and sudden metamorphosis as ruling only his own life, the Chorus broadens the theme to include all of life:

> O mirror of our fickle state,
> Since man on earth unparallel'd!
> The rarer thy example stands,
> By how much from the top of wondrous glory,
> Strongest of mortal men,
> To lowest pitch of abject fortune thou are fall'n!   (164-169)

When Samson specifies that his situation has been caused by a "deceitful Woman," the Chorus extends even this indictment to a generalization about women:

> Tax not divine disposal; wisest Men
> Have err'd, and by bad Women been deceiv'd;
> And shall again, pretend they ne'er so wise.   (210-212)

Milton uses the familiar trope of a shipwreck to describe Samson's and man's fall.[6] Samson says that he, like a foolish pilot, has shipwrecked his "Vessel" trusted to him "from above, gloriously rigg'd" (198-200). Later in the drama the Chorus, referring to the effect of women on men, says:

> What Pilot so expert but needs must wreck
> Embark'd with such a Steers-mate at the Helm?   (1044-1045)

Manoa takes up the theme of a change in fortune. In addressing the Chorus upon his arrival, he refers to "your once glorified friend,/ My Son now Captive" (334-335). As the Chorus extended illusion and deception beyond Samson's world, indeed, universally, Manoa now deepens it by interpreting it as something pernicious embedded deep within the human situation:

> O ever failing trust
> In mortal strength! and, oh, what not in man
> Deceivable and vain! Nay, what thing good
> Pray'd for, but often proves our woe, our bane?   (348-351)

Manoa does not entertain the theodical possibility that the opposite of what he says may also be true, i.e., that evil may prove our good. He never reaches that level of vision; only Samson does. However, Manoa almost stumbles on the truth when he implies that barrenness, which he thought a reproach, may, indeed, have been a blessing in view of what happened when his prayers for children were answered. Manoa offers two rather salty criticisms of God:

> Why are his gifts desirable; to tempt
> Our earnest Prayers, then, giv'n with solemn hand
> As Graces, draw a Scorpion's tail behind?   (358-360)

Alas! methinks whom God hath chosen once
To worthiest deeds, if he through frailty err,
He should not so o'erwhelm, and as a thrall
Subject him to so foul indignities,
Be it but for honor's sake of former deeds.   (368-372)

Samson immediately rejects these criticisms and takes all the blame on himself:

Appoint not heavenly disposition, Father,
Nothing of all these evils hath befall'n me
But justly; I myself have brought them on.   (373-375)

Still, as we shall see in a more detailed study of Samson's evolving attitude, he soon reverts to thinking of himself, at least in part, as a victim: "Then swoll'n with pride into the snare I fell/ Of fair fallacious looks" (532-533). Quite clearly, at this point in the drama Samson still thinks of the evil that has befallen him as just punishment rather than an integral part of the divine plan or an important aspect of his fulfillment. In some respects, Manoa's vision of God's hand in the Scorpion's tail is closer to the attitude Samson will eventually evolve.

Manoa seems to be convinced by Samson's rebuttal that he has been a traitor to himself; otherwise Manoa would not go on to devote his energies to prayers for further graces (Samson's ransom). However, his words will not be without their effect on Samson. In fact, the Chorus closes the encounter between Samson and Manoa with words echoing Manoa's declaration that he had found the source for sudden metamorphoses of Fortune (which render man's stature and reality a mere illusion) in God:

God of our Fathers, what is man!
That thou towards him with hand so various,
Or might I say contrarious,
Temper'st thy providence through his short course,
Not evenly, as thou rul'st
Th'Angelic orders and inferior creatures mute,
Irrational and brute.   (667-673)

Samson's facile dismissal of Manoa's accusations is not the final answer. In speaking of God's "elected," which of course includes Samson, the Chorus adds:

Yet toward these, thus dignifi'd, thou oft,
Amidst thir height of noon,
Changest thy count'nance and thy hand, with no regard
Of highest favors past.   (682-685)

The interview with Manoa ends with these solemn reflections on the mutability of God's favor. We may take the persistence of these words as an indication that Manoa's ideas, despite Samson's quick and only momentarily successful rebuttal, have been absorbed into, if not Samson's imagination, at least the theoretical structure of the play and will contribute to the development of its final attitude.

In none of the episodes are illusion and deception so clearly the subject matter as in Samson's encounter with Dalila. The most interesting aspect of this conflict is its effect on Samson, but I shall discuss that aspect later as well as Dalila's general relation to Samson with regard to the themes I am concerned with. Here I merely wish to underline the episode's obsession with illusion.

Even before Dalila presents herself, her deceptiveness is emphasized. Samson refers to her as "a deceitful Woman" (202) and "that specious Monster, my accomplisht snare" (230); while the Chorus names her "that fallacious Bride" (320). Samson also refers to her "Treason" (391) and "wiles" (402) and clearly evokes the Circe archetype in describing his fall into Dalila's snare ("into the snare I fell/ Of fair fallacious looks . . ." 532-533). Like the Armida episodes in *Gerusalemme liberata*, the Dalila encounter has the most concentrated references to illusion in Milton's drama. A simple glance at some of its diction indicates this: "Traitress" (725), "false" (749), "deceive" (740), "betray" (750), "feign'd" (752, 829, 872), "sorceress" (819), "betray'd" (840), "hypocrisy" (872), "false pretexts and varnish'd colors" (901), "snare" (931), "enchanted" (934), "sorceries" (937), "Deceivable" (942), "falsehood" (955) and "conceal'd" (998).

The Dalila episode adds considerably to the drama's general attitude toward illusion and deception. The Chorus broadens Samson's general statement of the theme; and Manoa deepens it to include consideration of illusion's ultimate source and meaning. Dalila's appearance adds an element of antithetical dichotomy and even some degree of ambiguity. Not only is there the possibility that Dalila is sincere (about which I shall say more later), but the episode dramatizes the conflict between the hero and his deception. Dalila pleads that she deceived Samson for the public good:

> . . . at length that grounded maxim
> So rife and celebrated in the mouths
> Of wisest men, that to the public good
> Private respects must yield, with grave authority
> Took full possession of men and prevail'd;
> Virtue, as I thought, truth, duty so enjoining.   (865–870)

Hinting at a major theme of the drama, Dalila also claims in her favor that "Love hath oft, well meaning, wrought much woe" (813). To this, Samson sets up a dichotomy between Love and Hate, insisting that what Dalila calls Love is Hate; while Dalila's judgment in choosing between the Philistines and her love for Samson is certainly subject to criticism, her sincerity about her own feelings, however much they fall short of what Samson is calling Love, is questioned within the drama only by Samson's own opinion. In analyzing the relationship between Dalila and Samson later in my essay, I shall discuss various hidden identities between them. In simply discussing the episode's obsession with illusion, one sees here a confusion of identities simlar to that pattern of opposition and affinity between Clorinda and Tancredi: Tancredi as Lover or Enemy? He turns out to be both and something else. Are Dalila's feelings Love or Hate? Or are they both, and do they have a purpose, hidden to both Samson and Dalila, a purpose beyond their reach to know?

Like Manoa's words, the conflict with Dalila is to have its latent effects on Samson, effects leading toward a resolution within Samson. However, it is inevitable that on the surface, at least, the encounter ends in a total dichotomy. Samson tells Dalila, "thou and I long since are twain" (929). This division is similar to his surrender to fate earlier in the play in a battle "Twixt God and Dagon" (462). The whole movement of the drama is toward a resolution of these dichotomies. Yet, at this point, Dalila is forced to see history as "double-fac't" and "double-mouth'd." Her divided vision is revealing and is ultimately related to the drama's struggle between good and evil:

> Fame if not double-fac't is double-mouth'd,
> And with contrary blast proclaims most deeds;
> On both his wings, one black, the other white,
> Bears greatest names in his wild aery flight.
> My name perhaps among the Circumcis'd
> In Dan, in Judah, and the bordering Tribes,
> To all posterity may stand defam'd,
> With malediction mention'd, and the blot
> Of falsehood most unconjugal traduc't.
> But in my country where I most desire,
> In Ekron, Gaza, Asdod, and in Gath
> I shall be nam'd among the famousest
> Of Women, sung at solemn festivals,
> Living and dead recorded, who to save
> Her country from a fierce destroyer, chose
> Above the faith of wedlock bands, my tomb
> With odors visited and annual flowers.   (971–987)

In the next encounter with Harapha, illusion continues to be dramatized in a binary mode. When the Chorus announces the arrival of Harapha as the approach of a "storm," Samson responds:

> Fair days have oft contracted wind and rain.   (1062)

The Chorus proceeds to point out the contradiction in Harapha's appearance ("His habit carries peace, his brow defiance," 1073), to which Samson, prefiguring the resolution which antithetical elements of the drama are eventually to find within him, answers:

Or peace or not, alike to me he comes.   (1074)

The episode centers on the irony of the contrast between the external signs of Harapha's strength and his inner weakness. Samson challenges him to a combat without "feign'd shifts" (1116) and states for himself: "I know no spells, use no forbidden arts" (1139).

This disavowal of any sort of trickery is notably different from the following episode of the drama in which Samson finally embraces the use of deception in achieving his own and God's ends. But I am not ready to discuss that central aspect of the drama's statement. At this point in my argument we can see in the final Chorus an echo and resolution of the various attitudes toward illusion I have been discussing:

All is best, though we oft doubt,
What th' unsearchable dispose
Of highest wisdom brings about,
And ever best found in the close.
Oft he seems to hide his face,
But unexpectedly returns
And to his faithful Champion hath in place
Bore witness gloriously.   (1745–1752)

This Chorus is modeled after the closing Choruses of several Greek tragedies.[7] One of the elements which distinguishes Milton's Chorus from his classical models is the muted reference to God's use of illusion: "Oft he seems to hide his face" (1749). With this Biblical theodical imagery which I discussed in my Prologue, Milton at once metaphorically resolves the dichotomies between the unfallen and fallen Samson and Dalila's "double-mouth'd" fame, answers Manoa's doubts and explains the discrepancy between appearance and reality which we feel throughout the drama and especially in the Harapha episode. The metaphor of God hiding his face bears the burden of these resolutions.

III. Race of glory / race of shame

The illusory aspect of appearance is, therefore, central to *Samson Agonistes*. It is the theme of *Mondo mutabile* in *Gerusalemme liberata*. Just as *Mondo mutabile* serves a more complex purpose for Tasso, so does the imagery of deceptive appearances which clusters around the *Shipwreck't* metaphor eventually reveal more significant patterns in *Samson Agonistes*. There is a tendency for the imagery and the world of *Gerusalemme liberata* to develop into symmetrical polarities. Not only does Erminia disguise herself, but she disguises herself as her opposite. She substitutes her identity as lover for that of an enemy warrior. The same is true of Tancredi. And this resolution of illusion into antithetical dichotomies is reflected in the larger patterns of the poem in the conflict between the Christians and pagans. Similar patterns are present in *Samson Agonistes* in a form less radical but nonetheless responsive to Saint Augustine's sense of the "eloquence of things" in the articulation of his theodicy.

The mutability of fortune which I have been discussing has the character of dramatic metamorphoses into opposites; the movement is from the highest to not merely one step down but to the lowest. To return to the opening soliloquy of the drama: Samson falls from the highest condition as hero to the lowest position as slave. His "glorious strength" is "Put to the labor of a beast." At the end of his soliloquy in which he mourns the even greater vulnerability to deception effected by his blindness, Samson refers to his "Life in captivity/ Among inhuman foes." At this instant, he hears approaching footsteps and imagines them to belong to his foes:

> But who are these? for with joint pace I hear
> The tread of many feet steering this way;
> Perhaps my enemies who come to stare
> At my affliction, and perhaps to insult,
> Thir daily practice to afflict me more.   (110–114)

Reversing the usual pattern, the supposed enemies turn out to be friends.

This tendency of Milton's drama to divide itself into antithetical dichotomies is as prevalent as the imagery of illusion and deception. We have already seen this in the ambiguity of the Samson-Dalila conflict. Love can not be merely faulty or misconceived; it is otherwise Hate. In the Samson-Harapha encounter, Samson confronts Harapha's hollow monument of strength with his own guilelessness and steadily augmenting inner strength. And, significantly, just before Samson enacts the most cunning deception of the drama, he has achieved the opposite ideal and describes himself to Harapha as innocent of "spells" and "forbidden Arts" (1139). Indicating a more complicated tendency of the drama which I shall discuss later, the inverse reflection of this last dichotomy is present in the fact that just at the point where Samson has achieved sufficient regeneration to be reinstated as the hero of God, he is called by Harapha a "Murderer, a Revolter, and a Robber" (1180).

The other major dichotomies of the drama are worked out in terms of the opposition between Israelites and Philistines, God and Dagon, blindness and vision, masculine and feminine, pitiful detachment and scorn, liberty and bondage, peace and defiance, inward and outward virtues. Indeed, the drama begins, symbolically, with the "choice of Sun or shade":

A little onward lend thy guiding hand
To these dark steps, a little further on;
For yonder bank hath choice of Sun or shade.[8]   (1-3)

In addition to words related to mutability, fraud and deception, one of
the most important words of the drama is "contrary" and its variants.
After the Dalila episode which emphasizes her relationship to fraud and
establishes the Love-Hate dichotomy, the Chorus relates the "Seeming"
of illusion to the themes of vain outward strength ("far within defensive
arms"), battle ("Adverse and turbulent"), bondage ("enslav'd"), corruption ("sense depraved") and self-guilt ("folly and shameful deeds").
These themes, so central to Samson himself and to the drama as a whole,
all revolve around the word "contrary." It is one of the many baroque
passages in Milton which combine both what Saint Augustine calls in his
theodicy the "eloquence of rhetoric" and the "eloquence of things":

Whate'er it be, to wisest men and best
Seeming at first all heavenly under virgin veil,
Soft, modest, meek, demure,
Once join'd, the *contrary* she proves, a thorn
Intestine, far within defensive arms
A cleaving mischief, in his way to virtue
Adverse and turbulent, or by her charms
Draws him awry enslav'd
With dotage, and his sense deprav'd
To folly and shameful deeds which ruin ends.   (1034-1043)

The Chorus has already described God's hand as "contrarious" (669), and
Samson described to Dalila the pagan goals as "the contradiction/ Of thir
own deity" (898-899).

The sense of contradiction is one of the most important elements of the
drama. Its greatest contradiction in terms of good and evil is, as we shall
see, embodied in Samson's final gesture. But this element can also be seen
in the smallest details. For example, Manoa points out to Samson that he
is using his strength for a purpose opposite to that for which it was
intended: "Wilt thou then serve the Philistines with that gift/ Which was
expressly giv'n thee to annoy them? (577-578). Samson pictures "every
woman false" as she debates whether to assail her husband's "virtue or
weakness" (756). The Chorus states that man is to hold despotic power
over a woman, "Smile she or lour" (1057). And, in one of the many
indications of a total reversal of roles (all of which are thematically
related to Samson's ultimate reversal), the Chorus describes Manoa as
reversing the roles of fathers and sons:

Fathers are wont to lay up for thir Sons,
Thou for thy Son art bent to lay out all;

> Sons wont to nurse thir Parents in old age,
> Thou in old age car'st how to nurse thy Son,
> Made older than thy age through eyesight lost.   (1485–1489)

IV. Thir Superstition yields

In *Gerusalemme liberata* the temporary resolution of conflicting identities and forces into antithetical dichotomies seems to be controlled by the poem's theodical concern with the ultimately beneficent purposes of evil. Good and evil are symmetrically enough divided that they become inverted mirror reflections of each other. To return again to the beginning of *Samson Agonistes*: the fact that Samson is deceived, through his blindness, into imagining his approaching friends to be enemies does not in any way seem to control the fact that his visitors are, indeed, friends who initiate the various currents of the play which will eventually result in Samson's regeneration and fulfillment. In other words, we do not necessarily feel that Samson had to imagine that his friends were enemies in order for their friendliness to come into being as we feel in *Paradise Lost* that Adam and Eve had to fall in order for their humanity to be fully realized. However, reading a little beyond Samson's initial confusion of friends and enemies, we realize that the identity of these opposites does lie in ambiguous darkness. I have already referred to Samson's observation on the duplicity of friends:

> Your coming, Friends, revives me, for I learn
> Now of my own experience, not by talk,
> How counterfeit a coin they are who friends
> Bear in their Superscription (of the most
> I would be understood); in prosperous days
> They swarm, but in adverse withdraw thir head
> Not to be found, though sought.   (187–193)

Samson's observation and his compliment to his friends seem to be (like so many elements of the drama) curiously inverted. What he should learn from the arrival of his friends, one would assume, is the nature of true friendship, its unswerving loyalty. Yet, he puts his observation in inverted terms. Their coming teaches him about the falseness of friends who did not come ("of the most"). But he is revived because what he has learned about false friends also points out, by implication, the nature of his present true friends. Although Samson does not define this, the context of the drama makes it clear. In this light, his initial mistaking of friends for enemies, the friend-enemy dichotomy, does not seem so simple. The true friend seems to grow out of his opposite. In any case, the contrast has enabled Samson to distinguish between the two. Before the end of the drama, the dichotomy will be expressed in more theodical terms.

There are other passages in *Samson Agonistes* which prefigure in this way a central concern with the justification of evil. Just as the initial "choice of Sun or shade" seems to anticipate the drama's various dichotomies, symmetries and contradictions, Samson's immediate reference in the first few lines of the drama to the irony of his release from labor because of a Philistine "solemn Feast" seems to initiate the theme of beneficent evil:

> This day a solemn Feast the people hold
> To Dagon thir Sea-Idol, and forbid
> Laborious works, unwillingly this rest
> Thir Superstition yields me.   (12-15)

There is a more immediate and obvious prefiguration here: before the end of *Samson Agonistes* the same Philistine feast will have resulted in the physical release of the Israelites and a metaphysical release for Samson.[9]

Many other elements of the drama reflect this major theme. Well before the Chorus' final observation that God often "seems to hide his face," in discussing Samson's unlawful marriage to a Philistine the Chorus argues God's ability to break "his own Laws" and prompt his hero toward a bride who is false and immersed in evil:

> For with his own Laws he can best dispense.
>   He would not else who never wanted means,
> Nor in respect of th'enemy just cause
> To set his people free,
> Have prompted this Heroic Nazarite,
> Against his vow of strictest purity,
> To seek in marriage that fallacious Bride,
> Unclean, unchaste.   (314-321)

Indeed, the marriage image with which the Chorus chooses to describe this quality of God expresses figuratively the central theme of *Samson Agonistes* with which I am concerned. Later in the drama Samson will receive a further prompting from God which will lead him into a figurative marriage with evil.

Another incident which touches this theme and prefigures much is Samson's description of his blindness as a blessing:

> Yet that which was the worst now least afflicts me,
> Blindness, for had I sight, confus'd with shame,
> How could I once look up, or heave the head.   (195-197)

If we read these lines in the light of the broader themes of the drama, we can see why blindness is such a central symbol. The lines imply that it is necessary for God to use mysterious ways, to "hide his face," and, consequently, necessary for his hero to act with blind faith. Were he confused with knowledge which is beyond reason and beyond his understanding, he could not lift himself to the task, as Samson eventually does. When he describes to Dalila the misfortune of husbands who are beguiled by the false pretenses of their wives, his own destruction is seen as a blessing because it prevents further fraud: "If not by quick destruction soon cut off/ As I by thee, to ages an example" (764–765). The major theme is also present here. The beneficent blindness has become speed; the redundance of "quick" and "soon" points this out. Since the quality of a beneficent fate can not be understood and frequently appears as its opposite, in order to avoid ignorant human opposition it must happen in blindness or with such speed that it will be unobserved and unopposed.

There are also minor episodes and elements of the drama which reflect this theme—sometimes ironically. After Harapha's departure, Samson implies that Harapha will have to use deception in order to save face:

> He must allege some cause, and offer'd fight
> Will not dare mention, lest a question rise
> Whether he durst accept the offer or not,
> And that he durst not plain enough appear'd.   (1253–1256)

We have seen that Dalila pleaded "public good" as an excuse for her betrayal of Samson. In his dialogue with Manoa, Samson indicates that he successfully delayed his present destruction through deception. He "deluded" Dalila three times:

> Thrice I deluded her, and turn'd to sport
> Her importunity, each time perceiving
> How openly, and with what impudence
> She purpos'd to betray me.   (396–399)

Samson fought deception with deception. Even this slight allusion prefigures the mirror imagery of the Dalila episode and, more importantly, the successful deception of Samson's final gesture.

V.   A rougher tongue

Eventually Samson is lead to the total identification of the dichotomies around which *Samson Agonistes* is structured and acknowledgment of the beneficent effects of evil. But the understanding which Samson achieves is not shared by the other characters in the drama—at least not until after he has enacted his sacrifice. All of the other characters come into contact with the same dichotomies and signs revealed to Samson. The obvious inadequacies of their responses serve to delineate more clearly and to emphasize Samson's ultimate resolution.

We have seen in the earlier, unregenerated Samson's descriptions of Dalila and his adverse fortune that he initially sees evil as an external, hostile force. Even if he finds it within himself *(Sole Author, I)*, he considers evil as, in some sense, foreign, having no definition in what he would acknowledge as his own being. Dalila, at least, sees a relationship between private misfortune and public good, but it is not a relationship of interdependent balance. She cannot convince Samson, nor even herself, that what she did was also for his benefit. Of necessity, she ends up with a rigid dichotomy.

Harapha has been studied as a type of *miles gloriosus*, descended from renaissance comedies.[10] But he can also be understood as a foil to Samson's powers of vision—especially as they have developed toward the end of the drama. Of all the characters in the drama, Harapha is the one least able to think paradoxically. His reaction to the dichotomy of Samson's former and present condition is to reject the former as incredible: "Much I have heard/ Of thy prodigious might and feats perform'd/ Incredible to me" (1082-1084). He bases his judgment totally on appearances:

> And now am come to see of whom such noise
> Hath walk'd about, and each limb to survey,
> If thy appearance answer loud report. (1088-1090)

The only way that Harapha can account for Samson's former greatness is through "black enchantments, some Magician's Art" (1133). For Harapha, God could not possibly be involved in a plan which leads to his hero's suffering and downfall. Any such connection, he declares, is merely Samson's assumption (1134-1135). He himself assumes what appearances tell him, that God has totally abandoned Samson:

> Presume not on thy God, whate'er he be,
> Thee he regards not, owns not, hath cut off
> Quite from his people, and delivered up
> Into thy Enemies' hand. (1156-1159)

Manoa, on the other hand, most closely approaches Samson's final vision. However, Manoa always remains on this side of irony.[11] Because the agonies created by the downfall of his son are so much worse than those he suffered from barrenness, Manoa implies that barrenness was something more or something less than it seemed:

> I pray'd for Children, and thought barrenness
> In wedlock a reproach; I gain'd a Son,
> And such a Son as all Men hail'd me happy;
> Who would be now a Father in my stead? (352-355)

He does not directly state that barrenness was a blessing in disguise; much less does he see Samson's downfall as anything other than its obvious physical reality. But Manoa is not as limited to appearances as Harapha. He does achieve some minimal resolution as well as balance of antithetical dichotomies. In describing his willingness to pay whatever ransom he can for Samson, he says, "much rather I shall choose/ To live the *poorest* in my tribe, than *richest,*/ And he in that calamitous prison left" (1478-1480). Manoa realizes that wealth and poverty could not be simply judged in these circumstances and that one may easily become its opposite. And we have seen that Manoa is conscious of a certain contradiction in God's treatment of his heroes. However, when Samson has ended his life in a moment which is both his fulfillment and defeat, Manoa asks, somewhat prosaically:

> How died he? death to life is crown or shame.   (1579)

The Chorus, while not sharing Samson's final intuitive intelligence, seems to help him arrive at it. There is something rather too facile in Samson's dismissals of the arguments presented by Manoa and Dalila and the threat presented by Harapha. In continuing to dwell on those arguments, the Chorus indicates that Samson's dismissals are not the whole story. We have seen that after Manoa's departure the Chorus keeps alive his theme of God's "contrarious" hand toward his heroes. Samson must still look further than a personal fault for the source of evil and misfortune. After the Dalila episode, the Chorus warns that "beauty, though injurious, hath strange power,/ After offense returning, to regain/ Love once possest" (1003-1005). When Samson dismisses this danger with a distinction between "Love-quarrels" and "wedlock-treachery" (1008-1009), the Chorus still continues for fifty lines (1010-1060) describing the seductiveness and treachery of women. Samson has still a further encounter with deception. When he adopts as his mode of action the very wiles he has condemned in Dalila, he is in a sense marrying her to greater effect than he had before. Finally, after Samson has scored an easy victory over Harapha, it is the Chorus who, upon seeing the advancing officer, first expresses the fear that "perhaps more trouble is behind" (1300).

VI. House of liberty

Among the effects of the structural—narrative and prosodic—identifications between love and war, lover and enemy, peace and battle, pagans and Christians and life and death in *Gerusalemme liberata* is that Erminia paradoxically finds peace among the war tents and feels *Securi fra l'arme*. Samson is also eventually motivated to find the blessing of freedom in his enslavement. Toward the end of his encounter with Dalila, when he considers her offer of hospitality and nursing love and care, he rejects her, saying:

> This Goal I count the house of Liberty
> To thine whose doors my feet shall never enter.   (949-950)

It is not unlike some of the poetic techniques employed in the more formally structured verses of *Gerusalemme liberata* that Milton balances

"This Goal" and "the house of Liberty" in one line rather than modifying his paradoxical statement by allowing them to flow into the next line where he indicates that he is speaking of the jail only in comparison with Dalila's home. By finding at least a relative good in evil, Samson is opening his vision toward a more specifically theodical perspective and is finally able to embrace fully the realities of his fall.

There are many ways in which Samson comes to acknowledge the fortuitous aspects of his fall. They are all departures from or grow out of the evil-good dichotomies of the drama. The overtones suggested in the friends-enemies dichotomy at the beginning of the drama are mild by comparison with the perspective Samson draws out of it toward the end. After Samson's encounter with Harapha, in which Harapha appears as an overwhelming example of the illusion of strength, Samson's remarks to the Chorus (1253-1267) follow a sequence similar to the one I have been following in my argument: deception, irony, paradox. Samson, as we have seen, states that Harapha will have to conceal his (Samson's) challenge to combat from the Philistines. He also refers ironically to the benefit Philistines derive from his labors:

> If they intend advantage of my labors,
> The work of many hands, which earns my keeping
> With no small profit daily to my owners.   (1259-1261)

He goes on from this ironic fruit of his tragedy to build something paradoxically positive out of the blackness of his situation:

> But come what will, my deadliest foe will prove
> My speediest friend, by death to rid me hence,
> The worst that he can give, to me the best.   (1262-1264)

Samson's earlier confusion between friends and enemies is no more accidental in terms of the themes of the drama than the confusion of Tancredi's role as lover and enemy is in *Gerusalemme liberata*. Because his situation can not be any worse, death and, therefore, his murder would be a blessing.

These are the more noticeable instances of Samson's inversions of good and evil. In general, his speech is increasingly paradoxical throughout the drama. While Manoa thinks in terms of *either* "shame" *or* "crown," Samson, again recalling poetic techniques in *Gerusalemme liberata*, joins "shame" and "glory" in the action of a single verb:

> My race of glory *run*, and race of shame.   (597)

He speaks of the loudness of mute speech:

> The deeds themselves, though mute, spoke loud the doer;   (248)

but he tells Dalila that her evasions further reveal her crime:

Or by evasions they crime uncover'st more.   (842)

And it is Samson who phrases paradoxically the weakness of the Israelites as being

> to love Bondage more than Liberty,
> Bondage with ease than strenuous liberty.   (270-271)

The most salient aspect of Samson's language in this regard is that he tends to find meaning and hope in disaster: liberty in slavery, friends in enemies. At the end of the speech in which Samson characterizes his "deadliest foe" as his "speediest friend," there is a faint echo of the love-hate dichotomy in his encounter with Dalila:

> Yet so it may fall out, because thir end
> Is hate, not help to me, it may with mine
> Draw thir own ruin who attempt the deed.   (1265-1267)

In saying that he will destroy his enemies even though what they intended as evil had a good outcome for him, Samson is at least acknowledging that hate can have the effects of love. This attitude can be seen as an inversion of Dalila's "Love hath oft, well meaning, wrought much woe." It is as if at this point in the drama Samson has more fully realized hidden dimensions in his relationship with Dalila and illusion in general. Inevitably, the resolution of the drama colors its episodes in a different light. The meeting with Dalila is not the simple encounter with an "accomplish't snare" it seems on the surface. Dalila, like fate itself, has hidden identities.

VII. Th' example

Modern criticism has observed the tendency of the allegorical hero to generate secondary characters.[12] To some extent Dalila demonstrates this relationship to Samson. Although most critics have tended to view Dalila as the stereotyped Circe or temptress, she, in fact, has a more complicated function in the drama. One critic has attempted to solve the problem by calling her a "debating Circe,"[13] but that is just a rough beginning.

In his encounter with Manoa, Samson seems to accept total responsibility for the evils which have befallen him; but his view of himself as "Sole author" of his misfortunes is quickly and repeatedly qualified by his many references to himself as the victim of deception and fraud in the "fair fallacious looks" of Dalila. The encounter with her brings Samson's guilt much closer home to him. In Dalila's fraud he discovers his own example. When she holds herself up as a mirror to Samson,

> To what I did thou show'd'st me first the way   (781)

Samson immediately recognizes his own reflection:

> I gave, thou say'st, th' example,
> I led the way; bitter reproach, but true,
> I to myself was false ere thou to me.   (822-824)

In a prosody rather more subdued but, nonetheless, related to the various modes Tasso used to balance the mirrored dichotomies of his verses, it is worth noting "I to myself" and "thou to me" balanced on the fulcrum of "false." Samson's encounter with Dalila is, in fact, full of binary polarities which identify them and comment on the rest of the drama.

Dalila, as we have seen, is characterized by fraudulence, deceptiveness and mutability, by all the qualities of illusion and evil. The Chorus concisely localizes her vices in the dichotomy between highly developed outward gifts and undeveloped inward gifts and specifies this imbalance as a feminine vice:

> It is for that such outward ornament
> Was lavish't on thir Sex, that inward gifts
> Were left for haste unfinish't, judgment scant,
> Capacity not rais'd to apprehend
> Or value what is best
> In choice, but oftest to affect the wrong?   (1025-1030)

The mirror or example image in the Dalila encounter is not a new or unique motif. But it does serve to clarify an important theme in the drama. Samson twice specifically refers to himself as effeminate. When he describes to Manoa his enslavement to Dalila, he says that "foul effeminacy held me yok't/ Her Bondslave" (410-411). The reference of "effeminacy" is ambiguous. Dalila was his captor, but, as the preceding lines make clear, so was a lack of manhood or a degree of effeminacy within Samson:

> At times when men seek most repose and rest,
> I yielded, and unlock'd her all my heart,
> Who with a grain of manhood well resolv'd
> Might easily have shook off all her snares:
> But foul effeminacy held me yok't
> Her Bondslave.   (406-411)

Later, addressing himself to the Chorus, Samson speaks of the vanity of his temperance when he could still be "Effeminately vanquished" (562). Again he refers ambiguously to both Dalila and his own weaknesses.

Indeed, much of the imagery in *Samson Agonistes* serves to characterize Samson before his fall as lacking in inner resolution despite his outward signs of strength. For example, Samson's opening soliloquy:

> O impotence of mind, in body strong!
> But what is strength without a double share
> Of wisdom?   (52-54)

or a later address to the Chorus:

> Immeasurable strength they might behold
> In me, of wisdom nothing more than mean;
> This with the other should, at least, have pair'd,
> These two proportion'd ill drove me transverse.   (206-209)

The lack of balance between outward and inward gifts in the female sex
is, therefore, very parallel to a similar imbalance within Samson. One of
the most typical images used for Samson is of a prison or an enclosed
space: "Prison within prison" (153). There is no flow or communion
between the outside and inside worlds. They remain barred to each other
even if these two worlds are merely different aspects of Samson. The
dichotomy between outward or ornamental strength and inward resolution in Samson dominates his third encounter (Harapha), and it is not
insignificant that the imagery has shifted in this third and last encounter
after Samson has seen himself mirrored in Dalila. The Harapha encounter is an inverse reflection of the Dalila encounter in which Samson sees
himself as outwardly strong and manly but inwardly weak and effeminate. This tendency of the drama to show inverse reflections of its dichotomies is one of the minor ways it works toward monism. (Unlike Tasso
and Calderón, Milton depends more on the articulation of Samson's
consciousness than on prosodic techniques.) But the description of Dalila, at the beginning of her episode, as a decorated "stately Ship" makes
the reader think of Samson before his fall and recalls the "Shipwreck't"
imagery:

> But who is this, what thing of Sea or Land?
> Female of sex it seems,
> That so bedeckt, ornate, and gay,
> Comes this way sailing
> Like a stately Ship
> Of Tarsus, bound for th' Isles
> Of Javan or Gadire
> With all her bravery on, and tackle trim,
> Sails fill'd, and streamers waving,
> Courted by all the winds that hold them play,
> An Amber scent of odorous perfume
> Her harbinger, a damsel train behind;
> Some rich Philistian Matron she may seem,
> And now at nearer view, no other certain
> Than Dalila thy wife.   (710-724)

Samson's deception is so well characterized as a shipwreck that it can
seem as if the wreckage occurs here when through blindness he sees his
own image in Dalila. It is in keeping with the central paradox of the
drama that the shipwreck and the deception and mutation it represents is,
in fact, Samson's salvation.

Dalila's four major addresses to Samson all echo his own situation. In her first speech she begins by pleading that the "other side" of her offense be looked at:

Yet hear me Samson; not that I endeavor
To lessen or extenuate my offense,
But that on th' other side if it be weigh'd
By itself, with aggravations not surcharg'd,
Or else with just allowance counterpois'd,
I may, if possible, thy pardon find
The easier towards me, or thy hatred less.   (766-772)

After pointing out that he was her model in treachery ("Ere I to thee, thou to thyself wast cruel" (784), in a sort of baroque image of infinitely receding mirrors Dalila protests that she herself was the victim of deception:

            I was assur'd by those
Who tempted me, that nothing was design'd
Against thee but safe custody, and hold.   (800-802)

The major excuse Dalila offers for her treachery in this first speech—in which the Love/Hate dichotomy and the plea that "Love hath oft, well meaning, wrought much woe" are contained—is that out of love she preferred the safety of having Samson at home as the prisoner of her love to the temptations and dangers liberty would offer him:

            I knew that liberty
Would draw thee forth to perilous enterprises,
While I at home sat full of cares and fears
Wailing thy absence in my widow'd bed;
Here I should still enjoy thee day and night
Mine and Love's prisoner, not the Philistines',
Whole to myself, unhazarded abroad,
Fearless at home of partners in my love.   (803-810)

The selfishness of Dalila's motivation here is too obvious to need comment. The applicability to Samson is less obvious. He is not only identified with Dalila but also with the Philistines and Israelites. Samson accuses the Israelites of being in bondage because they "love Bondage more than Liberty,/ Bondage with ease than strenuous Liberty" (270-271). But the resolution of the drama is delayed because Samson himself prefers, at least temporarily, bondage to the strenuous effort which will resolve the drama and grant him liberty. Until the end of the drama, Samson insists that the conflict is now "Twixt God and Dagon" and in so doing seems to "love Bondage more than strenuous Liberty"—reflecting Dalila's fear.

In formulating her second motivation for treachery, Dalila balances "public good" and "Private respects" as opposing forces:

> at length that grounded maxim
> So rife and celebrated in the mouths
> Of wisest men, that to the public good
> Private respects must yield, with grave authority
> Took full possession of me and prevail'd;
> Virtue, as I thought, truth, duty so enjoining.   (865–870)

Public good can mean private misfortune and that is what Dalila intends here. Although they remain totally separate entities for her, she sees public good growing out of private misfortune, reminiscent of the manner in which Samson's friends grew out of his enemies. Samson rejects Dalila's argument as "feign'd Religion" and "smooth hypocrisy." However, her argument seems to me to be more than an ironic version of the drama's central motif. Samson's vision is far from unclouded at this point, and, in an ironic way, Dalila seems to be closer to the final truth which will enable Samson to annihilate his private self for the freedom of the Israelites. Most likely, Dalila is closer to the truth only in that she allows herself so freely to become a pawn in the hands of fate. But the drama is constantly telling us that in some slavery and blindness there is greater freedom and light. The irony that Dalila and Manoa should at times seem to be closer to the truth than Samson is explained in that a measure of blindness or innocence is necessary in order to fulfill a fate which is hidden or beyond the powers of human comprehension. And in baroque literature innocence involves a Quixotic or Hamlet-like naive idealism in regard to the nature of evil which initially seems more attractive than the final mature and necessary vision.

Samson further responds to Dalila's second justification by saying that the unnatural demand of the Philistines that she betray her husband vitiated their stature as men and nation and that, indeed, her gods, whose hands are also in this, can not be gods:

> . . . if aught against my life
> Thy country sought of thee, it sought unjustly,
> Against the law of nature, law of nations,
> No more thy country, but an impious crew
> Of men conspiring to uphold thir state
> By worse than hostile deeds, violating the ends
> For which our country is a name so dear;
> Not therefore to be obey'd. But zeal mov'd thee;
> To please thy gods thou didst it; gods unable
> To acquit themselves and prosecute their foes
> But by ungodly deeds, the contradiction
> Of thir own deity, Gods cannot be.   (888–899)

It would be easy to over-read especially the last few lines in terms of theodicy. But theodicy is in one respect an argument against contradictions within God by revealing the illusion of apparent contradictions. Samson demonstrates a rigidity here which might explain why despite his intuitions of self-guilt he continues emphatically to accuse external snares. All the inadequacies of Samson's earlier attitudes as compared to the paradoxes he moves toward are present in this midway rejoinder to Dalila. At this point, Dalila gives up argument and appeals to a "forgiveness" beyond reason. Certainly, Samson's final action in the play also abandons reason and seeks a higher knowledge and motivation.

The dualism with which the Dalila episode ends, fame as "double-fac't" and "double-mouth'd," seems inevitable for Dalila considering the reception she has received. Love must always be understood as hate by some. But at this point a certain dualism also seems inevitable for Samson, and the schism Dalila feels between the worlds of Judah and Gath reflects the difference which Samson still has not reconciled between the angelic heralding of his birth and his present misery. It also contains the seeds of a Manicheism which, however, Samson successfully evades before the end of the drama.

VIII.   *These two proportion'd*

It is not only Dalila who reflects Samson's situation. Both the Israelites and the Philistines mirror different aspects of Samson's individual conflicts. The drama is structured around the visits of three characters: one, Manoa, totally identified with the Israelites, another, Harapha, totally identified with the Philistines, and Dalila, in the middle, reflecting Samson's involvement in both worlds. In fact, the most important manifestation of that aspect of the drama's imagery which divides itself antithetically and later finds a paradoxical resolution—revealing "the eloquence of things"—is the opposition between Israelites and Philistines and its reflection in Samson.

Samson's identification with the Israelites is the more obvious because he is one of them. We have seen that Samson's criticism of the Israelites for preferring easy bondage to strenuous liberty is applicable to Samson himself. The same metaphor is used to describe both bondages. Samson speaks of the promise that he "Should Israel from Philistian *yoke* deliver" (39) and that he now finds "Himself in bonds under Philistian *yoke*" (42). The association between Samson's responsibility for his bondage and his seeming preference for that bondage is made clear when he says that "foul effeminacy held me yok't/ Her Bondslave" (410–411). The basis of Samson's accusation of the Israelites is that they failed to recognize him and to support him as their deliverer. When the Chorus points out to Samson with the obviously implied criticism that "Israel still serves with all his Sons" (240), he responds:

That fault I take not on me, but transfer
On Israel's Governors, and Heads of Tribes,
Who seeing those great acts which God had done
Singly by me against their Conquerors
Acknowledg'd not, or not at all consider'd
Deliverance offer'd: I on th' other side
Us'd no ambition to commend my deeds,
The deeds themselves, though mute, spoke loud the doer;
But they persisted deaf, and would not seem
To count them things worth notice.   (241-250)

The accusation of the Israelites as deaf plays with our awareness of
Samson's blindness, not only his present blindness but his greater blindness to the snares of Dalila which after all had been strongly foreshad-
owed in the deceptiveness of the woman of Timna. In fact, in an earlier
passage, Samson mentions the woman of Timna and his own failure to
"begin Israel's Deliverance" (225). Samson has failed as deliverer and has
himself been failed by the Israelites. A good deal of the tension in
Milton's drama comes from the fact that until the very end of the action
Samson externalizes his own contest as a Manichaean battle "Twixt God
and Dagon." The failure of the Israelites to recognize their deliverer in
Samson is in a sense a projection of Samson's own failure to fully
recognize himself. It at least serves to make this point clearer for the
audience.

The same speech further develops this tendency of Milton's drama to
mirror its hero's moral and psychological qualities, difficult to perceive
in themselves, in more obvious external events. Samson goes on to describe how the Israelites "to prevent/ The harass of their Land" (256-
257) betrayed him "to the uncircumcis'd a welcome prey" (260). This
prefigures Dalila's betrayal, but, as Dalila points out, it also echoes
Samson's self-betrayal. From this perspective, all of Samson's accusations
against Dalila and the Israelites could be directed towards himself.

Samson's identification with the Israelites is most important at the end
of the drama. The servile punishment which both Samson and the
Israelites suffer is ended with Samson's death, but it is only the Israelites
who are literally freed from servitude. It is to the same end as those we
have just been considering that Samson's body ("Prison within Prison")
is associated with the "yoke" and servitude that he and the Israelites
jointly endure. With Samson's death comes release from servitude for
himself as well as the Israelites. It is possible to see the chains fall from
the Israelites; Samson is buried with the Philistines "Soak't in his enemies' blood" (1726). If, as one of the Israelites, Samson is liberated by the
destruction of the Philistines, he also dies with them. It is as if Samson's
blind sepulchral body and Dagon's temple were totally identified as the
grave of both Samson and the Philistines.

Samson's identification with the Philistines is in many ways paradoxical and more difficult to define than his identification with the Israelites. But it is this paradox which places their identification at the heart of the drama and my concern with theodicy. In *Gerusalemme liberata* the identification between the opposing camps was achieved through ambiguity of syntax, the parallel development of the Christian and pagan camps or individual Christian and pagan warriors, and the confused or disguised identities of characters like Erminia and Clorinda. All of these elements are less ostentatiously present in *Samson Agonistes*.

While Milton's syntax is characteristically clear, there are several instances in which the oscillation of fortune between Samson and the Philistines is stated in terms which are sufficiently abstracted and balanced to indicate, as with similar effects in *Gerusalemme liberata,* a degree of identification. Milton creates this purposive strain in his verse in describing the oscillation of fortune between Samson and the Philistines. For example, Manoa describes the Philistine feast to honor Dagon who has delivered them from Samson:

> To Dagon, as their God who hath deliver'd
> Thee, Samson, bound and blind into thir hands,
> *Them* out of thine, who slew'st *them* many a slain.   (437–439)

In the context of the drama Dagon as deliverer of the Philistines parallels Samson as deliverer of the Israelites. Just as Samson joins his "race of glory" and "race of shame" in the word "run," the adverse and bright sides of the Philistines' fortune are identified in the word "them"; i.e., "them" is used for those slain by Samson as well as those freed from him. Its use creates a bridge between the good and evil fortune of the Philistines—and in so doing mirrors an important thematic element of Samson's fate. In a related technique, when Manoa responds to the noise of the simultaneous destruction of Samson and the Philistines, he declares in reference to the Philistines: "they have slain my Son" (1117). The Chorus' response is almost a perfect inverse mirror reflection: "Thy Son is rather slaying them" (1118).

The significance of these parallel and inverse reflections in the drama's syntax are perhaps most clearly seen in Samson's last long address to Harapha. As Samson is approaching his fulfillment as the deliverer of the Israelites, the most negative accusations of the drama are directed against him by Harapha: "Murderer, a Revolter, and a Robber" (1180). It is as if the drama's tendency to articulate antinomies requires here a ritual verbal evocation of the opposite of the role Samson is moving toward. It is only the Philistines' identification of Samson in the role of murderer, revolutionary and thief that places Samson between the sun and shade of the Philistine arena. After Harapha has specified his accusation by referring to Samson's murder and the robbery of thirty Philistines at Askalon, Samson replies by evoking the familiar friend-foe dichotomy:

> Among the Daughters of the Philistines
> I chose a Wife, which argu'd me no foe;
> And in your City held my Nuptial Feast:
> But your ill-meaning Politician Lords,
> Under pretense of Bridal friends and guests,
> Appointed to await me thirty spies,
> Who, threat'ning cruel death, constrain'd the bride.   (1192-1198)

As usual the dichotomy appears in a context with specific reference to deceptiveness. In these lines its ambiguity is heightened by the fact that friend is referred to negatively as "no foe" and foes are evoked as the "pretense of Bridal friends." Samson goes on not to accuse the Philistines directly as enemies, but to say that he acted toward them *as if* they were enemies:

> • When I perceived all set on enmity,
> As on my enemies, wherever chanc'd,
> I us'd hostility, and took thir spoil
> To pay my underminers in thir coin.   (1201-1204)

"To pay my underminers in thir coin" expresses metaphorically Samson's identification with or even disguise as the Philistines. It is the first indication in the drama of the possibility that Samson will consciously or deliberately use evil toward his ends, and it is interesting that he feels the necessity to justify it here. When he deliberately, fully and finally embraces deception, evil and death, he offers no justification other than claiming that he was inspired by God. A related aspect of Samson's identification with the Philistines is that he considers his own being as jailer and prison. It is the complement to his growing awareness of self-responsibility for his fall. Even the Chorus refers to Samson as "Dungeon of thyself" (156). While in *Gerusalemme liberata* theodicy is most forcefully articulated through the epic's imagery of "aesthetic plenitude" in harmoniously balanced antitheses, in *Samson Agonistes* the theodical balance is achieved within Samson's—and even the reader's—mind. I return to this dimension of the drama.

Apart from the imagery and syntax of the drama, there are more specific ways in which Samson is identified with the Philistines. Dalila arrives at an irreconcilable schism between the worlds of Judah and Gath, and my reading of the Dalila episode suggests that this dualism is a reflection of Samson's Manichaean struggles before the final resolutions of the drama. Samson himself brings the reader to this interpretation. When Manoa accuses him of being directly responsible for the day's feasts which are glorifying and magnifying Dagon while blaspheming God,

Samson accepts the responsibility as his "chief affliction, shame and sorrow" (457). He describes himself as performing precisely those services for Dagon and disservices for God that the reader would imagine the property of a Philistine:

> Father, I do acknowledge and confess
> That I this honor, I this pomp have brought
> To Dagon, and advanc'd his praises high
> Among the Heathen round; to God have brought
> Dishonor, obloquy, and op't the mouths
> Of Idolists, and Atheists.   (448–453)

The ambiguity of Samson's role as the hero of both Dagon and God is reflected in the basic paradox that the hero of God is finally fulfilled on one of Dagon's feast days.

Samson's most striking identity with the Philistines, as with the Israelites, is achieved at the end of the drama. In terms of imagery and thematic and symbolic content, nothing has been more endemic to Samson than his blindness. In one of the last choruses, the Philistines are described as calling upon their own destroyer "with blindness internal struck." The Semichorus describes God:

> Among them hee a spirit of frenzy sent,
> Who hurt thir minds,
> And urg'd them on with mad desire
> To call in haste for thir destroyer;
> They only set on sport and play
> Unwittingly importun'd
> Thir own destruction to come speedy upon them.
> So fond are mortal men
> Fall'n into wrath divine,
> As thir own ruin on themselves to invite,
> Insensate left, or to sense reprobate,
> And with blindness internal struck.   (1675–1686)

All the major themes associated with Samson are evoked here. Samson's self-responsibility ("thir own ruin on themselves to invite") and his victimization by deception ("Unwittingly") are strongly echoed. There is even a sense of his despair ("Insensate left, or to sense reprobate").

Samson's identification with the Philistines is perhaps most clearly seen in one of those mirror speeches which, as I have described them, while discussing one specific aspect of the drama seem to comment on more general themes. It is Manoa's speech interrupted by a noise that "tore the Sky," i.e., the last words of the drama before Samson, offstage, is fulfilled. Manoa describes the types of Philistines he has encountered in seeking Samson's release. The three types, proud, self-seeking, magnanimous, reflect—in the proper sequence—the various aspects of Samson we have known:

> Some much averse I found and wondrous harsh,
> Contemptuous, proud, set on revenge and spite;
> That part most reverenc'd Dagon and his Priests:
> Others more moderate seeming, but thir aim
> Private reward, for which both God and State
> They easily would set to sale: a third
> More generous far and civil, who confess'd
> They had enough reveng'd, having reduc't
> Thir foe to misery beneath thir fears,
> The rest was magnanimity to remit,
> If some convenient ransom were propos'd.
> What noise or shout was that? it tore the Sky.   (1461–1472)

The "contemptuous, proud" Philistines remind the reader of Samson before his fall and as he is reflected in Harapha. The Philistines seeking "private reward" reflect Samson at least in his identification with Dalila and with the Israelites who betrayed him for their own gain. The magnanimous Philistines are mentioned at the instant when Samson is himself being most magnanimous. This seems to be the point of ritual magic in the drama. It is as if the fact that Samson has finally achieved true magnanimity in his ultimate sacrifice forces this magnanimity on even the negative aspects of his character of which the Philistines are a reflection. And the destruction of the antithesis through total imitation seems to create the explosion which tears the sky. Paradoxically, as I shall now go on to consider, it is by imitating the forces of evil, the decision to "try thir Art" in more senses than one, that Samson has destroyed them by making them at one with himself and no more than the inversion of his own magnanimity.

IX. Unmoved

Although throughout the drama Samson has been increasingly able to perceive relative qualities of good in evil and to identify evil as an aspect of his own nature, this is still a considerable step removed from a theodical acceptance of evil as justifiable and necessary. But this acceptance will be implied in Samson's final gesture. Of the many symmetrical polarities developed in *Samson Agonistes*—friend/foe, Israelites/Philistines, inward/outward, insight/blindness, masculinity/feminity[14]—one of the most important is the dichotomy between immutability and mutability, between resolution and inconstancy. Milton's use of this polarity seems to echo Saint Augustine's articulation of his theodicy in the *Einchiridion*. In the first passage quoted in my Prologue, in the middle of his discussion of evil as an aspect of the good, Saint Augustine makes a distinction between the immutability of God and the mutability of fallen creatures:

> The cause of evil is the defection of the will of a being who is *mutably* good from the Good which is *immutable.*

An instructive contrast will be gained by considering briefly the manifestations of mutability and immutability in *Paradise Regained* and *Paradise Lost* before returning to *Samson Agonistes*.

Several critics have undertaken comparisons of *Paradise Regained* and *Samson Agonistes*. Michael Krouse analyzes Samson as a prototype of Christ. He makes an analogy between the three temptations of Christ and the Manoa, Dalila and Harapha encounters.[15] In an essay on *Paradise Regained* in *The Return of Eden,* Northrop Frye compares Christ's temptation on the pinnacle to Samson's refusal to go to the Philistine festival after he has beaten off Manoa, Dalila and Harapha.[16] But this is a similarity with a difference since Samson gives in. In general, recent criticism has found the differences between the two heroes more essential than the similarities. William G. Madsen says of Samson that "his significance for the Christian reader lies primarily in his inability to measure up to the heroic norm delineated in *Paradise Regained*." Although he states that *Samson Agonistes* could be regarded as a "companion piece" to *Paradise Regained* and is possibly contemporaneous, he sees a basic distinction between them in terms of "action vs. passion and letter (or flesh) vs. spirit (or word)."[17]

One of the most striking parallels between *Paradise Regained* and *Samson Agonistes* is finally resolved in strongly opposite terms. It is a similarity and then difference which are significant for an understanding of Milton's baroque theodicy. Both Christ and Samson have the possibility, and potentiality, of releasing a captive people from bondage. Christ rejects the possibility; Samson accepts it. I shall try to argue that while Christ, who, as one critic has said, is *in* this world but not *of* it,[18] rejects as a necessity the use of evil toward beneficent ends, Samson, who is very much *of* the world as well as *in* it, must immerse himself in evil in order to achieve his fulfillment.

Milton has chosen to interpret Satan's second temptation of Christ with "all the Kingdoms of the world" and "the glory of them" as, in part, the possibility of using the aid of either Rome or Parthia in order to free the ten Tribes of Israel: "Deliverance of thy brethren, those ten Tribes/ Whose offspring in his Territory yet serve" (III, 374–375). In rejecting this offer, that is, in deciding to leave the Israelites in bondage, Christ first points out the mutability of Satan's own attitude, reminding him that whereas he now appears to want to aid the Israelites he had once stood against them:

> Where was it then
> For Israel, or for David, or his Throne,
> When thou stood'st up his Tempter to the pride
> Of numb'ring Israel, which cost the lives
> Of threescore and ten thousand Israelites
> By three days' Pestilence? Such was thy zeal
> To Israel then, the same that now to me.   (III, 407–413)

Christ's refusal to aid the Israelites is based on his judgment that they were and are the cause of their own plight: "As for those captive Tribes,/ themselves were they/ Who wrought their own captivity" (414–415). The time will come when God "may bring them back repentant and sincere" (435), and this will lead to their freedom.

There are several motifs here which are important for my reading. The most important is that Christ remains "unmov'd" (386) by Satan's temptation. Christ's constant immutability throughout *Paradise Regained* is symbolic and is in direct contrast to Satan who is as shifting of attitudes and appearances as he is in *Paradise Lost*. Satan's disguises and mutability are as symbolic of his evil nature in the later poem as in the earlier. It is to this end that Christ specifically points out Satan's reversal of roles in regard to the welfare of the Israelites. "Unmov'd" is used to describe Christ not only in this episode but throughout the poem. For example, at the end of Christ's first encounter with Satan in the "First Book," the poem refers to the Savior's "unalter'd brow" (493), while the "Second Book" describes the deleterious effect of riches as they "slacken Virtue" (455).

In remaining immutable to the assaults of Satan, Christ is rejecting evil, its use for good ends and its inevitability (for him at least) in a world which is fallen and corrupted. This is specifically presented in the episode I am discussing by the proposed alliance with either Rome or Parthia. As I shall demonstrate, Samson, in a sense, aligns himself with the Philistines in order to save the Israelites. The implication is the use of evil toward beneficent ends. Samson's attitude toward mutability and deception is neither that of Christ (total rejection) nor of Satan (total identification). Samson's attitude is ambiguous—like Rinaldo's in *Gerusalemme liberata*—and it responds perfectly to the baroque theodical myth I am attempting to delineate. Christ's divine nature allows him an attitude which, as we shall see, Samson learns to appreciate and understand, but which remains unattainable for him except through its opposite.

A brief glance at a single episode in *Paradise Lost* may serve to introduce the ambiguous attitude toward mutability which is also to be found in Milton's drama. Raphael tells Adam, "God made thee perfect, not immutable" (V, 524). Eve does not remain steadfast in her pledge to Adam and to God. In succumbing to Satan's specious argument, she bends to his will. Adam, in turn, bends to Eve's fallen will. Upon gaining full consciousness of the fall and its implications, Adam repudiates Eve. In Book X, however, there is a reconciliation scene between Adam and Eve which is extremely important because it prefigures man's eventual reconciliation with God, his gaining of "the Paradise within" and, by so doing, is involved in Milton's metaphysic of the justification of evil and "the Fortunate Fall."[19]

After the fall, Adam regains a certain intransigence toward Eve. In repudiating her, he makes it clear that her own lack of steadfastness and her fall have made her as one with the evil and fraud which are Satan:

> Out of my sight, thou Serpent, that name best
> Befits thee with him leagu'd, thyself as false
> And hateful; nothing wants, but that thy shape,
> Like his, and color Serpentine may show
> Thy inward fraud, to warn all Creatures from thee
> Henceforth; lest that too heav'nly form, pretended
> To hellish falsehood, snare them. But for thee
> I had persisted happy, had not thy pride
> And wand'ring vanity, when least was safe,
> Rejected my forewarning, and disdain'd
> Not to be trusted, longing to be seen
> Though by the Devil himself, him overweening
> To over-reach, but with the Serpent meeting
> Fool'd and beguil'd, by him thou, I by thee,
> To trust thee from my side, imagin'd wise,
> Constant, mature, proof against all assaults,
> And understood not all was but a show
> Rather than solid virtue, all but a Rib
> Crooked by nature, bent, as now appears,
> More to the part sinister from me drawn,
> Well if thrown out, as supernumerary
> To my just number found.   (X, 867–888)

The imagery of deception ("false and hateful," "inward fraud," "hellish falsehood," "fooled and beguiled") and mutability ("*wand'ring* vanity," "*imagin'd* wise,/ Constant, mature proof against all assaults") in this speech defines Eve's fall as the opposite of the virtue of steadfastness defined by Christ in *Paradise Regained*. However, Eve pleads with Adam for forgiveness, and it is their reconciliation which evolves an ambiguous attitude toward immutability:

> She ended weeping, and her lowly plight,
> Immovable till peace obtain'd from fault
> Acknowledg'd and deplor'd, in Adam wrought
> Commiseration; soon his heart relented
> Towards her, his life so late and sole delight,
> Now at his feet submissive in distress,
> Creature so fair his reconcilement seeking,
> His counsel whom she had displeas'd, his aid;
> As one disarm'd, his anger all he lost,
> And thus with peaceful words uprais'd her soon.   (X, 937–946)

The "immovable" of this speech can be read to refer to: 1) Adam, who remains inflexible until Eve's confession of her fault brings peace between them,[20] 2) Eve, who is now as inflexible in her quest for forgiveness as she was flexible in her former vows, 3) Eve's plight, which must remain until change metamorphoses it into peace. This ambiguity of reference is carried over into the quality of immovability itself. In the first place, we feel that Adam is regaining some of his lost stature by his present hardness and inflexibility of attitude toward Eve, and Eve seems to gain strength by showing that she is at least capable of steadfastness. However, it is only by breaking the steadfastness that reconciliation and peace are finally achieved. Adam and/or Eve's *immovability* is rewarded when it reverses itself and becomes *movable*. This prefigures the action God himself must take, as Adam later tells Eve:

> Undoubtedly he will relent and turn
> From his displeasure.   (X, 1093-1094)

The ambiguity is clear when we recognize that the step being taken here by Adam toward "the Paradise within" is precisely the same step he took toward his fall. Here again Adam is "disarm'd" by the "Creature so fair," i.e., too fair, as Michael had warned him. However, the theme of reconciliation causes the reader to understand that this time Adam's action, although it mirrors the action of Adam's fall, is virtuous and is a step toward regeneration. Milton's psychology in the development of Adam and Eve, as well as in his control of the reader's attitude, is extraordinarily subtle at this point in the epic. Although something of our reaction to the passage may remain subconscious, if we react at all to the parallels between the reconciliation and the fall, our reaction must be ambiguous.

This ambiguity is present in Samson's final gesture. Throughout the drama change and mutability are identified with weakness and evil, and resolution and immutability are identified with strength and virtue. *Samson Agonistes* contains what could almost be called an ethic of immutability. It would be redundant to review all of the imagery associated with mutability. The "Shipwreck't" metaphor is central to the drama, from the simplest reference to "wand'ring thought" (302) to the most inconclusive confession by Samson of revealing God's "holy secret" (497). In the crucial episode in which Dalila points to Samson as the example of her weakness—"Let weakness then with weakness come to parle" (785)—she specifically accuses Samson of mutability:

> I saw thee mutable
> Of fancy, fear'd lest one day thou wouldst leave me
> As her at Timna, sought by all means therefore
> How to endear, and hold thee to me firmest.   (793-796)

In fact, mutability, as in the relationship between Adam and Eve, is a major theme of the episode. One of its strongest impressions is that Samson's character has undergone considerable regeneration, marked by the degree to which he is immutable in his resolution against succumbing to Dalila's will a second time. When Dalila pleads with Samson not to be "inflexible" with her, there is a good deal of irony present:

And Love hath oft, well meaning, wrought much woe,
Yet always pity or pardon hath obtain'd.
Be not unlike all others, not austere
As thou art strong, inflexible as steel.
If thou in strength all mortals dost exceed,
In uncompassionate anger do not so.   (813-818)

We feel that Samson must perform the opposite of Dalila's wish if he is to
redeem his situation. But the irony here is not at all simple. Samson, for
the most part, does remain inflexible toward Dalila. In fact, at the end of
the episode the Chorus attacks Dalila and her sex because it is her nature
to have "of constancy no root infixt" (1032). This condemnation, i.e., the
lack of constancy, contrasts with Samson's constancy and underlines his
achievement. Although Samson's full reversal of his immutability and
inflexibility does not come until the end of the drama, there is a prefiguration of Samson's final gesture within the episode. When Dalila approaches Samson for reconciliation, he forgives her "at distance."

> DALILA. Let me approach at least, and touch thy hand.
> SAMSON. Not for thy life, lest fierce remembrance wake
>   My sudden rage to tear thee joint by joint.
>   At distance I forgive thee, go with that.   (951-954)

Almost all the physical realities in *Samson Agonistes*—blindness, bodies,
sepulchres—have other dimensions, and here it is possible to think of the
"distance" Samson refers to as the indirect way in which his final gesture
will be a realignment with Dalila.

Samson expresses a revulsion similar to that with which he reacts to the
thought of Dalila's touch when at the beginning of the drama he considers the possibility of seeing his own degenerate state:

> Yet that which was the worst now least afflicts me,
> Blindness, for had I sight, confus'd with shame,
> How could I once look up, or heave the head.   (195-197)

He sees this function as belonging to his enemies: "Made of my Enemies
the scorn and gaze" (34). Just as Samson prefers to keep Dalila at a
distance, at that point in the drama he remains blind to certain aspects of
his nature.

X.   Sole Author, I

As close as Samson comes to making himself the "Sole Author" of his
circumstances and consciously accepting evil as a purposive dimension of
his existence, this commitment is always somewhat curtailed. And although in the Dalila encounter Samson sees himself as her "example" in
treachery, the following episode shows that he is still far from accepting
how "inevitably" bound good and evil are. He imagines that a single

combat between himself and Harapha can resolve the dichotomy with which Dalila left him:

> In confidence whereof I once again
> Defy thee to the trial of mortal fight,
> By combat to decide whose god is God,
> Thine or whom I with Israel's Sons adore.   (1174-1177)

Critics have been quite right in underlining the chivalric character of Samson's challenge to Harapha.[21] What should also be pointed out is its contrast with the guileful method Samson is about to embrace.

In the course of the drama and especially toward the end, Samson seems to be immersed in two mutually exclusive currents. On the one hand he is developing the sureness, resolution and steadfastness which he lacked before the beginning of the action of the drama. If weakness and mutability and their cognates seem to dominate the Dalila and earlier episodes, toward the end the drama echoes with resolution. The Officer refers to both Samson's "resolution" (1344) and "stoutness" (1346). Samson's frequently echoed "I will not come" implies a sureness of values and strength which, on the other hand, his increasingly paradoxical language seems to negate. If Samson truly cannot distinguish between foe and friend ("my deadliest foe will prove/ my speediest friend"), such resolutions seem weakly founded. In fact, Samson's conflicting attitudes come together at the end of the drama in what is its strongest paradox, and the energy of their collision provides the resolutions of the drama. When Samson like Adam reverses himself and tells the Officer that he will go with him, the Officer responds:

> I praise thy resolution.   (1410)

In fact, Samson has dissolved his resolution, and even the Officer—however unconsciously—is applying the word "resolution" to both Samson's negation and acceptance.

In the final moments of *Samson Agonistes* everything seems to be reversed. The rigidity and stoutness—the immutability—which Samson has been developing seem to have been a preparation for his final flexibility. In Samson's final gesture, unlike the straightforward challenge to Harapha, he employs all the wiles and deception which he has condemned in Dalila and his former self, but here he seems to embrace these in full consciousness as a positive good. Toward the end of the drama almost every line, especially Samson's lines, seem to have a double sense. When Samson first tells the Officer "Return the way thou cam'st, I will not come" (1332), he gives a command the essence of which he is about to follow himself. As Milton is at some pains to underline, Samson had fallen to his servile state through deception and wavering resolution, and it is precisely that road which he follows back toward his final victory over the Philistines. He breaks his resolution not to further humiliate himself by performing at their festival, and he deceives the Philistines with compliance knowing full well that he intends their destruction. What Milton's drama achieves at this point is not "harmony in spite of conflict" but "harmony because of conflict."

Many minor motifs of the drama are echoed as Samson returns to victory on, if not the same, at least a mirror reflection of the road that led him to defeat. The imagery of a tempest was used several times in describing the cause of Samson's shipwreck; and at the end of the drama it is the same "force of winds and water pent" which causes his simultaneous final destruction and victory:

> As with the force of winds and waters pent
> When Mountains tremble, those two massy Pillars
> With horrible convulsion to and fro
> He tugg'd, he shook, till down they came, and drew
> The whole roof after them with burst of thunder
> Upon the heads of all who sat beneath,
> Lords, Ladies, Captains, Counsellors, or Priests,
> Thir choice nobility and flower, not only
> Of this but each Philistian City round
> Met from all parts to solemnize this Feast.
> Samson with these inmixt, inevitably
> Pull'd down the same destruction on himself;
> The vulgar only scap'd who stood without.   (1647–1659)

Samson is never more fully identified with the Philistines than here: "Samson with these *unmixt, inevitably/* Pull'd down the same destruction on himself." The placing of "inevitably" at the end of the line subtly indicates that Samson not only inevitably destroyed himself with the Philistines, but that he was inevitably identified ("inmixt") with them. The image is as binding as those describing Tancredi and Argante in their final duel. The Chorus makes it clearer. To be "in death conjoin'd" with foes is an almost eerie transcendence of the drama's friend-enemy dichotomy:

> Among thy slain self-kill'd
> Not willingly, but tangl'd in the fold
> Of dire necessity, whose law in death conjoin'd
> Thee with thy slaughter'd foes in number more
> Than all thy life had slain before.   (1664–1668)

The "burst of thunder" which announces the Philistines' and Samson's joint deaths seems to be an echo of the sound heard in praise of Dagon when Samson first appears in the theater:

> At sight of him the people with a shout
> Rifted the air clamoring thir god with praise.   (1620–1621)

Samson's lowest and highest points are echoed in the same sound. Another landmark on both of Samson's roads is the breaking of a law. Just as he had broken a law against gentile marriages, he is breaking a law in presenting himself at the Philistine festival:

> Thou knowst I am an Ebrew, therefore tell them,
> Our Law forbids at thir Religious Rites
> My presence; for that cause I cannot come.   (1319-1321)

In both cases Samson is prompted to break the law by an "intimate impulse" (223) or "rousing motions" (1382) which argue God's involvement in using hidden methods toward unknown beneficent purposes. Finally, if in his downfall Samson had been Dalila's example, on the road toward his final victory Samson allows Dalila to be his model. Samson characterizes his presenting himself at the Philistine festival as:

>   . . . a greater sin
> By prostituting holy things to Idols;
> A Nazarite in place abominable
> Vaunting my strength in honor to thir Dagon?
> Besides, how vile, contemptible, ridiculous,
> What act more execrably unclean, profane?   (1357-1362)

In criticizing Dalila for breaking her marriage vows to him, he had accused her precisely of "prostituting holy things to Idols." Therefore, in deciding to present himself at the Philistine festival, Samson is again following Dalila's example. The breaking of resolution, the use of deception and the tendency toward self-destructiveness implied in Samson's final gesture are all, in a sense, a regression to the "Effeminacy" which Samson had so detested in himself. However, Samson is now fully aware and accepts and undertakes the inevitability of his actions.

Samson's final ambiguous statements grow out of the antinomies of the drama, his increasing awareness of paradox and the almost inevitable, in its context, metamorphosis of his growing resolution into its opposite. The structure of antitheses is forcefully multiplied during the drama's final moments. The Chorus tells Manoa that he is reversing the usual pattern of filial relationships in wanting to nurse Samson ("Sons wont to nurse thir Parents in old age,/ Thou in old age car'st how to nurse thy Son" (1487-1488). Samson invokes the friend-enemy dichotomy in voicing his fluctuating associations with Israelites and Philistines and his fallen glory:

> Brethren farewell, your company along
> I will not wish, lest it perhaps offend them
> To see me girt with Friends; and how the sight
> Of mee as of a common Enemy,
> So dreaded once, may now exasperate them
> I know not.   (1413-1418)

In expressing the fact that Samson has achieved his victory at the point of death, the Chorus puts it in antithetical terms: "Living or dying thou hast fulfill'd/ The work for which thou wast foretold" (1661-1662). And the Messenger voices dualistically the inevitable simultaneity of Samson's victory and defeat:

> Inevitable cause
> At once both to destroy and be destroy'd.   (1586-1587)

It is in this context that we hear the full ambiguity of Samson's final statements.[22] The most significant of these is his acceptance of the Philistines' commands:

> I could be well content to try thir Art,
> Which to no few of them would prove pernicious.
> Yet knowing thir advantages too many,
> Because they shall not trail me through thir streets
> Like a wild Beast, I am content to go.
> Masters' commands come with a power resistless
> To such as owe them absolute subjection;
> And for a life who will not change his purpose?
> (So *mutable* are all the ways of men)
> Yet this be sure, in nothing to comply
> Scandalous or forbidden in our Law.   (1399-1409)

Since Samson is here using Dalila's and the Philistines' devious methods, we can understand his "try thir Art" in a double sense. This also effects a final identification with them. Undoubtedly Samson is thinking of the "commands" of another master, but it is significant that the will of the Philistines and God are consonant at this moment and that Samson unifies them. Further emphasizing Samson's acceptance of his own responsibility is the Messenger's description of the horror of the *sight* of Samson's final victory:

> O whither shall I run, or which way fly
> The sight of this so horrid spectacle
> Which erst my eyes beheld and yet behold?
> For dire imagination still pursues me.   (1541-1544)

Samson, we remember, had expressed a similar horror of sight in contemplating his own responsibility for his downfall. But here it is the Messenger who expresses the horror; Samson has embraced it.

Various conjectures about the nature and meaning of offstage actions inform the last scene of the play with a special irony. The most obvious example of this is Manoa's conjecture at the noise that Samson's eyesight has been "by miracle restor'd" and that he "now be dealing dole among his foes,/ And over heaps of slaughter'd walk his way" (1527-1530). Most significant in this regard is the Messenger's account. Immediately upon saying that after Samson had performed feats of strength none dared to appear "antagonist" (1628), he describes Samson walking over to the pillars:

> And eyes fast fixt he stood, as one who pray'd,
> Or some great matter in his mind revolv'd.   (1637–1638)

Samson has become his own "Antagonist" and is finally able to look at and through his own destiny. Manoa's final speech at the end of the drama recalls its mirror patterns. This time it is not "weakness with weakness," or Samson and Dalila, or Israelites and Philistines or Samson and Harapha which are reflected but "Samson" with "Samson" and "heroicly" with "Heroic." The progress the drama has made is clear. Antinomies—most essentially good and evil—have been balanced in perfect "aesthetic plenitude" to the point of total identity:

>   Samson hath quit himself
> Like Samson, and heroicly hath finish'd
> •A life Heroic, on his Enemies
> Fully reveng'd hath left them years of mourning,
> And lamentation to the Sons of Caphtor
> Through all Philistian bounds. To Israel
> Honor hath left and freedom, let but them
> Find courage to lay hold on this occasion;
> To himself and Father's house eternal fame;
> And which is best and happiest yet, all this
> With God not parted from him, as was fear'd,
> But favoring and assisting to the end.   (1709–1720)

We feel in these lines that Samson has acquitted himself fully both "on his Enemies" and "To Israel." It is in this speech that Samson is described as "Soak't in his enemies' blood" (1726). Despite the horror of this sight, the struggle is one which seems to have been so totally resolved within Samson's mind that there is nothing strained in the lines directly preceding it:

> Nothing is here for tears, nothing to wail
> Or knock the breast, no weakness, no contempt,
> Dispraise, or blame, nothing but well and fair,
> And what may quiet us in a death so noble.   (1721–1724)

Samson himself had voiced the paradoxical quality of his tragedy when he asked the Officer whether he should "in my midst of sorrow and heart-grief/ To show them feats, and play before thir god" (1339–1340). The confused identities so crucial to the entire drama are here achieving expression as the union of joy and sorrow. It is hardly avoidable in a world where, as the Chorus tells us in the concluding lines of the drama, God himself "seems to hide his face."

XI. Inmost mind

The isomorphic imitation of antithetical worlds has a special character in Milton. The Philistines and the Israelites are identified in that they are both closely associated with Samson *(These two proportion'd)*. This in itself creates an allegoric structure similar to the *Un sol punto* in *Gerusalemme liberata*. Samson is the focus of the conflict between the Philistines and the Israelites, and their conflict mirrors a conflict of forces within Samson. Milton's sympathy for this allegoric attitude is clearly seen in Book XII of *Paradise Lost* in which Michael describes external tyranny as resulting from the lapse of reason within man:

> Therefore since hee permits
> Within himself unworthy Powers to reign
> Over free Reason, God in Judgment just
> Subjects him from without to violent Lords;
> Who oft as undeservedly enthral
> His outward freedom: Tyranny must be,
> Though to the Tyrant thereby no excuse.   (89–96)

We are reminded of this attitude when Samson, the bound victim of the Philistines, describes his torments which do not remain as "body's wounds and scores . . . But must secret passage find/ To th' inmost mind" (606–611). He continues:

> Thoughts my Tormentors arm'd with deadly stings
> Mangle my apprehensive tenderest parts,
> Exasperate, exulcerate, and raise
> Dire inflammation which no cooling herb
> Or med'cinal liquor can assuage,
> Nor breath of Veneral Air from snowy Alp.   (623–628)

The most effective symbol for this outward-inward balance in *Samson Agonistes* is Samson as his own prison ("Prison within Prison," 153); he is jailor (Philistines) as well as prisoner (Israelites), and when he destroys himself in the Philistine theater, he both destroys the prison (the Philistine yoke and his physical life) and releases the prisoner (Israelite bondage and his own return "Home to his Father's house" 1733). But there is more varied imagery in *Samson Agonistes* which tends to see Samson as the focus, container or prototype of the world around him.

Samson is described as an army (346), a fort (236), a camp ("his hair/ Garrison'd round about him like a Camp/ Of faithful Soldiery," 1496–1498) and a walled city ("What boots it at one gate to make defense,/ And at another to let in the foe," 560–561). He is described carrying on his shoulders the "Gates of Azza," just as Hercules bore up heaven (146–150). Samson describes the number and greatness of his miseries as "So many, and so huge, that each apart/ Would ask a life to wail" (65-66). His strength is such that it "Might have subdu'd the Earth,/ *Universally* crown'd with highest praises" (174-175) and is "Equivalent to Angels" (343), and the Chorus describes him as the "Image" of God's strength (706).

More importantly, in addition to the Dalila encounter, Samson is described throughout the poem as a prototype or example to others. The chorus describes him as a "mirror of our fickle state" (164). Samson observes that he was not a "private person" (1208-1213). At one point, during his encounter with Manoa, Samson describes himself as not only bringing doubt to "feeble hearts" but also affecting both Dagon and God so that his influence extends even to the divine worlds:

> Father, I do acknowledge and confess
> That I this honor, I this pomp have brought
> To Dagon, and advanc'd his praises high
> Among the Heathen round; to God have brought
> Dishonor, obloquy, and op't the mouths
> Of Idolists, and Atheists; have brought scandal
> To Israel, diffidence of God, and doubt
> In feeble hearts.   (448-455)

After Samson's death, Manoa anticipates his "Monument" (1734) and "Legend" (1737):

> Thither shall all the valiant youth resort,
> And from his memory inflame thir breasts
> To matchless valor, and adventures high.   (1738-1740)

Corollary to this are the many events or legends to which Samson's own legend is compared—Gideon (277-281), Jephtha (282-289), the Phoenix (1699-1707)—so that he becomes a monadic archetypal symbol encompassing more than his own world.[23]

Samson dies at the hour of noon (1612), the hour which earlier had been used to describe metaphorically the height of heroic development (682-686); it is an hour which has archetypal connotations as an epiphany containing and revealing all the other hours. And when Samson dies there is a "universal groan/ As if the whole inhabitation perished" (1511-1512).

As we shall see, in Calderón's radically allegoric *autos*, the monadic symbol of *Un sol punto* or the *Inmost mind* is very specifically the mind of the central hero or a focal point which contains all of reality so that the whole antithetical dichotomy between demonic and beneficent worlds seems to be nothing more than the reflection of the hero's moral condition—his choice between good and evil, strength and weakness, life and death. Apart from the imagery I have been discussing, there is at least a hint of this specific monadic symbolism in *Samson Agonistes*. We are told by the Messenger that when Samson was in the theater none dared "to appear Antagonist" (1628). Samson has become his own "Antagonist," and there is an indication that the conflict between the antithetical forces in the drama is resolved—as would be the conflict between good and evil within a saint—in Samson's mind:

> And eyes fast fixt he stood, as one who pray'd,
> Or some great matter in his mind revolv'd.
>
> (1637-1638)

XII. *Intimate impulse*

Just as with the *Segni ignoti* in *Gerusalemme liberata*, however much the concerns of theodicy may be articulated in the narratives and prosody of *Samson Agonistes*, an element of mystery prevails. Samson describes his motivation to marry the woman of Timna—which act he knew to be against the Hebrew law—as having come from an "intimate impulse" (223) that "motion'd was of God" (222). This, Samson tells us, is to the purpose "that by occasion hence/ I might begin Israel's Deliverance, the work to which I was divinely called" (224-226). The sense here of an intuited purpose which is beyond the understanding of reason is clear. Subsequently, the Chorus makes this point emphatically in a speech (293-325) which insists that the "ways of God" are "justifiable to Men," chastises those who doubt God ("they walk obscure") and mocks those who find contradiction in God:

> They ravel more, still less resolv'd,
> But never find self-satisfying solution.
>   As if they would confine th' interminable,
> And tie him to his own prescript,
> Who made our Laws to bind us, not himself,
> And hath full right to exempt
> Whom so it pleases him by choice
> From National obstriction, without taint
> Of sin, or legal debt;
> For with his own Laws he can best dispense.
>
> (305-314)

The Chorus ends by—in effect—dismissing reason as an instrument to understand the mysterious ways of God:

> Down Reason then, at least vain reasonings down.
>
> (322)

There are several references in the drama to the "unsearchable dispose" (1746) of God. In what we have discovered to be Samson's final embrace of deception and all that this implies, it is clear that he is responding to the same "intimate impulse":

> I begin to feel
> Some rousing motions in me which dispose
> To something extraordinary my thoughts.   (1381–1383)

This note of mystery is also expressed through one of the most interesting antithetical dichotomies in *Samson Agonistes*. Like the other dichotomies in the drama it resolves itself into paradox.

During the early Manoa episode, the Chorus praises Samson's temperance with wine (as opposed to women):

> Desire of wine and all delicious drinks,
> Which many a famous Warrior overturns,
> Thou couldst repress, nor did the dancing Ruby
> Sparkling, outpour'd, the flavor, or the smell,
> Or taste that cheers the heart of Gods and men,
> Allure thee from the cool Crystálline stream.   (541–546)

Samson subscribes to this praise, and the Chorus goes on to generalize the dichotomy between wine and "the cool Crystálline stream":

> Wherever fountain or fresh current flow'd
> Against the Eastern ray, translucent, pure,
> With touch ethereal of Heav'n's fiery rod
> I drank, from the clear milky juice allaying
> Thirst, and refresht; nor envied them the grape
> Whose heads that turbulent liquor fills with fumes.
>   CHORUS. O madness, to think use of strongest wines
> And strongest drinks our chief support of health,
> When God with these forbidd'n made choice to rear
> His mighty Champion, strong above compare,
> Whose drink was only from the liquid brook.   (547–557)

I quote these lines at length in order to emphasize the number of lines Milton devotes to this binary image. Few of the drama's other essential dichotomies are as fully developed. Like the friend-enemy dichotomy, it appears again.

At the end of the drama, when Samson has been described as "inmixt, inevitably" (1657) with the Philistines, they are described as bringing on their destruction "Drunk with Idolatry, drunk with Wine":

> While thir hearts were jocund and sublime,
> Drunk with Idolatry, drunk with Wine,
> And fat regord'd of Bulls and Goats,
> Chanting thir Idol, and preferring
> Before our living Dread who dwells
> In Silo his bright Sanctuary:
> Among them hee a spirit of frenzy sent,
> Who hurt thir minds,
> And urg'd them on with mad desire
> To call in haste for thir destroyer;

They only set on sport and play
Unwittingly importun'd
Thir own destruction to come speedy upon them.
So fond are mortal men
Fall'n into wrath divine,
As thir own ruin on themselves to invite,
Insensate left, or to sense reprobate,
And with blindness internal struck.   (1669–1686)

Samson himself can be described as fallen into a "wrath divine" because
he also brings destruction on himself. We have seen in the imagery of
"Prison within Prison," etc., how specifically the action is meant to be
simultaneous. It is not accidental that Samson's identity with the Philistines is evoked in this Semichorus when the Philistines are described in
terms of blindness: "And with blindness internal struck." In his last
speech, as reported by the Messenger, Samson describes himself as moving from reason ("I have perform'd, as *reason* was, obeying") to an action
inspiring an amazement which is complementary to the drunkenness of
the Philistines:

"Hitherto, Lords, what your commands, impos'd
I have perform'd, as *reason* was, obeying,
Not without wonder or delight beheld.
Now of my own accord such other trial
I mean to show you of my strength, yet greater;
As with amaze shall strike all who behold."   (1640–1645)

Clearly, the inspiration for Samson's final act does not come from "the
cool Crystálline stream"; rather, just as Samson's final action is accom-
modated by the Philistines' drunkenness, it is inspired in something
beyond reason, "something extraordinary." This turning from the cool
stream of reason is corollary to Samson's sudden reversal from his immutability and his final embrace of deception.

CALDERÓN

Y está claro que si la tierra os pareció como
un grano de mostaza y cada hombre como
una avellana, un hombre solo había de cu-
brir toda la tierra.

Don Quijote, Cervantes

El mayor encanto amor; de D. P.º Calderon de la barca

Personas de ella

Ulises —	floro —	astrea —	vna dueña —
antistes —	clarin —	libia —	vn criado —
arquelao —	arsidas —	yris —	brutamonte —
Lebrel —	lisidas —	casimira —	aquiles —
Polidoro —	circe —	tisbe —	vn soldado —
timantes —	florida —	galatea —	musica —

Tocan vn clarin y descubrese vn nabio y en el Ulises, antistes arquelao, lebrel, polidoro, timantes, floro, y clarin;

anti   en vano forcejamos
        quando Rendidos a la suerte estamos
        ┌ entra dos elementos
arg   │ omicidas los mares y los vientos
        └ oy seran nra Ruina
timan   siza el trinquete
pol   larga la bolina
flor   grande tormenta el vracan promete
anti   ala xicia:
 eb   a la escota
clar   al chafalbete
Ulis   jupiter soberano
        ┌ que resollo en espumas desesperano
  s   │ yo boto a tu deydad aras y altares
        └ si la colera aplacas de estos mares
antis   ┌ sagrado dios neptuno
        │ griegos ofendes a pesar de sumo
arg   │ causando esta desmayos
        └ el cielo en Relampagos y Rayos

Manuscript page: Courtesy of The Hispanic Society of America.

In many respects illusion and beneficent evil is a more obvious theme in Calderón than in either Tasso or Milton. Calderón makes *engaño* and *desengaño* the central theme of many of his plays; major and minor characters debate and soliloquize about it at great length. The theme is very much Calderón's own, and there is not the strong derivative relationship to an earlier literature such as we noticed between Tasso and renaissance epics. Neither is the theme of *engaño* subservient in Calderón as it seems to be in Milton to the subtle analysis of the development of character. It is very much in the foreground of the plays. One sees this merely by looking at the list of Calderón's plays. Many of their titles, such as *En esta vida todo es verdad, todo mentira, Darlo todo y no dar nada* and *Amado y aborrecido,* could serve as epigraphs for the different sections of my analysis. At the same time Christian doctrine, the biblical theme of man's fall and redemption through sacrificial death and Christian symbolism are closer to the surface or at least more specifically and analytically treated in much of Calderón than in either *Gerusalemme liberata* or *Samson Agonistes.*[1] For this reason, I have deliberately chosen to discuss, for the most part, plays based on pagan myth so as to keep a closer parallel with my discussions of Tasso and Milton in which a theodical interpretation of the theme of illusion and beneficent evil is present only by implication. In analyzing Calderón's reinterpretation of classical myth, one seems to see more clearly his own most essential myth. Furthermore, one has the feeling that Calderón's virtual obsession with *engaño* and the paradoxical nature of good and evil was both—in an artistic paradox—less conscious and more inventive than his concern with Christian doctrine.

In my discussion of both Tasso and Milton, I indicate that the nature of a beneficent evil is communicated in the mode essential to tragedy which dictates that the moment of the hero's highest fulfillment is also the point of his lowest decline, i.e., the moment in which he identifies with the antagonist or his opposite element. Most of Calderón's work and all of the plays I shall consider, even *La vida es sueño,* are essentially untragic. The theodical nature of a beneficent evil is communicated more—in an Augustinian "aesthetic plenitude"—through the symmetrical balancing of good and evil. While the heroes' embrace of *engaño* is essential for their fulfillment, that fulfillment is not precisely identical with their surrender to *engaño*. *Engaño* is presented in clearly ambiguous terms, but between *engaño* and *desengaño* there is a pause which is filled by a *deus ex machina* who performs the miracle of metamorphosing *engaño* into *desengaño*, evil into good. On the other hand, in Calderón's *autos* we find a more perfect representation of the *Un sol punto* and the *Inmost mind* symbolism I discussed in Tasso and Milton because in the *autos* the action is totally allegorical. Indeed, it is all specifically represented as taking place within a spaceless and timeless mode of being.

The theme of *engaño* has been more specifically discussed in Calderónian criticism than in Tasso and Milton. Therefore, I refer to the existing criticism more specifically here than I do in my other essays. However, there has been no specific discussion of the relationship in Calderón between the themes of *engaño*, the transitoriness of life, *sueño*, etc., and theodicy or a metaphysics of beneficent evil. It is to this relationship that I devote my attention.

In form, this essay is closer to my essay on Tasso, in which I analyze separately individual episodes of *Gerusalemme liberata*, than to my essay on Milton, in which I analyze in some detail only *Samson Agonistes*. In discussing theodicy in Calderón, I use different plays to illustrate the various points of my argument. But, as in my discussion of *Gerusalemme liberata*, there are many cross references, and as Rinaldo and Armida evolve as the focus of my Tasso essay, in this Calderón essay *La vida es sueño* serves as a central point of reference.

At this point the steps of my argument should be familiar. My introductory section on Tasso *(Docere delectando)* and my initial discussion of the Olindo and Sofronia episode in *Gerusalemme liberata (Volto ascoso al volto)* and my introductory remarks about *Samson Agonistes (Changest thy count'nance)* serve essentially to introduce the themes and nature of my argument. In the present essay, I begin *(Fingir y disimular)* with an analysis of Calderón's *El mayor encanto, Amor*, a play based on the Circe myth. All of the major themes and elements I discuss in Tasso and Milton as well as Calderón—the Circe myth, narcissistic mirror imagery, ambivalence and antinomies, dichotomies, ambiguity, paradox, allegorical division of the central character—are present in this play. Its elaborate development of the specific type of *engaño* involved in *fingir* and *disimular* I find revealing as to both Calderón's generally ambiguous presentation of *engaño* and the particular pattern of *engaño-desengaño* which Calderón constantly uses. In my next section *(Síncopa del día)*, I begin my discussion of *La vida es sueño*. There I point out the ambiguous and paradoxical imagery which dominates the play. Rosaura, particularly in her use of disguise and the androgynous references made to her, is centrally associated with this imagery. Here there are many echoes of the use of disguises in *Gerusalemme liberata (Sotto mentito aspetto)* and the stylistic and conceptual paradoxes of *Samson Agonistes (Race of glory/ race of shame)*. Continuing my discussion of *La vida es sueño (Confuso laberinto)*, I investigate the relationship between concealment and revelation and *engaño* and *desengaño*. Their close identification and rather confused identity are like the ambivalent and shifting nature of reality in Tasso *(Mondo mutabile)* and Milton (Shipwreck't). The pattern which eventually becomes evident between *engaño* and *desengaño (Sangrienta lengua que enseña)*, indicates, as similar modes of ambiguity did in Tasso *(Adorno inganno)* and Milton *(Thir Superstition yields)*, a paradoxical beneficence in deception and illusion and the evil of which they are an emanation. True to this pattern and in a mode very similar to Milton's Samson, Segismundo fully and consciously embraces *engaño* and its concomitant evil. However, previous to the embrace there is a strong tendency to evade *engaño-desengaño*. This evasion and its unfortunate consequences are more clearly seen in Calderón's *Eco y Narciso (Anteviso el daño)*. The inability of some of Calderón's minor characters—and in the case of *Eco y Narciso* the protagonist—to accept the theodical benevolence of *engaño* is like the lesser accomplishment of Tancredi *vis à vis* Rinaldo in *Gerusalemme liberata (L'un l'altro guarda)* and the relationship of all the minor characters to Samson in *Samson Agonistes (A rougher tongue)*. In this respect, Calderón is making subtle use of narcissism in *Eco y Narciso* in contrast to the androgyny of *La vida es sueño*. The particular interpretation of the Circe myth which I considered in Tasso and Milton *(Narciso, Th'example)* is also at work in Calderón. In the next section *(La luz del desengaño)*, I examine more specifically in the play based on the Psyche myth, *Ni Amor se libra de Amor*, the pattern of *engaño-desengaño*. Their paradoxical identity is like the identity between war and peace *(Securi fra l'arme* in *Gerusalemme liberata)* and the identity between his prison and freedom *(House of liberty)* which Milton's Samson finds. Therefore, *engaño* in Calderón responds to a metaphysical justification of evil as illusion and deception do in Tasso *(Colpe umane)* and Milton *(Unmov'd)*. Toward this purpose, the metamorphosis of good and evil into each other and their total isomorphic imitation of each other, which I discuss in Tasso *(Movon concordi)* and Milton *(These two proportion'd)*, are also in evidence in Calderón *(Tan presto tan otro)*. This metamorphosis of antitheses is clearest in *La estatua de Prometeo*. In this play *engaño*, i.e., disguises, deceptions, ambiguous reality, a paradoxically beneficent evil, is almost totally replaced by a process of metamorphosis in which a *deus ex machina* transmutes antinomies, including good and evil, into each other. In the baroque myth I am delineating, metamorphosis seems to be the agent of transmission between an Irenaean suffering mode and an Augustinian aesthetic mode of theodicy. This leads me to my final seciton *(El gran teatro del mundo)* in which I discuss *engaño* and evil in Calderón's *autos*. In these allegorical works, *engaño* is totally replaced by metamorphosis and the entire landscape of the play becomes no more than a totally mutable reflection of man's spiritual condition. We noticed this phenomenon in Tasso *(Un sol punto)* and Milton *(Inmost mind)*. In Calderón's *autos* the tendency of allegorical literature to present the objective world as a reflection of man's inner landscape is completely realized. Finally, I save my summary remarks on Calderón for an Epilogue in which I summarize my conclusions and indicate the possibility of even more displaced modes of theodicy in baroque literature.

I. Fingir y disimular

In almost any one of Calderón's plays, whether *Dramas* or *Autos Sacramentales* or even the *Comedias de capa y espada*,* the reader can find evidence of his obsession with *engaño* and *desengaño*. By way of introduction to his development of this theme, I could select almost any one of his hundreds of plays. But inasmuch as my discussions of Tasso and Milton to some extent center on Armida and Dalila as Circe figures and a major theme of this essay will be to discuss Rosaura in *La vida es sueño* as a related figure, it seems sensible to begin by analyzing Calderón's felicitous treatment of the Circe and Ulysses** myth in *El mayor encanto, Amor.*

Apart from *La vida es sueño,* most of the *dramas* and *autos* that I shall discuss are based on classical myths. The medieval and renaissance vogue for allegorizing classical myths seems to have influenced Calderón considerably. In writing about the myths, while he does not allegorize the *dramas* nor follow slavishly standard Christian interpretations in the *autos,* he does seem to be prompted toward a consideration of good and evil in theodical terms. In most of the plays I discuss I will be interested in analyzing only those themes which are pertinent to my interest in theod-

---

*All my Calderón quotations are taken from the three-volume Aguilar *Obras Completas*: (1) Pedro Calderón de la Barca, *Obras Completas*, I-*Dramas*, ed. Angel Valbuena Briones (Madrid, 1959); (2) II-*Comedias*, ed. Angel Valbuena Briones (Madrid, 1960); III-*Autos Sacramentales*, ed. Angel Valbuena Prat (Madrid, 1952). I quote only from the *Dramas* and the *Autos Sacramentales*. Since most of my quotations are from the *Dramas*, I give only the page references when I quote from that volume. When I quote from the *Autos Sacramentales*, I also include "*Autos*." There are innumerable typographical errors in the Aguilar editions of Calderón. I have corrected them in my quotations, but there are a few cases in which I was in doubt about a variant seventeenth-century spelling. I left these as printed in the Aguilar.

**In deference to style, I anglicize the major classical names, but not those of minor characters.

icy. It therefore seems to be appropriate to begin with a relatively complete and full reading of *El mayor encanto, Amor,* showing the richness of Calderón's inventiveness in treating the Circe myth. In so doing I will underline the themes which I shall be discussing in the other plays. *El mayor encanto, Amor,* like so many of the mythical dramas, is an extremely well written play. Its poetry is lovely and varied, and its structure is intricately and subtly wrought. The major and minor plots, the imagery, the comic episodes and the interweaving of the various themes all work toward a well-conceived whole. In reading it, one senses what happy affairs these plays must have been as they were presented with their elaborate *son et lumière* staging in the Buen Retiro.

The opening lines of *El mayor encanto, Amor* sound one of the most important themes in Calderón's treatment of *engaño*: surrender to an adverse fate.

> En vano forcejamos
> cuando rendidos a la suerte estamos,
> contra los elementos.   (1598)

Calderón has revised the Ulysses myth to his own purposes in that it is a threatening storm which brings Ulysses to Circe's island. This storm is the harbinger of another impending storm or the symbol of an adverse fate with which the hero must come to terms. (It also appears in his rendering of the Psyche legend.) As Ulysses sets foot upon the island, his first words sound another major theme, the dichotomy of two opposing fates, beneficent and malefic:

> Saluda el peregrino,
> que en salado cristal abrió camino
> la tierra donde llega,
> cuando inconstante y náufrago se niega
> del mar a la inconstancia procelosa.   (1599)

The earth succors while the sea opposes. In most of the other mythical plays, this dichotomy is seen in terms of two opposing gods, such as Minerva and Pallas in *La estatua de Prometeo.* In all cases it is not until the opposing forces are resolved that the hero's fate is fulfilled. In *El mayor encanto, Amor,* as in the other plays, these opposing forces are deliberately ambiguous. It is Circe's island which soon becomes the greatest threat to Ulysses and his men; the sea which finally provides help and escape.

Soon all of Ulysses' men disappear into the "triste oscuro centro" (as it is described by one of them, Clarín, 1599) of the island in order to explore it. Ulysses remains with the *gracioso* figure, Clarín, who will eventually reflect in a comic mode Ulysses' own adventures on the island. The "triste oscuro centro" is a constant symbol in the plays. It is the center of *engaño* which the hero must penetrate before he experiences *desengaño*. In *La vida es sueño* there is Segismundo's prison, in *Ni Amor se libra de Amor* Cupid's darkened bedchamber, and caves appear, prominently, in *Eco y Narciso* and *La estatua de Prometeo*.[2]

Almost immediately the men reappear, having been metamorphosed into animals. One who escaped transformation, Antistes, tells Ulysses about Circe and what has happened. By referring to man as the source of his own danger, he openly hints at the allegorical content of the play:

> del mar pensamos que el cielo
> nos había dado amparo,
> nos había dado puerto;
> mas iay triste! que el peligro
> es de mar y tierra dueño,
> porque en la tierra y el mar
> tiene el peligro su imperio.
> . . .
> pues el hombre en tierra y mar
> • lleva el peligro en sí mismo.   (1600)

When Ulysses has heard Antistes' story, he expresses the dichotomy of adverse forces on which the play centers in terms of the traditional conflict between Juno, who favors the Greeks, and Venus, who opposes them. He asks for protection against the one from the other. Juno's messenger, Iris, arrives with the branch which will protect him. The rest of the first act is taken up by Ulysses successfully resisting Circe, both telling their stories, and the introduction of some of the plot and subplot elements for the rest of the play. Calderón brings a good deal of Dante's *Inferno* (XIII, 16ff.) or Virgil's *Aeneid* (III, 39ff.) into play here. Ulysses requests that two trees which are metamorphosed human beings be restored—"a la luz restituídos"—because he has unknowingly wounded them with his sword. Circe explains that they are Flerida and Lisidas, handmaiden and foreign prince, who have been thus transformed because they had profaned Circe's palace with carnal love. She also speaks disdainfully of Arsidas, who is in love with her. When he appears begging her favor, she informs him that his complaints, in fact, serve only to demonstrate that she is accomplishing her purpose.

In the second act, Calderón takes over the legend with his favorite themes. It begins with the discovery of Circe in tears by her handmaidens. Circe confesses to Flerida that she loves Ulysses and engages her aid in a bed trick: "que quiero a Ulises, y no/ quiero que Ulises lo entienda" (1609). She wants Flerida to enamor Ulysses by day, and she will replace her at night. Flerida, introducing the central theme of the play, protests that Circe is imposing a double burden on her: Flerida, who loves Lisidas, must dissemble her love for him ("disimular") and at the same time feign ("fingir") love for Ulysses:

Yo amo a Lisidas, y tú
cruel, señora, me ordenas
que *disimule* el amarle;
yo no amo a Ulises, e intentas
qua *finja* amarle. ¿Pues cómo,
a dos afectos atenta,
quieres que olvide a quien quiero,
y que a quien olvido quiera?   (1609)

This double aspect of *engaño* (*disimular* and *fingir*) is played with
elaborately in the drama. When Flerida asks Circe why she does not
engage the services of one of the women who will at least not have to
disimular, she responds that Flerida's having to *disimular* is a protection
in her eyes. Circe can not possibly be jealous of someone who she knows
loves another: "de manera/ que tu no me daras celos,/ y otras sí" (1609).
For the first time, a specific virtue is attributed to *engaño*.

At this point Clarín and Lebrel appear. Circe decides to overhear their
conversation. Clarín thoroughly maligns Circe; Lebrel tries to protect
her. When Circe suddenly appears, Clarín pretends that he has been
defending her against the abuses of Lebrel. Circe orders Lebrel's punishment and Clarín's reward. Flerida, who has heard the real debate with
Circe, asks in astonishment about the inverted justice:

¿Cómo castigas, señora,
al que te defiende, y premias
al que te ofende?   (1610)

But Circe is answering deception with deception. This inverted punishment and reward will again be reversed. Clarín, like the Clarín in *La vida
es sueño,* runs right into disaster by his rapid fluctuations in trying to
avoid it.

In the next scene Ulysses begins to show signs of involvement with
Circe. He can neither forget nor love her: "es imposible olvidarla/ y es
imposible quererla" (1610). As the characters seat themselves around
Circe's garden, Flerida, fulfilling her mistress' wishes, seats herself next
to Ulysses. Lisidas sees her advances toward Ulysses and immediately
becomes jealous. When Flerida is asked to initiate some debate with
which to pass the early hours of the afternoon, hoping to relay a message
to Lisidas, she asks whether it is more difficult to feign or to dissemble:
"¿cuál es más dificultoso?/ ¿Fingir o disimular?" (1611). A debate ensues
between Arsidas, who is in love with Circe, and Ulysses. Arsidas says that
fingir is more difficult, while Ulysses insists that *disimular* is. Ulysses
argues that he who must pretend not to love always carries with him the
burning passion of his love; Arsidas argues that he who pretends to love
must fight oblivion. Interestingly, in terms of the drama's resolution,
Ulysses characterizes the pretense of love as a "batalla sin enemigo"

(1610). Circe finally attempts to resolve the question by asking Ulysses to pretend *(fingir)* to love her (since he thinks it is so easy) and Arsidas to pretend not to *(disimular)*. In this way she will get the attentions of Ulysses, which she so much desires, and will be rid of Arsidas. They both agree. The scene ends with the very Calderonian note of Circe wishing that illusion and reality were reversed, i.e., that Ulysses really loved her and that Arsidas did not:

> ¡Oh si este amor, si este olvido,
> uno no fuera fingido,
> y otro fuera verdadero! (1613)

In the next scene, Flerida approaches Ulysses as she has been commanded to do. Both Lisidas and Circe watch the scene unobserved. In his response, Lisidas delineates a structure which is common to the plays I shall be considering: the dual role of the baroque hero discussed in my Prologue. (Hamlet is both the avenger of his father's murder, and the object of Laertes' revenge for his own father's murder.) Lisidas says that Ulysses gives him both life and death: he effected his release from enchantment as a tree, and yet now he is stealing Flerida from him. In *La vida es sueño* this is Clotaldo's position in relation to Astolfo who both saves him from Segismundo's death stroke and dishonored his daughter. It is, in fact, the same theme brought to a human, circumstantial level of an adverse and protective god ("tierra" and "mar" or Juno and Venus), and there is an important evolution in the theme here in that the antinomies are embodied in one figure, Ulysses.

The other observer, Circe, finds Flerida's deception all too real: "Bien que fingiese quisiera,/ no que fingiese tan bien" (1613). She tells Flerida to stop because in this instance, reversing her previous desire, she does not wish illusion to be too real: "no quiero celos fingidos/ que sepan a verdadero" (1614). At this point there is no doubt that we are well into the particular territory of Calderón's own myth. The special dialect is unmistakable, and classical Greece has been left far behind. When Circe leaves Flerida, Lisidas appears to his beloved. Here another particular Calderonian theme with which I shall be concerned is introduced. Lisidas tells Flerida that he has witnessed both her flirtation with Ulysses and her scene of reproach with Circe so that he realizes that the former was feigned. Flerida responds:

> . . . que este fingimiento,
> si fué causa de mi engaño,
> también, también desengaño
> *ha de ser de mi tormento.*[3] (1614)

Deception is a source of *engaño,* but also of *desengaño.* Similarly, Samson's regeneration was from illusion but it was accomplished *through* illusion. The same, as we shall see in terms of *fingir* and *disimular*, is true of Ulysses. However, another theme (or part of the same theme) just as important for Calderón is immediately introduced. Lisidas tells Flerida that he cannot accept this paradoxical identity of good and evil. He believes only the scene that he witnessed between Flerida and Ulysses:

> De un triste el rigor es tal,
> que aunque mal y bien estén
> iguales, duda del bien
> el crédito que da al mal.   (1614)

This inability to accept the identity of antithetical forces acts as a foil to the greater vision of the hero. I discussed this phenomenon in *Samson Agonistes* under the title *A rougher tongue* and in Tancredi as opposed to Rinaldo in *Gerusalemme liberata*. The theme and contrast is present in many of the plays I shall discuss. Only in *Eco y Narciso* does the limited vision afflict and condemn the hero himself.

In the following comic scene, Clarín goes to collect his reward and receives his *desengaño*. He is metamorphosed into a monkey. Immediately following, Ulysses and Circe, retiring from the hunt, reappear. Ulysses protests his love for Circe. She asks him to stop pretending *(fingir)*, but Ulysses makes it known to her through an elaborate image involving the hunt of a heron that he now is really in love with her. The only thing that is feigned is that he feigns to love her when he in fact does ("sólo esto es fingido en ser fingido" 1619). At this moment the other members of the court hunt arrive and Circe tells Ulysses that he must for the moment pretend not to love her (*"disimular"* 1619). This comic reversal of the sitaution prefigures a more important reversal in the plot. Ulysses has learned to love Circe through *engaño (fingir)*, but his final escape from her also will be accomplished through *engaño (disimular)*. He will escape from illusion *through* illusion. When Ulysses has fully embraced Circe and come to see her as a reflection of his own weakness and effeminacy (like Samson), he will dissemble the strength not to love her and thus escape by feigning virtue.

The second act closes with another debate about *fingir* and *disimular*. There is a sudden eruption of warlike sounds. It seems that the giant Brutamonte, who had earlier tormented Clarín and who as a cyclops hates the Greeks, has decided to attack them in Circe's palace. There is a general rush to battle. But Circe quickly halts the action with the announcement that the attack has been staged by her in order to test the reactions of her feigned and real lovers. The debate between Arsidas and Ulysses about whether the nobler course lies in acting like or unlike a lover is so fierce that Circe has to end it by invoking a storm.

The second act seems to concentrate on establishing the theme of confused identities, a theme which, as we shall see, is even more elaborately developed in *La estatua de Prometeo*. Just as Ulysses is both a giver and a taker of life for Lisidas, through *fingir* and *disimular* his and Arsidas' roles as lover and non-lover are confused and identified with each other. In fact, in the third act Arsidas becomes the enemy besieging Circe's palace, with Ulysses, the lover, within. There is, of course, a surface and thematic similarity here to Tancredi and Clorinda in Tasso, i.e., in the confused identities of enemy and lover. The third act expounds on the nature of Ulysses' enchantment by Circe. Mirror imagery is very prominent, and the echo from Tasso here is of Armida.

Act III begins with a discussion among Ulysses' men. Having noticed his immediate response to Circe's staged war, they are going to stage another such scene in order to get him away from Circe. They describe Ulysses in Circe's gardens in terms of narcissistic mirror imagery:

> . . . Ulises anda
> estos jardines, que hermosos
> narcisos son de esmeralda,
> y enamorados de sí,
> se están mirando en las aguas.   (1622)

This theme is taken up in the next scene when we see Ulysses and Circe in the garden. In describing the garden, to the notes of mirror imagery Circe adds harmonies of resolved antitheses ("tan contrariamente hermosas,/ y hermosamente contrarias") and illusion and reality ("cuál es la yerba o el agua"):

> En esta florida margen,
> desde cuya verde estancia
> se juzgan de tierra y mar
> las dos vistosas campañas,
> tan contrariamente hermosas,
> y hermosamente contrarias,
> que neutral la vista duda
> cuál es la yerba o el agua,
> porque aquí en golfos de flores,
> y allí en selvas de esmeraldas,
> unas mismas ondas hacen
> las espumas y las matas,
> a los suspiros del Noto,
> y a los alientos del aura,
> puedes descansar, Ulises,
> las fatigas de la caza
> en mis brazos.   (1623)

The mirror imagery has the same thematic purpose as in the Armida episode of *Gerusalemme liberata* where Rinaldo recognizes himself in Armida. When Ulysses finally decides to flee Circe and is asked what he is fleeing from, he responds: "De mí mismo" (1630).

The plot of Ulysses' men fails. It awakens a debate between war and
love within Ulysses:

> Aquí guerra, amor aquí
> oigo, y cuando así me veo,
> conmigo mismo peleo:
> defiéndame yo de mí.   (1625)

But love wins. Ulysses remains lost to "olvido" in Circe's "prisión" and
"sepulcro." These terms (1625) all correspond to Segismundo's forgotten
and imprisoned situation before he finally embraces *engaño* with moral
awareness. Ulysses has not yet recognized Circe as a reflection of his own
weakness. That comes later in the act.

The scene immediately after Ulysses' surrender to his love for Circe
again begins with war noises. Circe thinks that it is another Greek plot,
but Flerida informs her that this time the threat is real. Arsidas and
Lisidas, the two jealous lovers, have left Circe's island and are now
returning from across the sea with armies. The approach from the wide
horizons of the sea ("vi . . . una confusa apariencia,/ que era, al perspicaz
examen/ de la vista, neutral duda,/ mezcla de nubes y naves" 1626)
contrasts rather vividly with the "triste oscuro centro" of Circe's island in
which we have just left Ulysses. In Calderón the center and circumference
have antithetical values, but these values are reversed and identified with
each other. Arrival by sea heralded Ulysses' fall into Circe's enchantment,
and now it heralds his release from it. Once again, the same symbol takes
on antithetical values.

We learn from a conversation between Arsidas and Lisidas that Lisidas
has experienced *desengaño*. He is no longer jealous of Ulysses but realizes
that Flerida's love for the Greek hero was feigned under constraint ("un
cauteloso amor, amor fingido"). He wants only to free Flerida from
Circe. This subplot *desengaño*, of course, prefigures Ulysses'. When
Arsidas and Lisidas and their army encounter a deadly "selva umbría"
(1638) and the soldiers wish to turn back from the dark forest, Arsidas—
Rinaldo-like—points out the illusion: "que esos monstruos incultos/ son
fantásticas formas" and leads the army through. Another prefiguration of
Ulysses' *desengaño* involves Clarín, who has been turned into a monkey.
In an amusing scene between Clarín ("de mona") and Lebrel, who plans
to train and exploit this clever monkey as a public attraction, Clarín is
released by his enchantment by seeing himself in a mirror.

Ulysses' *desengaño* comes in the form of a visit from the spirit of
Achilles. This episode and the closing scenes of the play strongly suggest
the influence of *Gerusalemme liberata* on Calderón. Antistes and some of
Ulysses' other men decide to take advantage of the siege of Circe's island
in order to sneak into his retreat and place at his feet, as a more effective

reminder of Ulysses' other self than the earlier staged battle, the armor of
Archilles. After they have done this, Ulysses awakes from a lethargic sleep
("ni bien vida, ni bien sueño" 1629). This is precisely the pattern followed in *Gerusalemme liberata* by Carlo and Ubaldo in bringing to
Rinaldo the magic shield in which he is to see his reflection. Ulysses sees
the armor as another symbol of the defeat within himself of Mars by love:

> Bien está a mis pies, por que
> rendido a mi amor se juzgue
> y segunda vez en mí
> amor de Marte se burle.   (1629)

But the spirit of Achilles appears to chide Ulysses for his present effeminacy:

> Y tú, afeminado griego,
> que entre las delicias dulces
> del amor, de negras sombra
> tantos esplendores cubres.   (1630)

Ulysses decides to heed the warning even if it is an illusion ("aunque
soñada, es bien/ que la crea y no la dude" 1630). This particular theme is
significant in that it is *engaño* which both victimizes (in the feigned-
turned-true lover for Circe) and frees Ulysses; however, it is not fully
developed in this play. Realizing that there is no simple victory over love,
i.e., over himself, but that once before the "fingido" has passed over to the
"verdadero" in his love for Circe, Ulysses feigns a virtue, as it were, and
runs away from love in an action which is obviously related to the
dissembling of love *(disimular)* in the play:

> Huyamos de aquí; que hoy
> es huir acción ilustre,
> pues los encantos de amor
> los vence aquel que los huye.   (1630)

Here we understand a little more clearly Ulysses' earlier argument that
disimular is a battle with an enemy, i.e., Circe or the part of himself
which Circe represents.

The play's final scene with Circe reminds one very strongly of the
defeat of Armida and Solimano in *Gerusalemme liberata*. In *El mayor
encanto, Amor* Circe does not lose the battle. This makes her final defeat
all the more symbolic. She is, in fact, victorious over Arsidas and Lisidas.
Circe informs Lisidas (repeating a by-now familiar theme, i.e., the malig-
nant and benevolent effect of one and the same phenomenon) that if he
has come to this pass on Flerida's account, she will also free him on her
account:

Pues si preso estás por ella
también por ella estás libre.   (1631)

When Circe hears of Ulysses' flight, she comments on the fact that her
suffering aids his escape:

¿Quieres que me queje humilde?
Escucha. Mas, ¡ay triste!,
no llore quien te pierde, ni suspire,
si te dan, para hacer mejor camino
agua mis ojos, viento mis suspiros.   (1631)

Like Armida (XX, 63-64), she debates between revenge on her escaped
lover and destroying herself. But when Galatea, owing a debt of gratitude
to Ulysses, impedes her attempts to stop Ulysses, Circe, like Argante, who
falls by his own weight (XIX, 24), and Solimano, who seemed to be
paralyzed against the Christian (XX, 106), turns inward and destroys
herself:

                . . . si no puedo
vengarme en quien huye libre
en mí podré.   (1632)

Circe's palace disappears into the sea. In my essay on Tasso, I read this
self-destruction as allegorically representing Rinaldo's and the Christians' conquering weaknesses within themselves. The same reading lends
itself to *El mayor encanto, Amor* even if in a more comic vein.

If it is *engaño (fingir)* which leads to Ulysses' enchantment, it is also
engaño (disimular) which helps him to escape. Ulysses moves from
feigning love toward dissembling love, not only in the scene at the end of
the second act when the interruption of Circe and Ulysses by the other
courtiers makes him arrest his confession of love and feign his original
indifference, but also in the course of the whole play. It is to this thematic
end that so many antinomies are balanced in the play: Ulysses is a source
of both life and death for Lisidas; Flerida is a source of freedom and
imprisonment for Lisidas; Ulysses and Arsidas—as well as Circe herself—
as both lover and enemy; the approach by sea as a fall into and an escape
from the "triste oscuro centro" of *engaño*; the metamorphosis or confusion between "verdadero" and "fingido," jealousy and love; and the antithetical values which the land and the sea take on. An allegorical reading
of the play might see these balanced dichotomies as the theodical identity
of good and evil in a metaphysics which understands the beneficent
purposes of evil. It is through Circe that Ulysses conquers himself.
However, these themes are present in *El mayor encanto, Amor* almost like
unresolved musical themes. While the play serves as an excellent intro-

duction to Calderón's treatment of illusion and beneficent evil, it is essentially a grand and elaborate entertainment. The metaphysical implications of the themes are more clearly evident in *La vida es sueño*.

II. Síncopa del día

In the past several decades, *La vida es sueño*, like Calderón's work in general, has received increasingly enlightening criticism. Menéndez y Pelayo's markedly wrong objections to the play on the basis of (1) a lack of continuity in Segismundo as a plaything of passion and as an ideal prince and (2) an extrinsic subplot have been many times superseded.[4] E. M. Wilson's essay "On *La vida es sueño*" is one of the earlier examples of this recent criticism.[5] In answer to Menéndez y Pelayo's first objection he demonstrates the many "possibilities of redemption" which Segismundo exhibits from the very beginning of the play: "pity," "wit," "the [correct] matter of his speeches," and "the wish to know."[6] In answer to Menéndez y Pelayo's second objection, Mr. Wilson points out that Segismundo's experiences are reflected in those of other persons in the play:

> Pride comes before a fall, and from the fall the proud man may become humble and prudent. Segismundo is not the only man to be humbled; Clarín, Basilio, Astolfo, a servant, and the rebel soldier have also to learn how to submit to the inevitable.[7]

Each one of them undergoes a "disillusion," "expresses too much confidence in his own powers, deeds or position" and "is humbled." Rosaura and Clotaldo, on the other hand, are purposefully contrasted with Segismundo and these other characters:

> Clotaldo and Rosaura subordinated their lives to principles; they saw they had difficulties to face and the world was confusing and untrustworthy. They faced their problems with constancy, unselfishness, and prudence. For this reason they did not ride to a fall as the others did.[8]

In his essay "The Structure of Calderón's *La vida es sueño*," A. E. Sloman further demonstrates the relationship between the plot and subplot by showing how both Rosaura and Segismundo initially are "dogged by misfortune" and how their fates are worked out through interdependent action.[9]

Nevertheless, there is a great deal as regards Rosaura's role and function in the play that has not been fully illuminated. This is particularly true when we consider the function and use of illusion and the presence of theodicy. In general, criticism has associated Rosaura with Segismundo's redemption. Federico Michele Sciacca argued that Rosaura revealed to Calderón's hero a form of Platonic beauty.[10] In a brief essay, "Rosaura's Role in the Structure of *La vida es sueño*," William M. Whitby further argued that Rosaura is associated with Segismundo's self-enlightenment and his "respect for the rights of others."[11] These interpretations are correct as far as they go. But they seem to me to ignore an important aspect of the play. The Circe figures in Tasso and Milton, Armida and Dalila, were also associated with the heroes' enlightenment and were, therefore, clearly ambiguous. They were beneficent as well as destructive agents. Even Circe in *El mayor encanto, Amor* is the impetus whereby Ulysses passes from *engaño* to *desengaño* and becomes sufficiently enlightened to conquer his own failings. Calderón's critics have understandably tended to emphasize Rosaura's beneficent effects. The heart of the play is, after Segismundo's conquest of an adverse fate, the fortuitous growth of his character and his redemption, and Rosaura does play an important role in these developments. But critics have, I think, tended to overlook the precise way in which Segismundo does conquer his adverse fate. Rosaura is also a Circe figure and, therefore, as ambiguous as Armida or Dalila. The fact that in the *auto* version of *La vida es sueño*,[12] which I shall discuss later, Rosaura's role is taken by Sombra, the shade of death and sin, is in itself an indication of the paradoxical nature of her redeeming qualities.

In general, criticism has not fully addressed itself to the function of illusion and paradoxes—much less to their relationship to theodicy—in *La vida es sueño*. For example, while Angel Valbuena Prat discusses the structure of the whole play (he calls it an "orden barroco")[13] and Dámaso Alonso discusses the antithetical structure of the verse,[14] neither one of them associates it with a metaphysical theme within the play. Undoubtedly one reason for this is the existence in the criticism of Spanish literature of the ready-at-hand term "conceptismo," a "juego de palabras" or "ingenio," which, whenever the ambiguities and paradoxes appear, can be invoked without explaining their meaning or function, if, indeed, it is believed by the critics that they have a function in the play. "Conceptismo" also exists in Tasso and Milton in such phrases as "trovando ti perdo eternamente" (XIX, 105) and "my deadliest foe will prove/ My speediest friend" (1262–1263). But they are expressive of a metaphysical truth their authors are trying to communicate. This is no less true of Calderón. As an example of the one-sided view of Rosaura, William M. Whitby quotes the following lines of verse while discussing Rosaura as "bringing light to [Segismundo's] sleeping consciousness" and her presence as "equivalent to light":

Ojos hidrópicos creo
que mis ojos deben ser;
pues cuando es muerte el beber,
beben más, y desta suerte,
viendo que el ver me da muerte,
estoy muriendo por ver.   (368)

These lines are spoken by Segismundo in order to describe his reaction to Rosaura, and yet in quoting this beautiful and powerful "hidrópicos" metaphor, Mr. Whitby does not mention death. I shall be interested in discussing Rosaura's negative qualities as well as her beneficent nature. But before I analyze in what sense Rosaura is a Circe figure and is related, for Segismundo, to death, some analysis of the ambiguous imagery and paradoxical language of the drama is necessary.

The light which characterizes Rosaura and which is an important symbol for the play is the ambiguous "luce incerta" of dawn or sunset, qualities of light "quinci notturne e quinde mattutine," with which we are already familiar through Tasso. It is, as we shall see in my discussion of Calderón's drama based on the Cupid and Psyche legend, *Ni Amor se libra de Amor,* like the brilliance of the good Cupid shrouded in the dark night of Psyche's love. *La vida es sueño* begins at "anochecer" with the appearance of Rosaura. Segismundo's prison, from which the action in all three acts emanates, is, like "anochecer," a particularly ambiguous symbol. It is situated in a tower "cuya planta baja sirve de prisión." The tower and the cave, both important symbols for the particular theme of Calderón I am discussing, are joined here. Rosaura appears at the height ("en lo alto") of the surrounding mountains and descends ("baja") to the bottom level of the tower. Significantly enough, the timorous light of nightfall is immediately associated with illusion:

> Mas si la vista no padece engaños
> que hace la fantasía,
> a la medrosa luz que aun tiene el día,
> me parece que veo
> un edifico.   (366)

The doubtful light which Rosaura notices in Segismundo's prison is described in even more paradoxical terms in that it is said to add to the obscurity:

> ¿No es breve luz aquella
> caduca exhalación, pálida estrella,
> que en trémulos desmayos,
> pulsando ardores y latiendo rayos,
> hace más tenebrosa
> la oscura habitación con luz dudosa?   (366)

In the second act, Segismundo specifically associates this ambiguous light with Rosaura when, imploring her not to depart immediately upon her arrival in his presence, he refers to "la síncopa del día":

> Oye, mujer, detente;
> no juntes el ocaso y el oriente,
> huyendo al primer paso;

que juntos el oriente y el ocaso,
la lumbre y sombra fría,
serás, sin duda, síncopa del día.   (381)

This "luz dudosa" has many echoes in the play.[15] Almost all of its
imagery is expressed in terms of ambivalence, ambiguities and paradoxes;
something which is neither dark nor light, a mixture of both, or, paradoxically, both one and the other. Indeed, Segismundo's reaction to
Rosaura is consistently ambiguous. In the first moment of their encounter he is violent ("entre mis brazos/ te tengo de hacer pedazos," 367), but
two lines later he is all tenderness ("tu voz pudo enternecerme"). And this
pattern does not vary throughout the play. When Clotaldo first recognizes the sword Rosaura is carrying as his own, he does not know whether
to believe that the events he is witnessing are "illusiones o verdades"
(369). When Basilio interrupts the duel between Astolfo and Segismundo
and asks what is happening, Segismundo echoes Astolfo's "Nada" with
"Mucho" (382). When Rosaura announces to Clotaldo that she intends to
revenge herself on Astolfo, they each define her action in perfectly balanced opposites; "despecho"-"honor," "desatino"-"valor," "frenesí"-
"ira" (392). But these antitheses have been well demonstrated by Calderón's critics. One antinomy which touches more closely my concern with
a beneficent evil occurs at the end of the play when Segismundo announces to Rosaura that in order to be truly "piadoso" with her, he must
now be "cruel" (395). And, finally, when Rosaura approaches Segismundo in the third act and describes her previous contacts with him, he
expresses his astonishment by describing truth in terms of illusion and
reality:

> . . . Pues ¿tan parecidas
> a los sueños son las glorias,
> que las verdaderas son
> tenidas por mentirosas,
> y las fingidas por ciertas?   (394–395)

Rosaura is not the only character in the play who embodies a dual role
for another. The way in which she does this for Segismundo is rather
subtle, and it is revealed only gradually in the course of the play. But
Astolfo becomes for Clotaldo in a very concrete and conscious way both
the source of dishonor and life. He has dishonored Clotaldo's daughter,
Rosaura, but also has saved him from death at the hands of Segismundo.
Clotaldo expresses this ambiguous relationship in terms of a dual obliga-
tion to Rosaura and to Astolfo:

> Y así, entre los dos partido
> el afeto y el cuidado,
> viendo que a ti te la he dado,

y que dél la he recibido,
no sé a qué parte acudir,
no sé qué parte ayudar.
Si a ti me obliqué con dar,
dél lo estoy con recibir.   (391)

The antithetical verbs "dar" and "recibir" are, in fact, continually echoed
in the play. But the ambiguity of Clotaldo's relationship to Astolfo is
clearly symbolic of larger themes in the play. It embodies Segismundo's
relationship to Rosaura and to fate in general.

An aspect of the play's imagery which is more revealing in regard to
Calderón's central concern with *engaño* and *desengaño* is the life-death
dichotomy. *La vida es sueño* abounds with expressions such as "vivo
cadáver," "esqueleto vivo" and "animado muerte." Segismundo's prison
is called "cuna y sepulcro," and birth and death are frequently compared:
"el sepulcro vivo/ de un vientre—porque el nacer/ y morir son pareci-
dos" (372). Just as Samson's blindness and imprisonment reversed for
him the roles of friends and enemies, so does Segismundo's imprisonment reverse the blessings and misfortunes of life and death:

pues dar vida a un desdichado
es dar a un dichoso muerte.   (368)

When Clotaldo examines Rosaura's sword which is supposed to bring
her support in the Polish court, he, mindful of the king's condemnation
of anyone who has seen Segismundo, realizes that instead the sword will
be a warrant for her death:

si quien la *trae* por favor,
para su merte la *trae*.   (369)

These lines, particularly in the repetition of "trae," approach the prosodic balancing in Tasso and Milton. The idea that life may be death and
death life is strongly echoed when Rosaura tells Clotaldo that the life
without honor she has received from him is not life:

pues vida no vida ha sido
la que tu mano me dió   (391)

Any doubt that this "vida no vida" is related to death is quickly erased
when Rosaura announces that she shall consequently seek her death
(resulting in the debate of opposites I have just quoted). Very suggestive
of the function of illusion in *La vida es sueño* and its relation to Calderón's ultimate concern with theodicy is Clotaldo's description of the sleep
which transports Segismundo from his cave to his father's palace as a
feigned death: "muerte fingida" (376).

Another important dimension of this imagery in *La vida es sueño* is the androgyne. Anthropology has long been interested in archetypal images of the androgyne as a symbol for the resolution of contraries and the abolition of contradictions, a metaphysics in which good and evil are illusory and relative as all other pairs of opposites—hot-cold, long-short, etc. This archetypal imagery is, of course, very evident and important in Clorinda, the disguised Erminia and the narcissistic imagery related to Armida and Rinaldo, and it is implicit in Samson's effeminacy. Androgynous imagery is very explicit in Calderón's development of Rosaura, who, like Erminia and Clorinda, wears a disguise.

Disguise is the most important symbol for *engaño* and *desengaño* in *La vida es sueño*. Rosaura's particular disguise is to be dressed as a man. She reveals her disguise to Clotaldo with words which could be used to describe fate and reality as they are gradually revealed in the play: things are not as they seem.

> que es este exterior vestido
> enigma, pues no es de quien
> parece: juzga advertido,
> si no soy lo que parezco.   (375)

Her disguise is no more simple than the disguise of opposites in Clorinda, Tancredi and Erminia—the lover hidden under the appearance of the enemy warrior. Rosaura herself elaborates on her androgynous quality in her lengthy revelation and plea to Segismundo for help in the third act. In a tripartite structure, this speech restates the major themes of the play. Rosaura begins by comparing Segismundo's exit from prison in order to win his princedom to "la Aurora" (392), the complementary opposite of the "anochecer" with which the play began. She tells Segismundo that he has seen her three times: (1) as a man in prison, (2) as a woman amid the majesty and pomp of the palace and (3) now as an ambiguous phenomenon: "monstruo de una especie y otra":

> La tercera es hoy, que siendo
> monstruo de una especie y otra,
> entre galas de mujer,
> armas de varón me adornan.   (393)

This "monstruo"—the resolution of her opposite sexes—is equivalent in terms of the play's imagery to the "luz dudosa" of dawn and sunset which is, again, a strange resolution of dark and light. The speech reiterates and plays with the theme of the purposeful resolution of opposites. Rosaura describes her mother as unfortunate as she was beautiful ("según fué desdichada,/ debió de ser muy hermosa"), as if this misfortune and blessing were necessary corollaries of each other. She describes the adulterous intercourse from which she was born in equally ambiguous terms:

> . . . maldado nudo
> que ni ata ni aprisiona,
> o matrimonio o delito,
> si bien todo es una cosa.   (393)

Finally, Calderón's *conceptismo*—which so easily can be passed over as mere ornament without seeing its relation to the thematic material of the play—comes out when Rosaura describes the loss of her betrothed, Astolfo, to Estrella:

> ¿Quién creerá que habiendo sido
> una estrella quien conforma
> dos amantes, sea una Estrella
> la que los divida ahora?   (393)

This star is to Rosaura what Astolfo is to Clotaldo. It is a star which both unites and separates in any number of senses. In gaining Astolfo, Estrella separates Rosaura from him. And it is a different phase of the same fate which separates Astolfo from Rosaura and joins him to Estrella and will later rejoin him to Rosaura. In concluding her speech, Rosaura joins her opposite identities toward a single purpose:

> Mujer, vengo a persuadirte
> al remedio de mi honra;
> y varón, vengo a alentarte
> a que cobres tu corona.
> Mujer, vengo a enternecerte
> cuando a tus plantas me ponga,
> y varón, vengo a servirte
> cuando a tus gentes socorra.   (394)

III. *Confuso laberinto*

In revealing her misfortunes to Segismundo in the third act (392-394), Rosaura also mentions two fortuitous circumstances. One is the aid which her disguise afforded her ("para que a menos costa/ fuese") and the other is the aid she derived from disclosing her disgrace to her mother when she told her that she had been betrayed by Astolfo. Concealment and revelation are very subtly related in *La vida es sueño*, and they provide the most prevalent imagery in the play for *engaño* and *desengaño*. They both have individual beneficent effects, although they are frequently dependent on each other and, most importantly, upon occurring or being resorted to in a specific order. They are very much like *fingir* and *disimular* in *El mayor encanto, Amor. Engaño* is the descent into an underworld of evil and deception from which *desengaño* is the release; although *engaño* is the only road toward that restoration. As in *Gerusalemme liberata,* the fact that *desengaño* can be achieved only through *engaño* and that *engaño* has its own momentary beneficent effects leads to the eventual theodical acceptance of *engaño* as a necessary evil. It is in the confusion of *discovering* the *disguised* intruder to be his daughter that Clotaldo calls the situation, in which, in a sense, all of the play's major characters find themselves, a "confuso laberinto":

> ¿Qué confuso laberinto
> es éste, donde no puede
> hallar la razón el hilo?   (375)

Disguise has many expressions in *La vida es sueño* apart from Rosaura's male costume. Clotaldo hides his identity as her father from Rosaura so that if fate should not present an opportunity for salvaging her honor, his own honor will not be soiled. This is, of course, the subplot parallel to Basilio's concealment of his ancestry from Segismundo. Further, Segismundo is hidden in prison just as Rosaura hides herself. In fact, the play contains several passages in which Segismundo's prison and the use of disguise are related. When Segismundo and Rosaura first see each other in the palace, their reactions are exactly parallel. Segismundo intuits having seen her beauty before, and Rosaura remembers seeing Segismundo who is now released from the strictures of his prison. In both there has been release from constrictive forces (Rosaura's disguise and Segismundo's prison) and flowering (Rosaura's beauty and Segismundo's princedom):

> SEG. (Yo he visto esta belleza
>   otra vez.)
> ROS. (Yo esta pompa, esta grandeza
>   he visto reducida
>   a una estrecha prisión.)   (381)

In Rosaura's speech to Segismundo, she describes the disclosure to her mother of the secret of her disgrace by Astolfo as a breaking out of prison ("rompió la prisión"). Her description also contains a veiled allusion to the Pandora myth which has an interesting parallel, as we shall see, in Calderón's treatment of that myth in *La estatua de Prometeo*:

> Violante, mi madre, ¡ay cielos!
> rompió la prisión, y en tropa
> del pecho salieron juntas,
> tropezando unas con otras.   (393)

As we shall see, the ultimate effect of Rosaura's revelation of her "penas" to her mother is helpful to her.

In *La vida es sueño*, breaking out of prison or disclosing secrets is also identified, paradoxically, with the embrace of illusion. The two, concealment and revelation, are so closely related that it is not always clear which is which or in which order they occur. When Segismundo first comes out of prison for his reign as king-for-a-day, he is constantly reminded that he may be dreaming and that all he is experiencing may be no more than an *engaño*. When Rosaura disclosed her disgrace to her mother, she was embracing *engaño* in a very different sense by bringing to the light of day the "penas" she had been hiding. One of the most important themes in the play is the tendency to hide or to hide from adverse fortune. Yet, it is only when this fortune is fully accepted and embraced that the individual characters really experience *desengaño* and are freed from tyranny.

Although many of the characters in Calderón's play attempt to hide (or to hide from) the negative effects of an adverse fate—Clotaldo will not reveal Rosaura's identity lest it soil his honor, Clarín, the fool, attempts to escape the battle and, most notably, Basilio hides Segismundo in his tower-cave—Segismundo himself demonstrates the most revealing attempted escapes, and, of course, it is when he reverses this tendency to escape and embraces *engaño* with his cry "soñemos, alma soñemos" (389) that the whole action of the drama is resolved.

Very early in the play Segismundo reveals a tendency to hide his weaknesses and misfortunes. When, at the beginning of the first act, he learns that he has been discovered in his prison by an intruder, he reacts with the lines which are typical of the whole drama:

> Pues la muerte te daré,
> porque no sepas que sé
> que sàbes flaquezas mías.   (367)

Francisco Ayala has observed the mirror imagery in these lines which he considers typical of the baroque.[16] The reflection of consciousness in the "you-know-that-I-know-that-you-know" is especially interesting because the intruder is Rosaura, who reflects and is involved in so many aspects of Segismundo's fate. Segismundo is afraid of having his weakness come to light—perhaps even to the light of his own consciousness. Later in the play, in the second act, Segismundo again threatens death, this time to Clotaldo, who keeps reminding Segismundo that his present power as king may be no more than an illusion:

> A rabia me provocas,
> cuando la luz del desengaño tocas.   (382)

The revelatory phrase "la luz del desengaño" is crucial. Segismundo prefers to keep his mind clear of the possibility of disillusionment. This is most clearly indicated later in the play, when, in the third act, the soldiers come to take him out of prison again and to engage him in battle for his rights to the kingdom. Segismundo refuses to join them because he is afraid of further disillusionment. Again, he echoes the mirror imagery of his initial response to Rosaura by expressing horror at the possibility of *seeing himself* subject to his adverse fate:

¿Otra vez queréis que toque
el desengaño o el riesgo
a que el humano poder
nace humilde y vive atento?
Pues no ha de ser, no ha de ser:
miradme otra vez sujeto
a mi fortuna.   (388)

In initially turning his back on the soldiers and retreating to his prison, Segismundo is, in a sense, turning his back on life itself. In the *auto* version of *La vida es sueño*, Man is released from the chaos of non-being when he is created and placed in the "alcázar" which is the equivalent of Basilio's palace:

A sacar me determino
de la prisión del no ser
a ser este oculto Hijo,
que ya de mi Mente ideado
y de la Tierra nacido,
ha de ser Príncipe vuestro.   (*Autos*, 1391)

Segismundo is not the only character for whom simply the knowledge of possible disillusionment and personal disaster is painful and who, therefore, turns his back on it. In the second act, Estrella, who has been trying to extract from Astolfo the miniature portrait he had worn during their first encounters, suddenly reverses her request and asks to be spared the portrait because she does not want to remember: "no quiero con tomarle, que me acuerdes/ que te le he pedido yo" (385). It is precisely at this point in the play that Segismundo has been returned to his prison, i.e., Basilio's disguise of or deception about his son's fate, and Clarín— again paralleling life and death—advises him to remain concealed in sleep:

No acabes de despertar,
Segismundo, para verte
perder, trocada la suerte
siendo tu gloria fingida,
una sombra de la vida
y una llama de la muerte.   (385)

Estrella, we assume, is saved some pain by her self-willed blindfold; Segismundo's deception is imposed upon him. Nevertheless, the two are associated in that they are both a descent, consciously and unconsciously, into *engaño*. In his long first-act soliloquy, Basilio describes discovering the tragic divination concerning Segismundo as an act of suicide: "que a quien le daña el saber/ homicida es de sí mismo" (372).

As with Tasso and Milton, the more closely one analyzes the major scenes of Calderón's drama, the more allegorical they become. Calderón's *auto* version of *La vida es sueño* makes it quite explicit that at least in one sense the play can be read as an allegory of the fate of Man, and the various other characters in the play are reflections of this fate or of different aspects of the central character. If Segismundo—like other characters in the drama—is afraid that the mere consciousness of his weakness will be painful to him, we see in Rosaura, who is so closely identified with Segismundo, how bringing these weaknesses to light can be paradoxically both destructive and productive. At the very beginning of the drama, Rosaura falls victim to Basilio's edict that anyone who has discovered Segismundo must die. Her *discovery* will result in death. At the same time, another *revelation* has taken place which will redeem her. When Clotaldo brings Rosaura to Basilio, announcing that she (or "he," because Rosaura is still in disguise) has discovered the prince, Basilio responds that it does not now matter because he himself ("supuesto que yo lo digo") has already revealed his secret:

> No te aflijas, Clotaldo;
> si otro día hubiera sido,
> confieso que lo sintiera;
> pero ya el secreto he dicho,
> y no importa que él lo sepa,
> supuesto que yo lo digo.   (374)

Basilio has decided, at least provisionally, to face—if not embrace—his fate, and this acceptance, albeit temporary, of what has been prophesied as a negative fate has the effect of saving Rosaura's life. Rosaura—like Basilio's embrace of a destructive fate—is saved only temporarily. But what is important here is that the *discovery* of something hidden and secret—Segismundo in his prison—is simultaneously the source of condemnation and release from that condemnation. Of course, it is only within the context of the whole play—in which many similar revelations of evil have beneficent effects—that this aspect of the interaction between Rosaura and Basilio becomes clear. And it does not seem accidental that both in the *Old Testament* and in Calderón the phenomenology of concealment and revelation can be related to theodical concerns about good and evil.

IV. Sangrienta lengua que enseña

Under the title *Adorno inganno*, I discussed the innumerable passages of *Gerusalemme liberata* in which illusion or evil is used for or works toward a good purpose, thereby developing into a major theme. The same pattern is clearly developed in *La vida es sueño*. The play begins with a debate between Rosaura and Clarín which touches the theme comically. When Clarín complains that Rosaura does not include his own troubles in her long lament with which the play opens, Rosaura responds that she does not want to deprive Clarín of the pleasure of sounding his own complaints:

> Que tanto gusto había
> en quejarse, un filósofo decía,
> que, a trueco de quejarse,
> habian las desdichas de buscarse.   (366)

It is difficult to judge whether Rosaura is trying to be humorous or just tender and consoling toward Clarín. But it is significant that Clarín totally rejects her remark. Clarín, unlike the other characters in the play, militantly and consistently attempts to avoid any sort of adverse fate. The result is his death, as Clarín himself recognizes: "Soy un hombre desdichado,/ que por quererme guardar/ de la muerte, la busqué" (396). Indeed, Clarín's speech just before his death contains some of the most elegantly turned paradoxical phrases of the play, and it summarizes many of the themes I have been discussing: disguise or imprisonment can not help one evade death; he who most tries to evade it most directly encounters it; and, like Erminia "Securi fra l'arme," the surest escape from death is by embracing it in the midst of the battlefield:

> Soy un hombre desdichado,
> que por quererme guardar
> de la muerte, la busqué.
> Huyendo della, topé
> con ella, pues no hay lugar
> para la muerte secreto;
> de donde claro se arguye
> que quien más su efecto huye,
> es quien se llega a su efeto.
> Por eso tornad, tornad
> a la lid sangrienta luego;
> que entre las armas y el fuego
> hay mayor seguridad
> que en el monte más guardado;
> que no hay seguro camino
> a la fuerza del destino
> y a la inclemencia del hado;
> y así, aunque a libraros vais
> de la muerte con huir,
> mirad que vais a morir,
> si está de Dios que muráis.   (396)

Basilio takes Clarín's death as an example and moralizes upon it, enlightening the other characters in the play:

¡Que bien, ¡ay Cielos!, persuade
nuestro error, nuestra ignorancia,
a mayor conocimiento
este cadáver que habla
por la boca de una herida,
siendo el humor que desata
sangrienta lengua que enseña
que son diligencias vanas
del hombre cuántas dispone
contra mayor fuerza y causa!   (396)

Almost immediately after this speech, Basilio embraces his own adverse fortune by placing his white head at Segismundo's feet.

In discussing the parallel of concealment and revelation in Rosaura's long third-act confession to Segismundo, I indicated that both the *engaño* of her disguise and the *desengaño* of her confession to her mother are presented as beneficent. Rosaura describes her confession in Pandora-like terms of "penas" breaking out of prison. She goes on to elaborate the fact that her mother was able to be sympathetic toward the confession because of her own similar misfortune:

que a veces el mal ejemplo
sirve de algo. En fin, piadosa
oyó mis quejas, y quiso
consolarme con las propias:
juez que ha sido delincuente,
¡qué fácilmente perdona!   (393)

Not only does Rosaura derive benefit from embracing her misfortune in the sense of openly revealing it, but it is made clear that a similar misfortune in her mother's fate now reaches back over the years as a soothing balm. Furthermore, the mother, like Basilio moralizing over Clarín's death, learns from her own mistakes and is able to advise her daughter:

y escarmentando en sí misma
. . .
por mejor consejo toma
que le siga, y que le obligue,
con finezas prodigiosas,
a la deuda de mi honor.   (393-394)

The word *escarmentar* appears several times quite prominently in Calderón's development of *engaño-desengaño*. *Escarmentar* has overtones of purgation, i.e., it means (1) to punish rigorously in order to redeem someone who has erred and (2) to learn by experience. In the *auto* version of *La vida es sueño*, Poder, God the Father, uses it to describe his experience of the rebellion of Lucifer:

pues la criatura mejor
oponerse al Criador quiso,
escarmentando (bien puedo
en esta frase decirlo,
que no es baja voz, que a mí
me escarmientan los delitos)
quise, acudiendo a mis Ciencias,
consultarme a mí conmigo.   (*Autos*, 1390)

So that crimes ("delitos"), in an anachronistically modern tone, take on
the metaphysical reality of steps in the evolution of God, which if not
understood as a metaphor for theodicy would seem to refer to some
astounding heresy.

The beneficent effect of one character's misfortune on another character is strongly present in Rosaura's initial encounter with Segismundo.
She says that the heavens have guided her to Segismundo's cell as a
consolation:

si consuelo puede ser
del que es desdichado, ver
a otro que es más desdichado.   (368)

She goes on to describe a paradoxical metamorphosis of sorrows into
joys:

hallo que las penas mías,
para hacerlas tú alegrías
las hubieras recogido.   (368)

The imagery here is close to the *Autos sacramentales* in which, as we
shall see, joys and sorrows, good and evil, etc., are readily metamorphosed one into the other according to the moral choice of the hero.

In the course of the play, Segismundo's "penas" are metamorphosed
into "alegrías" and Rosaura is a central agent of this metamorphosis.
But, as the theodical basis of the play requires, she is a paradoxical agent.
Rosaura cannot merely be seen, as some critics would have it, as Segismundo's telescope for Platonic Beauty[17]—a concept which seems, in any
case, rather far removed from the "confuso laberinto" of the play. It is,
after all, Rosaura who in the second act incites Segismundo's excesses:

Harás que de cortés pase a grosero,
porque la resistencia
es veneno cruel de mi paciencia.   (381)

This perfectly parallels the role of Sombra in the *Auto sacramental*; she
incites Man to bite into the forbidden fruit. And just as Rosaura returns
in the third act to inform Segismundo that he has seen her before, so does
Sombra return to Man after his fall. In the *auto* the clear function of

Sombra's return is to allow Man the opportunity of using his free will to reject her this second time. Thus, Sombra, by providing the occasion for Man's exercise of his free will, is the agent of both his fall and his redemption, depending on how Man's will is exercised. In this respect, Sombra's function in the *auto* is ambivalent, and in this she resembles Rosaura. Her second (as a woman) encounter with Segismundo is more ambiguous than in the *auto* because she initially appears to further incite Segismundo to his rebellion; however, he finally does reject his passion for Rosaura. Segismundo does this because in a previous action he has accepted and embraced life as an illusion, and he is, therefore, free to "obrar bien" for eternal verities. The dual function of Rosaura (and Sombra) as an agent of both a fall and a redemption parallels the role of Circe or *fingir-disimular* in *El mayor encanto, Amor,* Dalila in *Samson Agonistes* and Armida in *Gerusalemme liberata.*

When the soldiers approach Segismundo in the third act in order to persuade him to leave his prison and to lead them in a battle for his rights to the kingdom, Segismundo refuses for much the same reason that he had reacted violently to Rosaura's exposure of his weakness and to Clotaldo's constant reminder of "la luz del desengaño." There has been a change in Segismundo in that he now considers himself "desengañado ya":

> Ya os conozco, ya os conozco,
> y sé que os pasa lo mesmo
> con cualquiera que se duerme;
> para mí no hay fingimientos,
> que, desengañado ya,
> sé bien que la vida es sueño.   (389)

However, he is still retreating. His subsequent sudden reversal has, like Samson's similar reversal when he decides to present himself at the pagan feast, something of the *deus ex machina* about it. Segismundo pretends to be influenced by the soldier's argument that his former experience was not an illusion but an omen of what is to come now. Nevertheless, Segismundo announces his decision with "soñemos, alma, soñemos" (389). His decision is clearly to embrace illusion with the difference that he is clearly aware that it *is* illusion:

> pues que la vida es tan corta,
> soñemos, alma, soñemos
> otra vez; pero ha de ser
> con atención y consejo
> de que hemos de despertar
> deste gusto al mejor tiempo.   (389)

This decision is not unprepared, nor is it without echoes in the play. We have seen some of the most important in Clarín's sudden revelation at

death that one should rush into battle in order to escape death and
Basilio's moralization on Clarín's death. Rosaura also heralds Segismundo's final embrace of illusion. Toward the end of the second act of *La
vida es sueño* there is confusion resulting from disguised identities,
involving Estrella, Astolfo and Rosaura, which is like that of some of
Shakespeare's comedies. What happens is that Estrella asks Rosaura to
take from Astolfo the portrait of a woman which he had been wearing
earlier. The portrait is of Rosaura herself, Astolfo's former beloved,
whose identity, at the request of Clotaldo, has not as yet been revealed to
Astolfo or anyone else. The action begins with the central theme of the
revelation of a long-held secret. Just as Basilio's decision to reveal his
secretly hidden son to the light of the kingdom actually exposes Segismundo to what he will come to consider a world of illusion, so does
Estrella's decision to confide ("fiar") in Rosaura the secret ("lo que aun
de mí muchas veces/ recaté") of her betrothal to Astolfo and her anxiety
over a portrait he had worn hurl Rosaura into her own "confuso laberinto" from which she is finally saved through *engaño*. Estrella tells
Rosaura:

> me atrevo a fiar de ti
> lo que aun de mí muchas veces
> recaté.   (383)

When Estrella says that Rosaura must know well what love is ("bien
sabrás lo que es amor"), Rosaura responds (after Estrella has left) that she
would she did not ("¡Ojalá no lo supiese!"), thus echoing the play's
theme of the desire to escape from pain and the knowledge of pain.
Rosaura goes on to describe her never-ending army of multiple "desdi-
chas":

> pues siempre van adelante,
> y nunca la espalda vuelven.   (383)

And she asks whether she is to "disimular" or "fingirlo" in order to get
out of her present dilemma. She finally runs—almost imitating her
misfortunes by never looking back—headlong into deception or *engaño*
and refuses to acknowledge to Astolfo, who recognizes her, that she is
Rosaura. When Estrella appears, she fabricates a tale to the effect that
Astolfo has taken from her her own portrait which she had been reminded of by Estrella's confession and had taken out to examine while
she waited for Astolfo to appear with the other portrait. Astolfo describes
for us Rosaura's surrender to *engaño* in his accusation: "Pues que
quieres/ llevar al fin el engaño" (384).

I said that Rosaura runs into *engaño* and not that she decides to use
engaño because she describes herself as merely surrendering to fate:

¿Qué haré? ¿Mas para qué estudio
lo que haré, si es evidente
que por más que lo prevenga,
que lo estudie y que lo piense,
en llegando la ocasión
ha de hacer lo que quisiere
el dolor?   (384)

It is fate which provides her resolution, and her fate is pain:

Y pues a determinar
lo que ha de hacer no se atreve
el alma, llegue el dolor
hoy a su término, llegue
la pena a su extremo, y salga
de dudas y pareceres
de una vez; pero hasta entonces
¡valedme, cielos, valedme!   (384)

This description by Rosaura of what will, in fact, turn out to be a rather grand deception as the "término" of pain and "pena a su extremo" is interesting for the rest of the drama because Segismundo's final willingness to embrace *engaño* also leads to the fulfillment of all the worst prophecies which Basilio has feared, including treason and finding himself at Segismundo's feet. One of the critics of *La vida es sueño* has stated that at the end of the play the prophecies are invalidated: "queda invalidado el horóscopo."[18] But this is not the case. Everything is, in fact, tragically accomplished. Estrella's description of the battle in the third act makes this clear:

Tanta es la ruina de tu imperio, tanta
la fuerza del rigor duro y sangriento,
que visto admira, y escuchado espanta,
el sol se turba y se embaraza el viento;
cada piedra un pirámide levanta
y cada flor construye un monumento;
cada edificio es un sepulcro altivo,
cada soldado un esqueleto vivo.   (390)

The "sepulcro altivo" and "esqueleto vivo" significantly echo the death-life imagery of the first act. It is only through this destruction that both Segismundo and Basilio escape a more permanent catastrophe.

Just as Rosaura escapes "la pena a su extremo" by running into it through *engaño*, Segismundo's final embrace of "fingimientos" does, in fact, place Basilio and Rosaura at his mercy, but it also allows him to transform these conquests into occasions for redemption. He does this by conquering himself ("vencerme a mí," 398). He surrenders himself to his father and gives Astolfo's hand to Rosaura. As Ulysses in *El mayor encanto, Amor* arrived through "fingimientos" at the abilty finally to *disimular* his interest in Circe, so Segismundo, at the end of *La vida es sueño*, has learned to *disimular* his propensities to fulfill his adverse fate. This is seen most clearly in his rejection of Rosaura. However, victory and peace are achieved only after Segismundo and his father have conquered their desire to hide adverse fate in Segismundo's prison and have, instead, embraced it: Segismundo, like Rosaura, by giving himself up to it, and Basilio, quite literally, at Segismundo's feet.

La vida es sueño remains somewhat allegorical. The adverse fate which the characters embrace is merely a potentiality which tests their resolution and exercises their free will. In the *auto* version of the play this is totally the case. Perhaps this is Calderón's way of avoiding Manichaean implications in plays involving prophecy and the sense of a too-rigid predetermination. However, in the *drama* there is some sense of the paradoxical tragedy which we felt in *Gerusalemme liberata* and *Samson Agonistes*, i.e., the sense that the moment of the heroes' greatest fulfillment is the moment of their destruction. Even Clarín's death affects us as no more than instructive—like Segismundo's embrace of *engaño*. But the sentencing of a soldier at the end of the play to a lifelong imprisonment strikes a different note. After Segismundo has rewarded Clotaldo for remaining loyal to his father, the soldier asks what his reward will be for having aided Segismundo in his rebellion. Segismundo answers by condemning him to lifelong imprisonment in Segismundo's former tower-prison. We have seen Segismundo's identity with so many of the characters in the play. Just as at the end of *Hamlet* we feel that Hamlet in some way participates in Fortinbras' victory,[19] there seems to be some indication at the end of *La vida es sueño* that a part of Segismundo remains condemned to prison. If all of life is an illusion, as Segismundo has come to accept, then his restoration to Basilio's kingdom can be of little more comfort to him than his prison. The stars had predicted for Basilio that he would be the victim of treason and catastrophe, and we sense momentarily that the *engaño* which Segismundo embraced was as real and negative as Samson's death.

The paradoxical nature of Segismundo's *desengaño*, the patterns of retreat from *desengaño* because it can be achieved only through *engaño*, the final embrace of *engaño* and the allegorical content of these patterns all become much clearer when they are studied in several other *dramas* and *Autos sacramentales*. I will now turn to these other plays, keeping in focus the themes I have been discussing in *La vida es sueño*.

V.   Antevisto el daño

It seems to be a favorite exercise of Calderón criticism to discover Segismundos in all of Calderón's work,[20] and, indeed, the Segismundo myth is present in many of his plays. Up until this point we have seen the retreat from *desengaño* enacted only partially by the hero and fulfilled—tragi-

cally—in minor characters: Clarín, in *El mayor encanto, Amor,* metamorphosed into a monkey and Clarín, in *La vida es sueño,* killed in the
attempt to escape death. In *Eco y Narciso* Calderón has written another
play in which the hero is warned against a disastrous fate and attempts to
evade it. In this play, however, the retreat is fulfilled, and the hero makes
no decision to embrace the negative forces of his fate and, consequently,
desengaño comes only when it is too late. And since Eco sees his *engaño*
as totally negative, his *desengaño* reflects that vision. The similarities and
contrasts of the *engaño-desengaño* pattern with *La vida es sueño* are
quite striking.

As in the two other plays I have considered so far, ambiguities and
paradoxes are very much a part of the imagery and thematic material of
Eco y Narciso, and *engaño* and *desengaño* are manifested in every aspect
of the play. In developing the Narcissus myth, Calderón more or less
played down the arrogant pride of the hero of the legend, even though the
Spanish mythographers concentrated on this,[21] and exaggerated the warning which his mother, the Nymph Leiriope, received that "Narcissus will
live to a ripe old age, provided that he never knows himself."[22] In
Calderón, the legend is primarily that of a youth who attempts to avoid
the fulfillment of a negative prophecy about himself and in so doing
encounters precisely that disaster in death. All the minor elements and
characters of the play are concerned with this theme. It is as if Clarín were
the hero of *La vida es sueño* and the themes and characters of that play
were made to reflect his tragic fate.

The essential plot of *Eco y Narciso* is quite simple. Leiriope, like
Basilio, is hiding her son, Narcissus, in a cave in the mountains where he
has grown up having neither contact with the outside world nor an
awareness of the reason why he is being so sheltered.[23] One day on a
hunting expedition, Leiriope is discovered by some shepherds who cap-
ture her. She tells them her story of rape by the river god Cephisus, the
negative prophecy by Teiresias in regard to her son and her consequent
life of retreat and hiding. Among the shepherds is Silenius, Leiriope's
father, who rejoices in her recovery. But unlike the comfort which comes
from Rosaura's revelation to her mother in *La vida es sueño,* there is no
echo of Silenius' joy in the larger pattern of the play since Narcissus,
unlike Segismundo, persistently hides from his adverse fate. I mean to
underline the analogy here between revealing a shameful secret and
embracing a hidden, adverse fate. It is a coincidence of plot profoundly
embedded in the fabric not only of *La vida es sueño* and *Eco y Narciso* but
many of Calderón's dramas.[24]

In the second act, Leiriope and all the shepherds set out to search for
Narcissus, who has disappeared during his mother's absence. He is found
by Echo. As the play develops, Echo, who is loved by two shepherds,

Phebus and Silvius, herself falls deeply in love with Narcissus. He becomes very much attracted to Echo, but by this time his mother has told him Teiresias' warning of seduction:

> una voz y una hermosura
> solicitarán su fin
> amando y aborreciendo:
> guárdale de ver y oír.   (1965)

Narcissus associates Echo with this warning, and although he vacillates to some extent, he consistently avoids *desengaño* by renouncing Echo until it is too late. While Segismundo embraces *engaño* knowing that it is illusion and may lead him to *desengaño*, Narcissus unwillingly falls a victim to *engaño* in his own reflection. The images, language and patterns in which this story is told by Calderón are what reveal my interest in it.

While Leiriope and the shepherds are searching for Narcissus, they sing various lyrics about *engaño* and *desengaño* and pain:

> Es el engaño traidor
> y el desengaño leal,
> el uno dolor sin mal
> y el otro mal sin dolor.   (1968)

This lyric presents *engaño* and *desengaño* rather ambiguously with the reversal of "dolor sin mal" and "mal sin dolor" and the ambiguous reference of "uno" and "otro." Another lyric substitutes the life-death antinomy:

> Ven, muerte, tan escondida
> que no te sienta venir,
> porque el placer del morir
> no me vuelva a dar la vida.   (1968)

Were Narcissus to surrender to the pleasure of death ("el placer del morir") through Echo despite the threat of *desengaño*—and there is sufficient imagery in the play to indicate that his reaction to Echo is like that expressed in Segismundo's "ojos hidrópicos" speech—he might be saved from his tragic *engaño*. As is usual for Calderón, these paradoxical notes have many echoes in the play.

It is Echo's suitors, Silvius and Phebus, who argue the pros and cons of *engaño* and *desengaño* almost in a musical counterpoint throughout the play. Indeed, one is reminded frequently in Calderón's mythological plays of what Northrop Frye calls the "operative features of Shakespearean comedy," in which thematic "images and words echo and call and respond." "Such repetitions," Frye continues, "seem to have something oracular about them, as though arranging them in the right way would provide a key to some occult and profound process of thought."[25] At the beginning of the play Silvius and Phebus initiate their opposition by taking opposing views as to Echo's birthday. For Silvius it is a day of "alegría" merely because another year has been added to Echo's existence. For Phebus it is a day of "tristeza" because each year is one grace less: "cada año más es una gracia menos" (1957). The debate between *engaño* and *desengaño* is introduced in the first act when Silvius importunes Echo to keep her word by bestowing a ribbon she wears on her favorite of the two shepherds. From such pastoral trifles Calderón wrings metaphysics. When Silvius insists that he prefers *"desengaño"* to dying from doubt:

> que si a una duda rendido
> tengo de morir, que acuda
> es mejor mi fe desnuda
> de su desengaño al daño,
> por morir del desengaño,
> si he de morir de la duda.   (1963)

Phebus, on the other hand, states quite unequivocally that he prefers *engaño*. Since he knows that he cannot have what he wants ("no/ es posible tener yo/ la ventura que no espero"), the "duda" he prefers is equivalent to *engaño*.

When the debate is resumed, Phebus and Silvius have changed roles. Phebus now prefers *desengaño*, Silvius *engaño*. They express these feelings rather spontaneously at the beginning of the third act in balanced and interwoven verse dialogue which Dámaso Alonso calls "correlación"[26] and which I shall discuss in connection with the *Autos sacramentales*:

> SILVIO. ¿Quién llegó a mayor desdicha,
>   que el galán que llegó a ver
>   cara a cara un desengaño . . .
> FEBO.   ¿Quién llegó a más dicha, quién,
>   que el amante que llegó
>   un desengaño a tener . . .
> SILVIO.   . . . pues cuanto vivió engañado,
>   vivió contento, porquë
>   una cosa es ignorar,
>   y otra cosa es padecer?
> FEBO.   . . . pues cuanto engañado amó,
>   fué desdichada, porquë
>   no hay mal como el que encubierto
>   mata, sin saberse dél?
> SILVIO. ¡Oh quién engañado amara
>   toda su vida . . .
> FEBO.   ¡Oh quién
>   hubiera este desengaño
>   tenido antes . . .

SILVIO.   . . . para que
    nunca sintiera el dolor!
FEBO.   . . . para que siempre el cruel
    dolor hubiera sentido!
SILVIO.   ¡Que en un amor . . .
FEBO.   Una fe . . .
SILVIO.   . . . no hay cosa como ignorar!
FEBO.   . . . no hay cosa como saber!   (1979)

This is the major theme of the play displaced in rather abstract terms. But Narcissus' problem is being discussed here. Should he, like Segismundo, embrace the malefic fate to which he is so powerfully attracted in Echo or evade it? There are a few questions which arise from the passage. Why should Phebus and Silvius exchange roles so radically? And why does Calderón use such a radical form of his favorite technique of "correlación" here? Both questions have the same answer. As we saw in discussing *La vida es sueño, engaño* and *desengaño* have a certain interdependence. By reversing the attitudes of Phebus and Silvius and by interweaving the verse of their debate, Calderón underlies that identity. It is by embracing *engaño* that Segismundo achieves his *desengaño*. If, however, the character thinks of himself as sufficiently enlightened—Leiriope will speak, with tragic consequences, to Narcissus of "antevisto el daño"—he effects his own *engaño*. This latter Manichaean pattern, which Segismundo almost falls into but finally evades, is fulfilled by Narcissus.

Just as Rosaura discovered the hidden Segismundo—bringing light to his sinister fate—Echo, in this mythological play, is the one to discover the lost Narcissus. Rosaura's action of bringing to the surface a black secret is reflected in Segismundo's paradoxical "ojos hidrópicos" lines. Narcissus' initial reaction to Echo is equally paradoxical and reflective of her role. Even the same metaphor of the senses' drinking is used.

    ¿cómo de una sed y otra
    tanto has trocado el afecto,
    que en vez que labios y oídos
    beban agua y aire, has hecho
    que beban fuego los ojos,
    y tan venenoso fuego?   (1969)

Parelleling Rosaura's abandonment of her male disguise, at the second meeting between Narcissus and Echo a change of costume is commented on: "Mucho/ verte en este traje estimo" (1973). But Echo does not fully become a redeeming figure for Narcissus because he has heeded the warning against his danger. At their second encounter Narcissus wishes to leave immediately. When Echo asks him why, he repeats the prophecy:

> Como habiendo sido
> una voz y una hermosura
> mis dos mayores peligros,
> y concurriendo en ti entrambos,
> el huir de ti es preciso;
> que es un encanto tu voz
> y tu hermosura un hechizo.   (1973)

Significantly, Calderón has transformed Narcissus' motivation for avoiding Echo from his narcissism or pride, as the Christian mythographers would have it, to the desire to avoid a malefic fate. Narcissus associates this fate with *engaño* in using the words "encanto" and "hechizo." They pay tribute to Echo's beauty, but they also strongly suggest *engaño*.

Although at one point Narcissus apparently does come close to surrender to his love for Echo, he withdraws as soon as she anticipates him in confessing her love: "te dijera el amor mío/ si hubieras callado el tuyo" (1976). Both Segismundo and Ulysses speak of conquering themselves after they have surrendered—ritually, at least—to their weaknesses. Narcissus feels this surrender coming, but, with Leiriope's advice, he attempts self-conquest before a fall:

> NARCISO.   Yo te confieso que es justo
> el recelar y el temer;
> pero vencerse a sí mismo,
> di, ¿quién ha podido?
> LIRIOPE.   Quien,
> antevisto el daño, huye.
> NARCISO. Pues si eso basta, yo huiré.   (1981)

Ironically, after Narcissus has suffered the *engaño* of his own reflection, Echo attempts to awaken him from his deception (desengañar tu ignorancia," 1984), but Narcissus thinks that she is attempting to deceive him:

> Ya sé, Eco, que me engañas,
> porque disuadirme intentas
> de mi amor y mi esperanza.   (1984)

There is not the dramatic change in attitude (close to a *deus ex machina*) that we have been studying in Samson, Segismundo and the other protagonists. At the beginning of the encounter and at its climax, Narcissus consistently thinks of Echo as a source of illusion.

Like Clarín in *La vida es sueño*, Narcissus encounters precisely the fate he attempts to avoid. The double reflection (visual and auditory) involved in the myths of Narcissus and Echo are thematically exploited by Calderón. Echo is the reflection of Narcissus' own fate. His reaction to his own mirror image is similar to the venomous fire he encountered in Echo:

Beberé, pues, pero enojos,
porque en sus claros despojos
hallo contrarios agravios.   (1983)

But the fate in this reflection is one encountered against the will in an
attempt to run away from it. Narcissus is himself responsible for his own
fate which is totally malefic rather than both a victory and a defeat like
Samson's or Segismundo's. In this respect, the opposite of the hermaph-
roditic imagery of *La vida es sueño* is being exploited by Calderón in his
development of the Narcissus myth.

VI.   La luz del desengaño

While *Eco y Narciso* magnifies and helps us to understand Segismundo's
momentary attempts to evade *desengaño, Ni Amor se libra de Amor*
illuminates the particular involuted pattern which Calderón establishes
between *engaño* and *desengaño,* i.e., the way in which the two reflect
each other and *desengaño* is achieved through the embrace of *engaño.*
Calderón's recreation of the Cupid and Psyche myth in *Ni Amor se libra
de Amor* is in terms of *engaño* and *desengaño* and narcissistic mirror
imagery. Calderón does this by establishing the usual thematic patterns
of deception and disguise and creating an elaborately developed subplot
which comments on the major encounters between Psyche and Cupid.
Calderón not only writes Psyche's two sisters into his plot, but he also
gives them suitor-husbands. In addition, all four fall in love with either
Psyche or Cupid.

At the beginning of the play we learn that Lidoro and Arsidas, the
suitors of Psyche's sisters, Astrea and Selenisa, respectively, have come in
disguise ("desconocido y disfrazado," 1998) and secretly ("he venido/ de
secreto a la isla," 1998) to Guido where Psyche's father, Atamos, rules.
Their simple mission is to see for the first time and before the wedding
their respective brides. The fact that they are hidden and disguised is
emphasized; when a comic character, Friso, who had fought in their joint
armies, discovers them, he remarks: "¡Encubiertos/ en Guido y disfraza-
dos!" (2000). Both Lidoro and Arsidas define their desire to replace their
imagined impressions of Astrea and Selenisa with the real thing because
the imagination is subject to *engaño*:

lo que no pasa a los ojos,
porque no perciben ellos
el objeto imaginado
sino realmente el objecto.   (1999)

In other words, they are using *engaño* (i.e., their disguises) in order to
avoid *engaño* and achieve *desengaño.* They have arrived at Guido on a
feast day during which the populace visits Venus' temple in order to
make offerings. As the procession passes, both Lidoro and Arsidas fall in

love with the same beautiful girl. At their request, Anteo, who loves
Psyche, identifies the girl among Atamos' daughters. She is neither Astrea
nor Selenisa; she is Psyche.

A rather precise and obviously intentional mirror reflection of this
engaño-desengaño occurs when, in the next scene, the play turns to
Astrea and Selenisa. Just at the moment when they are confiding to each
other that they want to see their betrothed, the comic Friso interrupts
them. He is, in fact, searching for his beloved Flora, a servant to Guido's
daughters, but he tells them that he is there to announce that he has seen
Lidoro and Arsidas on the grounds of the palace. Flora is alarmed by
what she considers a deceptive excuse on her lover's part ("¿Dónde este
embustero halló/ la mentira que ha fingido?" 2005), but Astrea and
Selenisa get Friso to promise to bring Lidoro and Arsidas to a place where
they can see them secretly. They conceal themselves for this purpose ("las
dos os esconded," 2005). As Lidoro and Arsidas are passing before Astrea
and Selenisa, Cupid arrives in the garden in order to revenge Venus on
Psyche. (Calderón has the populace of Guido turn on Venus because of
her supposed jealousy of Psyche.) Cupid is also in disguise "por no ser/
en las señas conocido" (2006). Astrea and Selenisa fall in love with neither
Lidoro nor Arsidas; both of them fall in love with Cupid.

This quartet of Psyche's sisters and brothers-in-law has embraced *engaño* and has, consequently, achieved *desengaño*. But the quality of
desengaño is ambiguous. Although they all lament that they are in love
with one who is not their betrothed, they are in love with someone who is
more beautiful and worthy. To describe her attraction to Cupid Selenisa
uses images of poison and enchantment which recall both Narcissus'
reaction to Echo and foreshadow the attraction between Cupid and
Psyche which is to follow:

> ¿Qué veneno fué, qué hechizo
> el que diste al corazón?   (2008)

There are important and enlightening parallels in Psyche's own experience.

Psyche resorts to *engaño* almost immediately when she and Atamos
agree that in view of the hostility she has aroused in Venus, it is best that
she conceal herself:

> Si ha sido
> envidia de su hermosura
> por quien Venus la procura
> tanto rigor, ha elegido
> buen medio en que no la vea
> nadie en el mundo: quizá
> no viéndola, cesará
> la envidia en Venus.   (2003)

Later, in the second act, it is Atamos who must deceive Psyche and abandon her on a foreign and apparently wild island. In her bittersweet lament to the departing ship, Psyche (in describing the ship) refers to the *"engaños"* which have brought her to this plight:

es paladïon marino
que en sus entrañas engendra
tantas máquinas de engaños,
de traiciones y cautelas.   (2015)

When the nymphs of the island beckon Psyche to enter the cave which will lead her to Cupid, Psyche, like Segismundo, blindly embraces the illusion ("Sombra, ilusión o fantasma") whether it be beneficent or malefic ("favorable o bien contraria"):

Sombra, ilusión o fantasma,
que al humo y luz desatea
aun más deslumbras que alumbras,
seguirte quiero, o bien seas
favorable o bien contraria,
que nada mi vida arriesga,
pues si favorable alivias
o si contraria atormentas,
en nada va a perder quien
vivir o morir desea
tan a un tiempo, que no sabe
en cuál de los dos acierta.   (2017)

Psyche's conscious and willing embrace of illusion is later carried one step further in her assenting to look furtively at Cupid. In Psyche, therefore, *engaño* and *desengaño* are even more closely identified than in her sisters.

Psyche's fate is in many ways as ambiguous as her sisters'. In a sense she also does not possess Cupid. She loves him without seeing him or knowing who he is. Yet she seems able to accept or at least to perceive the ambiguity of her situation. When her father and sister visit her in Cupid's palace, she articulates the schism as two deities:

Sabréis que si en estrella tan avara
una deidad me ofende, otra me ampara.   (2026)

This attitude is like Segismundo's and unlike Narcissus'. It is sharply contrasted with the Manichaean stance of minor characters in *Ni Amor se libra de Amor* for whom Psyche is either in the possession of a demon or married to a god:

FRISO.   Apuremos el lance,
          pues es desdoblar la hoja
          que doblada quedó antes.

¿El aquí a Psiquis no trajo,
y porque no le mirase,
mató la luz? Luego es monstruo.
FLORA.   El ¿no la llenó al instante
de galas y joyas? Luego
es un Adonis, un ángel.
FRISO.   El todas las noches ¿no
aguarda que no haya nadie
que le vea? Luego es feo.
FLORA.   El todos los días ¿no hace
el gasto? Luego es hermoso.
FRISO.   El desde que el alba sale,
¿no se va y no vuelve? Luego
es horrible y formidable.
FLORA.   El ¿no se ausenta y no vuelve,
sin que aflija ni canse,
se contenta con sus horas?
Luego apacible es y amable.   (2029)

The parallel between Psyche and her sisters is very detailed. In the play's development of Psyche's fate, there is even a repetition of the parallel hiding scenes in which both the sisters and the brothers-in-law are disillusioned. When Cupid enters Atamos' garden in order to kill the sleeping Psyche, he instead becomes a victim of his own love poison ("muere a su mismo veneno," 2009) and falls in love with Psyche. Just when he is about to kill both himself and Psyche, Cupid drops his torch and Psyche awakens dreaming of a monster. She wounds the stunned Cupid. This scene is repeated when Psyche attempts to see Cupid. The mirrorlike parallel is made quite explicit:

¿Otra vez, cielo piadoso,
esta hermosura no vi,
queriendo matarme? Sí.
¿Quién eres, Joven, que estás
seguro al matarte, mas
que cuando matabas?, di.
Cuando quisiste matarme,
turbado te vi primero;
y cuando matarte quiero,
tú te vengas con turbarme.
Dormida fuiste a buscarme,
dormido hallarte pretendo;
¿qué extremos son que no entiendo,
los que hay en los dos, pues cuando
dormí estabas tú soñando,
y yo, cuando estás durmiendo?   (2031)

Calderón has taken from the Psyche and Cupid legend Venus' prediction that Psyche would marry a monster and her jealous sisters' conviction that she was, indeed, married to one and has rather emphasized these elements to fit his own theodical myth of ambiguous evil. Toward this end, Calderón makes use of the ambiguity of the word *"monstruo"* in seventeenth-century Spanish; it meant either something deformed or something extraordinary. Calderón certainly retains at least a connotation of the former. We recall that in *La vida es sueño* Rosaura's ambiguous quality is evoked in her reference to herself as a "monstruo de una especie y otra." Not only are the monster references of the legend present in Calderón's Psyche play, but he has Psyche dream of a monster at the moment when Cupid approaches her and falls in love and he has Psyche refer to him rather ambiguously as a "monstruo de hermosura" (2031). Even Cupid uses this description for himself. When he discovers Anteo on the island in search of Psyche, he tells him that Psyche is under the control of a monster. This might seem a simple tactic to put off Anteo—and it is in one sense—but Cupid also restates the whole Phebus-Silvius debate between *engaño* and *desengaño*:

> Pero ya que es igual daño
> el ignorar las desgracias
> que el saberlas, y hay quien quiera
> saberlas más que ignorarlas;
> sabed que esa dama tiene
> dueño ya; porque el dejarla
> aquí, a efecto fué de que
> se cumpliese la amenaza
> del vaticinio de Venus;
> y así, un monstruo es quien la guarda.   (2025)

It is difficult to know precisely how to interpret Cupid's words in regard to Psyche. The sense in which Astrea and Selenisa and Lidora and Arsidas are better off disillusioned about each other but awakened to their love for Cupid and Psyche is, at least, clear. From this one can perhaps assume in terms of the play's themes that as long as Psyche loves Cupid unknown in the dark he must remain, in some sense, a monster for her, the expression of a primitive passion, the heart of *engaño*. This would indicate that Calderón had anticipated modern psychological interpretations of myth, as some critics are fond of doing,[27] and this myth in particular.[28] It is only when Psyche brings this passion to the light of consciousness *(desengaño)* that her love will be truly fulfilled. But this fulfillment can come only through *engaño* in two senses: (1) it is preceded by her unconscious love and (2) she must break her bond of faith and deceive Cupid in order to achieve it.

The references to Cupid as a monster are practically the only ways in which Calderón retains the tragic dimensions of Psyche's fate in *Ni Amor se libra de Amor*. The tragedy is clearer in Astrea and Selenisa and Lidoro and Arsidas. In any case, immediately after Psyche's fall, Calderón introduces through Cupid a *deus ex machina* which not only fully restores Psyche to Cupid, but assures us as to the happiness and well-being of all the other characters in the play. About the only evil left in which we could look for a beneficent purpose is Cupid's statement that it is Psyche's sorrows ("lástimas") which have worked her salvation:

> Tus lástimas han podido
> obligar, no solamente
> a mí, que te adoro, pero
> a Venus.   (2033)

Calderón chose to compress the endless trials which Psyche endures in the legend into that one word: "lástimas." Indeed, the play does seem to be more about the pattern of *desengaño* through *engaño* than anything else. A paradoxical beneficent-adverse fate is seen in the love for Psyche and Cupid which is born in Lidoro, Astrea, Arsidas and Selenisa despite their *desengaño* in regard to their betrothed, and the ambiguous monster symbolism which defines Cupid. Once the desirability of *desengaño* has been established, as it is in Cupid's words to Anteo, then, of course, a general beneficence is found in the deceit of *engaño*. It effects a *desengaño* which is at once the end of love and the birth of a higher love.

VII.   *Tan presto tan otro*

The pattern of attaining *desengaño* through *engaño*, which is common to so many of Calderón's plays, is also present in the *drama* based on the Prometheus and Pandora myths, *La estatua de Prometeo*. In this play, in addition to the *engaño-desengaño* pattern there is perceptible an identification of *engaño* with the metamorphic quality of some hidden power or deity which ultimately works toward beneficent ends. This metamorphic power is present in Segismundo's final ability to conquer himself and thus metamorphose the fulfillment of a disastrous fate into a beneficent one, and it is more allegorically presented in the final metamorphosis of Psyche's "lástimas" into "dichas" by Venus and Cupid in *Ni Amor se libra de Amor*. The metamorphic power is identified with *engaño* in these plays essentially in that *engaño* is a necessary step toward that final metamorphosis. But, in *La estatua de Prometeo* the identification of *engaño* with this metamorphic power is more specific. In this respect the Prometheus play takes us closer to my final discussion of the *autos* in which the theodical burden of *engaño* is totally replaced by metamorphosis.

In *La estatua de Prometeo* the balanced antitheses which we have considered in the other plays are partially represented in two totally opposed and conflicting forces: Prometheus and Minerva, on the one side, and Pallas and Epimetheus, on the other. Their identities are frequently confused and, indeed, they are metamorphosed one into the other through *engaño*. As we shall see, this occurs against a background in which good and evil are constantly being metamorphosed into one another, and the agent of this metamorphosis is *engaño,* which is finally associated with a beneficent *deus ex machina* (Apollo). As in the other plays we have considered, this action and resolution is dependent on the protagonist's embrace of an antithetical world from which he has previously retreated.

La estatua de Prometeo begins with a long narrative by Prometheus of his past life. He speaks about the absolute disparity between him and his twin brother, Epimetheus, who is given to the hunt while he himself prefers the pleasures of study and science. Prometheus became particularly devoted to astrology in his attempt to investigate the mystery of two such totally different brothers being born under the same star. When he tried to advise his fellow citizens about the laws of government according to the fruit of his studies, he was rejected by them. This motivated him to retreat further in his devotion to science and its goddess, Minerva. The fruit of this retreat is that he has created a perfectly carved replica of the visions which he had of Minerva, and he now invites the populace to view this statue. Among the others, Epimetheus is profoundly impressed and immediately falls in love with the statue. He hides this emotion, but proposes that a temple be built for the statue. At this moment, there is an announcement that a wild beast is loose in the nearby mountains. Both Prometheus and Epimetheus go off in pursuit. In the next scene, Prometheus encounters the beast which immediately reveals itself to be Minerva in disguise. She has come to reward Prometheus for his labors and offers to take him to heaven where he may select whatever gift he wishes. In the meanwhile, the others, of course, have no success in their pursuit. But Epimetheus encounters, at the end of a cave, his own protective deity: Pallas. (In his irrepressible penchant for antinomies, Calderón has merely taken the Greek and Latin names for the same deity and given them antithetical identities.) She speaks to him in language directly antithetical to Minerva's address to Prometheus:

> quise abatirte a este abismo,
> en tanto que al cielo eleva
> ella a su alumno, oponiendo
> a su lisonja mi ofensa. (2089)

She orders Epimetheus to destroy the statue with which he is in love. Thus, Epimetheus finds himself in the position of Tancredi in relation to Clorinda or Erminia in relation to Tancredi or even Rinaldo in relation to Armida. He immediately resolves *engaño* in familar terms: "Yo he de fingir" (2090). The first act closes with the scene in heaven in which Prometheus steals a ray of light from Apollo.

At the beginning of the second act, Epimetheus and a comic minor character, Merlín, are on their way to steal and hide the statue. Epimetheus imagines that he can appease both his passion and Pallas in this way. When they arrive at the place where the statue has been left, they notice an approaching light. Epimetheus is convinced that it is Minerva aiding his love-theft in the dark night. It turns out to be Prometheus returning with the stolen fire. He places the torch in the statue's hand and leaves to summon the populace. The statue comes to life singing the praises of science:

Quien triunfa para enseñanza
de que quien da ciencia, da
voz al barro y luz al alma.   (2094)

Epimetheus, amazed and frightened, also leaves to convene the populace to see this live statue. When Prometheus returns there occurs the first in a series of many confused identities. He sees the animated statue carrying the torch and imagines it to be Minerva who for some reason has decided to negate his gift to the statue. He soon realizes his error.

After they have all celebrated the miracle of the statue, the irate Pallas and Discord appear. They plot to call the statue Pandora and to introduce through various disguises and deceptions the disastrous urn. After the urn is introduced, Pandora opens it; and, as the result, Prometheus is disenchanted with Pandora. Epimetheus still loves her, but she is interested only in Prometheus. The second act ends with Epimetheus swearing to revenge himself: "yo buscaré medio/ que me vengue della en él" (2102).

At the beginning of the third act, Apollo has been informed by Pallas of the theft of fire. He seeks revenge, but Minerva argues him into withdrawing from the battle between her and Pallas. When she returns to inform Prometheus of the good news, he initially confuses her with Pandora (they are visually identical). Just when he has properly identified Minerva, she is forced to disappear at the approach of Epimetheus. Minerva leaves her image behind which Epimetheus confuses for Pandora. (There seems to be some narrative ambiguity in that the statue seems to be transformed into Pandora by the fire and to exist, here at least, independently of her as a statue.) At this point Pandora appears. Epimetheus himself is confused, but resolves to stick to his revenge. When Prometheus reappears, he mistakes Pandora for Minerva. This extraordinary and involved multiple confusion of identities within the dark heart of *engaño* ends with Prometheus resolving to end his retreat and enter the battle.

In the middle of the battle Discord appears pretending to be a messenger from Jupiter who now demands the burning of Pandora and the
punishment of Prometheus. In an attempt to save both Prometheus and
Pandora, Minerva pleads to Jupiter that Prometheus' theft has now been
balanced by Discord's usurpation of authority:

> Tonante dios
> ¿cómo permites que enmiende
> a una culpa otra mayor? (2110)

She is successful. Apollo appears just in time to save Prometheus and
Pandora. The final note is one of reconciliation: Prometheus and Pandora plan to marry, and the enmity between the two brothers ends.

Confused identities and the use of *engaño* are clearly central to Calderón's re-creation of the Prometheus myth. But before we return to them, it
would be well to consider another element from which the drama derives
much of its motivating force. Prometheus begins his whole pilgrimage
with an attempt to understand what seems to him a paradox: the birth of
two such irreconcilably different brothers under one star:

> movido quizá de aquella
> razón de dudar que una
> estrella en un mismo instante,
> de un mismo horóscopo infunda
> dos afectos tan contrarios:
> con ansia de ver si apura
> el ingenio que una causa
> varios efectos produzca,
> me di a la especulación
> de causas y efectos, suma
> dificultad en que toda
> la filosofía se funda. (2083)

In discussing *Ni Amor se libra de Amor,* I mentioned briefly a contrast
between Psyche's ability to accept an ambivalent situation ("Sabréis que
si en estrella tan avara/ una deidad me ofende, otra me ampara," 2026)
and the inability of the minor characters even to countenance it ("¿El
aquí a Psiquis no trajo,/ y porque no le mirase,/ mató la luz? Luego es
monstruo." 2029). Silvius and Phebus in *Eco y Narciso,* Lisidas in *El
mayor encanto, Amor* and Clarín in *La vida es sueño* all share this
inability. Another of Calderón's most famous plays, *El mágico prodigioso,* begins specifically with the question of theodicy. Cipriano's devotion to study and science is motivated by an attempt to explain the
existence of evil in a totally good principle. He questions the pagan gods:

> Pues ¿cómo en suma bondad,
> cuyas acciones sagradas
> habían de ser divinas,
> caben pasiones humanas? (813)

Ironically, in the course of the play it is precisely Cipriano's involvement in human passions through his sudden and unexpected love for Justina that finally leads him to God: "el gran Dios que busco" (842). The same measure of irony is present in *La estatua de Prometeo*. Prometheus comes closer and closer to embodying those aspects of Epimetheus' personality which he considered antithetical to his own. And just as it is *engaño* which confuses the identity of the various characters in the play, it is a different mode of *engaño* which makes possible for Prometheus a final reconciliation with his brother.

The confusion of identities and metamorphoses which *engaño* effects in *La estatua de Prometeo* are all the more impressive if one is aware of the polarities involved. The contrast between the twin brothers, Prometheus and Epimetheus, is considerably more absolute in the context of the play. It is also embodied in the contrast between Pallas and Minerva. Although at birth and during youth they were indistinguishable ("de manera/ que ya hubo quien dijo/ que equívocas eran/ o Minerva o Palas/ una cosa misma" 2089), they grew into totally antithetical natures:

nacimos las dos conformes;
crecimos las dos opuestas
en los divididos genios
de nuestras dos influencias
blanda ella lo diga,
dígalo soberbia
yo, dictando lides,
dictando ella ciencias.   (2089)

This opposition is echoed throughout the play. Significantly the opposition appears not only between the two goddesses, but within each one. When the crowd is distracted from admiring the beauty of Prometheus' statue by the threat of the wild beast, Merlín, the comic minor character, explains that he is remaining behind because he does not wish to lose the beauty of the statue for the fierceness of the beast. ("Porque no me gusta,/ por ir a ver su fiereza,/ dejar de ver su hermosura," 2087). Of course, both the statue ("hermosura") and the beast ("fiereza") are Minerva in different modes of representation or disguise. When Prometheus encounters the wild beast which suddenly metamorphoses into the goddess Minerva, he asks the goddess to resolve the dichotomy: "¿lo que a un monstruo pregunto/ me responde una deidad?" (2087). On the other side, when Epimetheus is commanded by Pallas to destroy the statue of Minerva, he describes Pallas presenting herself to him as a protective deity only to make requests that reveal her as inimical to his welfare: "que se explique favorable/ para declararse adversa" (2090). When the statue comes to life, the reaction of the enamored Epimetheus is expressed in oxymora:

quien me descifre el enigma
de una escultura animada
y un inanimado fuego,
que con calidad contraria
abrasa como que hiela
y hiela como que abrasa.   (2095)

Even the life-death imagery so essential to *La vida es sueño* comes into play when Prometheus invites the populace to see the inanimate statue he has created while Epimetheus calls them to see the same statue animated by Minerva:

pues si él os convocó a causa
de ver a su estatua muerta,
yo de ver viva su estatua.   (2096)

This antinomy is also manifested within the two brothers. When Prometheus has confused Pandora for Minerva and then is enlightened, he has recourse to pain-remedy imagery: "te hallo como daño, cuando/ te busco como remedio" (2108). The opposition within the brothers is expressed mostly in their conflicting relationship to Pandora. Discord describes it in terms of love-hate:

. . . tú, Epimeteo,
amarás aborrecido;
tú al contrario, Prometeo,
aborrecerás amado.   (2101)

We come closer to the metaphysical *raison d'etre* of the antitheses in *La vida es sueño* in Pandora's description of the flame which has given her life. Her descriptive antinomies are informed by the war sounds which Discord has produced in order to interrupt the celebration of the animated statue:

Si ya no es que al ver mezclar
horrores y voces blandas,
jeroglífico es que diga
que pacífica esta llama
será halago, será alivio,
será gozo, será gracia;
y colérico será
incendio, ira, estrago y rabia;
y así, temed y adorad
al fuego, cuando le esparza,
o afable o sañuda, a toda
la naturaleza humana
La Estatua de Prometeo.   (2097)

The negative aspect of this description is realized after Pandora opens the urn and Discord neatly describes the natural consequence of smoke and fire:

> Si tenéis el fuego hurtado,
> ¿qué admiráis el humo, siendo
> tan natural consecuencia
> que haya humo donde hay fuego?   (2101)

Prometheus later echoes this imagery in terms of good and evil. When he has discovered his confusion of Minerva, and Pandora comments on his sudden metamorphosis from receptivity to hostility ("¡Tan presto tan otro!" 2107), Prometheus asks whether there is anything new about the alacrity of change:

> ¿De qué te admiras? ¿Es nuevo
> el que venga presto el mal?   (2107)

The antitheses of the drama are generally associated with good and evil and birth and death and the paradox of rebirth. At the end of the third act when Prometheus and Pandora have been condemned, he describes the metamorphosis of good into evil:

> ¡Ay de quien el bien que hizo
> en mal convertido vió!   (2110)

But this metamorphosis is balanced and reversed by the intervention of Apollo who sings:

> Tened, parad, suspended el rigor;
> veréis a mi voz
> el mal convertido en bien
> y el bien en mejor.   (2111)

During the lyrical scene in which Prometheus steals fire from Apollo, the song describing the setting of the sun is of death and rebirth:

> No temas, no, descender;
> que si en todo es de sentir
> que nazca para morir,
> tú mueres para nacer.   (2092)

The metamorphosis and balancing of all these antitheses is also expressed in terms of relativity in the third-act debate between Pallas and Minerva when they are trying to convince Apollo of the vice or virtue of Prometheus' theft. Minerva responds to Pallas' accusation of vice by saying that the vice's purpose metamorphosed it into virtue:

No es así, cuando
resulta en tan gentil
noble glorioso empleo,
que si suelen decir
que el sol y el hombre dan
la vida, y hoy por mí
claro lo ven.   (2103)

The antitheses of *La estatua de Prometeo* are centralized in the paired
opposites of Prometheus-Epimetheus and Minerva-Pallas, and, as is evident from my synopsis of the play, it is always *engaño* in the form of
disguise or the confusion of identities which resolves these antitheses or
metamorphoses them into each other. Just as Epimetheus attempts to
resolve his ambivalent conflict deriving from Pallas' command to destroy
Minerva's statue through *engaño* ("Yo he de fingir . . ."), Minerva hides
from Epimetheus when he interrupts her discussion in the third act, and
this leads to the series of confused identities in which the whole quintet
(including Pandora) is involved. Pandora, as the description of her ani-
mating fire indicates, resolved within herself both Pallas and Minerva. It
is for this reason that all of the confused identities of the third act involve
her. "Tan presto tan otro," Pandora's complaint to Prometheus, is a
phrase which, as we shall see, could well describe all of reality presented
in the allegorical *autos*. But for a moment in *La estatua de Prometeo* it
also seems to suit the reality presented. In his confusion of identities
through *engaño*, Prometheus is like Ulysses in *El mayor encanto, Amor*,
who is metamorphosed from non-lover to lover and back to non-lover
through *fingir* and *disimular*. The same themes are at work in both plays.
Engaño allows Prometheus openly to receive Pandora not only for the
moment when he confuses her with Minerva, but also permanently at the
end of the play. As it is the *engaño* of Prometheus' theft of the fire which
creates most of his difficulties, it is the *engaño* of Discord's usurping
Jupiter's voices which finally allows Minerva to prevail in her defense of
Prometheus: "Tonante dios/ ¿cómo permites que enmiende una culpa
otra mayor?" (2110). In these many ways, *engaño* acquires the paradoxical value which we have observed it almost always has in Calderón. And,
not unlike the balancing of Christians and pagans in *Gerusalemme
liberata* and the final embrace by Samson of the very deception which he
had so condemned in *Samson Agonistes*, *engaño* is conquered by *engaño*
or, in more theoretical terms, conflict is resolved and evil is defeated
through its total isomorphic imitation.[29]

Prometheus' relationship to this resolution is very much like the one
we have noted in Calderón's other heroes. The desire to retreat from
conflict is as strong within Prometheus as it was in Segismundo, but,

again like Segismundo and unlike Narcissus, it is not strong enough to prevail. In his preface to the play (2080), Valbuena Briones brings up the question of why Prometheus rejects Pandora since her connection with evil is one of life itself. Clearly Epimetheus represents a potentiality within Prometheus of accepting Pandora despite her ambiguous nature. Throughout the play Prometheus himself shows a tendency to retreat from the ambiguities of life. But it is after he stops retreating—at the moment he nobly attempts to defend Pandora when they are both threatened by Pallas—that the saving *deus ex machina* is set in motion and the final metamorphosis of "mal" into "bien" is assured.

Prometheus is motivated to retreat further into his natural inclination for study by the paradox presented in the union between him and his brother. The misunderstanding of his advice by his fellow citizens makes him even more of a recluse:

> pues ofendido de ver
> lo que un tumulto repugna
> la obediencia, interpretando
> el buen celo como culpa,
> a vivir conmigo en esta
> melancólica espelunca
> me reduje.   (2084)

When Pandora also presents Prometheus with conflicts, he twice turns his back on her as he has on his fellow citizens: (1) initially, after she opens the urn ("Mas nunca vengas/ tras mí, infausto monstruo bello,/ que al mirarte como causa/ de las ansias que padezco,/ te he cobrado tal horror," 2101) and (2) when he discovers that he has mistaken her for Minerva. In the second instance he reveals a clear ambiguity in his attitude toward her, as if Epimetheus' attitude toward Pandora also belongs to him:

> Pues si deidad te contemplo,
> te adoro; si hermosa, te amo;
> si discreta, te venero;
> si prodigiosa, te admiro,
> y si todo, te aborrezco;
> que hay otro yo que sin mí
> manda en mí más que yo mismo.   (2108)

Although Prometheus clearly reverses himself and asserts his autonomy ("yo que sin mí/ manda en mí"), it is Apollo who effects the final metamorphosis, not, as with Segismundo, the protagonist himself. And the metamorphosis is a magical one and not the Irenaean "ripening for immortality" of character. This is also true in *Ni Amor se libra de Amor* in which Cupid and Venus motivate the *deus ex machina*. The *engaño* of *La estatua de Prometeo* is also more allegorical than it is in *La vida es sueño*. While Segismundo and Rosaura are relatively paradoxical human realities, Prometheus remains divided between himself and Epimetheus, and Pandora is little more (or less) than a convenient meeting ground for Minerva and Pallas. The characters of the Prometheus play lose and gain identities with the artificiality of an allegorical mannequin. Indeed, in *La estatua de Prometeo* we are very close to the allegorical world of the *autos*. *Engaño* is so closely related to metamorphosis that the "tan presto tan otro" identities of the characters seem to define a metaphysics in which reality itself is an illusion that changes face and character upon the resolution of a divine or human will.

VIII. El gran teatro del mundo

In considering *Gerusalemme liberata*, we noticed that the poem contains several similes which compare the battle between Christians and pagans to a conflict within an arena or a theater. As an extension of this simile, many references in Tasso's poem place the entire action within *Un sol punto*, someplace within the mind or soul of the protagonist. I interpreted the allegorical strength of these images as referring to the moral choice of the hero so that, in a sense, Tasso's entire epic chronicles not only the crusades, but also Everyman's struggle with good and evil. This further developed Tasso's use of illusion in the conflict between good and evil in that the balanced opposites, antitheses and paired worlds of apocalyptic and demonic imagery were reflections of the hero's moral condition and were illusory in that they could rapidly metamorphose one into the other according to that condition. As we saw, there are, indeed, many descriptions of the rapid metamorphoses of beautiful landscapes into bloody battlefields and vice versa. Although I did not specifically discuss it in these terms, it is easy to see that there are three major landscapes in *Gerusalemme liberata*: (1) Erminia's pastoral scene, (2) the enchanted palace of Armida and the enchanted forest and (3) the battlefield, and they occur more or less in this order in the poem. *Canto settimo* records "Erminia tra i pastori," the sixteenth and eighteenth canti present the palace and forest and the great battles are in the nineteenth and twentieth canti. Illusion and enchantment are the bridge from the pastoral landscape to the battlefield, and it is illusion, or disguise, which allows the two to exist simultaneously: Erminia in armor, Tancredi as lover and enemy, etc. This tripartite structure is also present in *Samson Agonistes* in that the Manoa (Hebrew) encounter and the Harapha (Philistine) encounter are joined by the Dalila encounter with its mirror imagery. Samson is the still point embodying both worlds.

In the whole of Calderón's work there are innumerable metaphors comparing the action to a stage scene. In *La vida es sueño*, Segismundo, dreaming, sees his valor displaying itself in the great theater of the world:

"Salga a la anchurosa plaza/ del gran teatro del mundo/ este valor sin segundo" (386). And Basilio, in the final battle between the forces supporting Astolfo and those supporting Segismundo, speaks of it in terms which remind us of Solimano's famous description of the battle in *Gerusalemme liberata*:

> teatro funesto es, donde importuna
> representa tragedias la fortuna.   (390)

Indeed, in Calderón's *auto*, *El gran teatro del mundo* the whole of the action representing man's journey from birth to death and spiritual rebirth in the various stations of life is described as being staged within the mind of God. In his study of the *autos* A. A. Parker analyzes many of them in terms of this image and shows how they frequently represent the action as taking place within the mind of a central character.[30] While this is very helpful, it does not specifically work for all of the *autos*. I shall be more interested in analyzing them in terms of an image which corresponds to the *Un sol punto* of *Gerusalemme liberata*.

In any case, it is clear that in the allegorical *autos* all of life as it is represented in its various manifestations is illusory. The evil or demonic aspects of life as they are represented in the *auto* are nothing more, to use W. K. Wimsatt's terms referred to in my Prologue, than "a tensional element that is a part of the moral quality of experience."[31] Indeed, since the *autos* are in a sense taking place within the mind of God or the protagonist, the evil in them is not "evil itself, or division, or conflict," but rather it is "facing up to them, facing up to the human predicament."[32]

In the *autos* the balanced opposites which are so typical of the prosody and structure of the *dramas* are still present. In *El gran teatro del mundo*, for example, the sun and the moon are described with verses in which the prosody is an inverse mirror reflection:

> dos luminares, el uno
> divino farol del diá,
> y de la noche nocturno
> farol el otro.   (*Autos*, 204)

However, the antitheses in both the prosody and thematic material of the *Comedias* succumb in the *autos* to metamorphosis. All of reality readily metamorphoses from its demonic to its beneficent aspects according to the moral condition of the protagonist. For example, we saw that in *La vida es sueño* there was something ambiguous in the symbol of Segismundo's prison. It managed to contain the full height of a tower as well as the depth of a prison. The time was "alba" or "anochecer." In the *auto Psiquis y Cupido* as soon as Psyche looks on Cupid, her beautiful palace turns into a desert. Day becomes night, and summer changes to winter. As for my concern with the role of illusion, we shall see that whereas in the *dramas* it is *engaño* which joins the antitheses, in the *autos* the antitheses (all of the demonic and beneficent imagery) metamorphose into each other, and the illusion is in the things themselves.

The step from *La vida es sueño* and the mythological plays I have been discussing to the *autos* is not a long one. It is, in fact, quite logical and instructive. Calderón himself took the step with *La vida es sueño* and several of the plays. Apart from using the same legend in both modes of drama, some of the most arresting qualities of the *dramas* reappear in the *autos* in a different guise. We have seen how Calderón totally re-creates the myths he chose as the subject of his plays. Introducing *graciosos,* subcharacters and subplots, almost any myth becomes for Calderón the vehicle for re-creating his own myth of *engaño* and *desengaño*. In the *autos* these myths become the vehicle for theodical concerns. Instead of introducing sub-characters, Calderón introduces natural and human cycles in archetypal patterns of death and rebirth. The *dramas* tend toward archetypes in that almost any legend becomes the archetypal situation of the protagonist aided by one god and attacked by another (Prometheus and Psyche).

There is a further instructive similarity between the *dramas* and the *autos* in the phenomenon most characteristic of Calderón which Dámaso Alonso calls "plurimembración correlativa,"[33] i.e., several related strands of imagery or thematic material, such as the four elements or the debate between Odio and Amor in the auto *Psiquis y Cupido,* are developed independently by different characters. According to Dámaso Alonso the "correlación" is "identificativa" in the *dramas* while in the *autos* there is "diferenciación específica," i.e., in the *autos* Fuego, Aire, Agua and Tierra remain absolutely distinct elements of the *auto* throughout, while in the *dramas* the parallel strands of imagery'or thematic material overlap or are exchanged between the characters. We saw this in discussing the Shakespearean interrelation of all the characters and subplots in the plays. A painterly baroque whole is seen in the many parts. Dámaso Alonso describes it in these terms:

> La plurimembración termina, pues, en el indiferenciado
> coro; o el coro es el límite de la plurimembración.[34]

As we shall see, there is a corollary to this in the *autos* in the extraordinary development of what in Tasso I called *Un sol punto.*

The nature of reality in the *autos* as a mere reflection of man's moral condition which changes with the rapidity of a motion picture screen according to the dictates of that condition is hinted at in the *drama La vida es sueño.* Segismundo accepts both the misfortune of his prison and the pleasures of his father's palace as dreams and illusions. The only reality is the goodness or badness of his moral action. In the *auto La vida es sueño* Man is placed in a paradisiacal garden where, as long as he remains free from sin, the elements—Earth, Water, Air, Fire—serve him:

TIERRA.   Y yo, en fe de que lo admito,
   de los limos de la tierra
   con este polvo te sirvo,
   para su formación.
AGUA.   Yo,
   para amasar ese limo,
   te daré el cristal.
AIRE.   Yo luego,
   porque cobre el quebradizo
   barro en su materia forma,
   te daré el vital Suspiro,
   que hiriendo en su faz le anime.
FUEGO.   Yo yo, aquel Fuego nativo,
   que con natural calor
   siempre le conserve vivo.   (*Autos*, 1392)

However, when Man falls, the elements fall with him:

LUZ.   Si a humano modo te ajustas
   a preguntar lo que sabes,
   dígalo esta luz ya oscura.
FUEGO.   Dígalo la mía eclipsada.
TIERRA.   Díganlo mis flores mustias.
AIRE.   Destemplados mis alientos.
AGUA.   Mis claras corrientes, turbias.   (*Autos*, 1400)

The metamorphosis of nature is one of the ruling characteristics of the *autos.* Extremely elaborate patterns are worked out so that every aspect of nature has its good and beneficent aspect as well as its demonic antithesis. Calderón describes man's birth, fall and regeneration in terms of solar and seasonal cycles.

Many of the *autos* are built around one central symbol which like *Un sol punto* in Tasso seems to contain within itself all of time and space. For example, the palace to which Cupid takes Psyche in *Psiquis y Cupido,* and which becomes a rocky mountain once Psyche falls from grace, is described as symbolic of the whole world, the paradisiacal garden and the New Jerusalem:

Este murado Alcázar,
que con el capitel
toca al Sol, es tan grande,
tan dilatado es,
que aunque parece que hoy
fuera del Mundo esté,

tan grande es como el Mundo;
pues los términos de él
comprehende, porque aquese
pequeño, al parecer,
edificio, es la hermosa,
nueva Jerusalén,
que verás dibujada
del celestial pincel
en bosquejos si acaso
la *Apocalipsis* lees,
en ella no habrá cosa
que no merezcas ver
obediente a tu mando,
y a tu gusto cortés.   (*Autos*, 356)

This passage describes the palace as touching the sun and containing the whole world of the four elements. The animal world ("el ave, el bruto, el pez"), the solar cycle ("Primavera") and the vegetable world ("en fruto y flor") are specifically mentioned. Of course, when Psyche falls by losing her blind faith in Cupid, the demonic aspects of all the elements are so intimately related to the central symbol that their simultaneous metamorphosis is to be expected.

Many of Calderón's *autos* contain a similar central symbol within which the whole *auto* seems to take place and which seems to contain all of nature in both its good and evil aspects. In *El verdadero dios Pan* it is one shepherd and one flock. In that *auto* Pan promises to return the lost sheep, represented as Gentilidad, to the fold "cuando un pastor y un rebaño/ sea todo el mundo" (*Autos*, 1260). In *Andrómeda y Perseo* the central symbol is Andrómeda's mirror in which she sees the battle of winter and summer. And in *El divino Orfeo* it is Orpheus' harp with the sounds of which, at the beginning of the *auto*, he creates the whole world:

ORFEO.   ¡Ah de ese informe embrión!
    ¡Ah de esa masa confusa
    a quien llamará el Poeta
    caos y nada la Escritura!
            (*Dormidos.*)
TODOS.   ¿Quién será quien nos busca?
ORFEO.   Quien de la nada hacer el todo gusta.   (*Autos*, 1840)

Therefore, when at the end of *El divino Orfeo*, Orpheus is able to restore Eurydice to her unfallen state by the power of his song, we are not surprised, since Eurydice, or Man, is, in the first place, the product of Orpheus' song, and his harp is the symbol within which the whole *auto* is contained, including all the ups and downs of the cycles it represents.

EPILOGUE

That I am wretched
Makes thee the happier: Heavens, deal so still!

King Lear, Shakespeare

One of the monadic symbols from Calderón's *autos*, such as Andrómeda's mirror or Orpheus' harp or Psyche's palace, can be seen as a microcosm containing the most important steps in the development of my argument. They resemble, in the first place, the emblematic scenes in Tasso, such as the description of Olindo and Sofronia back to back at the stake or the Gildippe-Odoardo *liebestod*: Odoardo holding his slain beloved in one arm and avenging her with the other. The sudden metamorphoses and paradoxical identity of friends and enemies in *Samson Agonistes* is represented by these monadic symbols in the sudden mutation from an unfallen to a fallen world which they contain. In fact, they contain the whole world of mutability in its full cycles. The antithetical worlds of good and evil are also present in these cycles, and their metamorphosis into each other or their paradoxical identity is emphasized by the all-encompassing conciseness of the symbol which contains them. The Narcissus myth is clear enough in Andrómeda's mirror, and it is evident that the cyclical worlds represented in all of these symbols are reflections of a moral condition. Tasso's *Un sol punto* could not achieve a more expressive embodiment. Here, the Circe myth is totally enveloped in the Christian ideology of man's fall, and the level of mystery hinted at in *Gerusalemme liberata* and *Samson Agonistes* is clearly the mystery of man's redemption.

The similarity in these central patterns and the mythical presentation of illusion and beneficent evil in the three authors is indeed impressive. Even more impressive is the parallel presence in all three authors of minor themes and stylistic devices used to develop the theodical myth: (1) prosodic division into symmetrical halves; (2) a tripartite division into antitheses and an almost mystical point of union or total identity (evident in large patterns such as the battlefield-enchanted forest-pastoral landscape in *Gerusalemme liberata* and the division of episodes in *Samson Agonistes* so that the Hebrew Manoa and the Philistine Harapha are joined in the mirroring Samson-Dalila encounter, as well as in stylistic devices such as the use of a singular verb to join two totally antithetical subjects); (3) emblematic scenes or imagery which point toward a thematic unity in the work and have the character of "painterly" organic unity; (4) imagery of *engaño,* mutability and evil; (5) disguises and hidden identities; (6) love-war conceits and similes; (7) an allegorical tendency toward total isomorphic imitation of antithetical worlds; (8) mirror and narcissistic imagery; (9) and a strong differentiation in the awareness of various characters of the paradoxical complexities of the main theme so that total awareness becomes in itself an heroic trait. These similarities certainly point toward a theme central to Tasso, Milton and Calderón. It is, in fact, a literary mode of theodicy which is closely enough related to stylistic devices and thematic material endemic to the baroque and centrally enough present in three major authors who have been considered baroque to be thought of as one of the informing myths of baroque literature.

Almost any major author—not only literary but also religious and philosophical—of the late sixteenth and early seventeenth centuries could be read profitably in terms of the baroque myth of theodicy which I have delineated in this book. In my Prologue I indicated briefly how *Don Quijote* responds to the theodical view of evil. One might also consider Montaigne's focus on the labyrinthian fluctuations of human subjectivity burning through to an appreciation of a monistic human essence; the saving grace which Pascal finds in skepticism, contradiction and human limitation; the apotheosis of psychological suffering in Racine's heroines; and the florid structures of physical pain graphically depicted in D'Aubigné's *Les Tragiques.* Turning arbitrarily to almost any one of Shakespeare's plays, one is overwhelmed with analogies. In *Measure for Measure,* for example, it is precisely the isomorphic imitation by Angelo of Claudio's adultery which serves as the redemptive *deus ex machina* of the play. In the bed trick of the fourth act Isabella embraces evil by proxy. To buttress this, there are the Duke's disguise; the necessity (and, ultimately, beneficence) of his dissembling; the paradoxical balancing of antithetical dichotomies, such as rise and fall, benefactors and malefactors, tempter and tempted, sin and virtue and—most particularly—Angelo's response to the Duke's "Be absolute for death" speech ("to sue to live, I find I seek to die,/ And seeking death, find life") and the Duke's description of the power of music ("to make bad good, and good provoke to harm"); the many references to the testing of honor, so that evil is not real but as in Calderón's *autos* a "tensional" element; the Duke's beneficent purposefulness in keeping Isabella ignorant of "her good"; Mariana's description of men who "become much more the better/ For being a little bad." As one might expect with Shakespeare, one could go on endlessly in almost all of the plays.

But I would rather conclude with an introduction to a different way of looking at theodicy in baroque literature. The concept of memory might seem rather free of theodical overtones. Yet, Tasso began the Clorinda-Tancredi battle by articulating his wish to rescue the memorable ("memorande") encounter from oblivion ("l'oblio") XII, 54. Samson's strongest repression of Dalila is in terms of forgetting—"lest fierce remembrance wake/my sudden rage" (952-953), and his final reversal is described in imagery which is powerfully evocative of awakening memory (*"Intimate impulse"*). And in *La vida es sueño* we saw that the memory of Segismundo in his prison seemed to free Rosaura from the forces constraining her, and in the *auto* of *El mayor encanto, Amor* the personification of memory urges eternity by reminding of death. Recent interest in classical mnemonics and the Freudian conception of memory as a hidden blocking mechanism, barely available to consciousness much less to moral and ethical choice, have obscured for the twentieth century another view of memory which is part of Western humanism's original articulation of man's freedom of choice. In some ways this is a surprise because many modern approaches to memory and amnesia—Baudelaire's conception of memory as an evaluative principle (Great art is remembered art.) or Nietzche's and Ernst Bloch's sense of amnesia as a principle of hope (Only the fact that societies and individuals can forget past tragedies makes it possible to continue.)—seem closer to this view of memory than to Freud. Its *locus classicus* is in the tenth book of Saint Augustine's *Confessions*:

> And so I come to the fields and vast palaces of memory, where are stored the innumerable images of material things brought to it by the senses. Further there is stored in the memory the thoughts we think, by adding to or taking from or otherwise modifying the things that sense has made contact with, and all other things that have been entrusted to and laid up in memory, save such as forgetfulness has swallowed in its grave.

Saint Augustine goes on to describe the marvels of this internal landscape in which we can choose to remember a painful incident while not feeling (i.e., forgetting) its pain:

> My memory also contains the feelings of my mind, not in the mode in which the mind itself has them when it is experiencing them, but in a different mode, proper to the power of memory. . . . I remember past sadness yet am not sad. I remember past fears without fear, and past desire without desire. Sometimes the thing is exactly contrary—when I am joyful I remember past sorrow.

In going on to discuss the phenomenon of knowing that one has forgotten something, he denies proper existence to forgetfulness and describes it as the absence of memory rather than a thing in itself:

> When I remember memory my memory itself is present to itself by itself; but when I remember forgetfulness, then memory and forgetfulness are present together—forgetfulness which I remember, memory by which I remember. But what is forgetfulness except absence of memory?

What Saint Augustine is presenting in these pages is a literary version of his doctrine of theodicy; memory and amnesia are described as an exercise of human choice: to remember is to say yes, to forget is to say no (as to good and evil). And Saint Augustine's theodical concerns with human will, the metaphysical nonexistence of evil and "aesthetic plenitude" are evident. In fact, I have attempted to balance these passages from the *Confessions* with the quotations from the *Enchiridion* in my Prologue.

In my Prologue I described the way in which Dante makes his *Inferno* and *Purgatorio* inverse mirror reflections of each other. Dante is also aware of Saint Augustine's own allegory when he describes the souls on the top of Mount Purgatory as passing through the rivers of Lethe (forgetting) and Eunoë (memory) before entering paradisiacal bliss. At present, I am involved in a study of remembering and forgetting in Shakespeare's plays as a mode of theodicy which is a refocusing (more specific and more rhetorical) of this book. Although my interest is in explicating a thematic development within Shakespeare, the centrality of Saint Augustine to any concern with good and evil through the Renaissance, the wide availability of Saint Augustine's writings, both in Latin and in translation, during the Renaissance and, interestingly for my purposes, the play of this Augustinian sense of memory and amnesia in many of Shakespeare's sources (with specific verbal echoes in Shakespeare)—all this, I think, makes a discussion of Shakespeare's treatment of remembering and forgetting in comparison with Augustinian theodicy especially informative. Even a cursory glance at "remember" and "forget" in *The Harvard Concordance to Shakespeare* reveals thousands of entries (not including synonyms and rephrasings or dramatizations of the concepts). They range from almost giddy usage by Romeo and Juliet as they remember and forget their ecstatic and tragic situation (II, ii, 168–175) to more complex interweavings of destiny—past, present and future—in the teasing assurance of Henry V (formerly the licentious Prince Hal) to his Chief Justice, who had arrested him as a youth, that as King he can *forget* past transgressions against his person because he would have the Chief Justice *remember* the same laws should a future Prince (his son) break them *(King Henry IV, Part II, Act V, ii, 65–145)*. In a comic vein Shakespeare seems to make an ironic comment on Augustinian theodicy through Rosalind in *As You Like It*, who playfully tells her companion Celia that she cannot remember their childhood pleasure without forgetting her banished father (II, i, 1–15). This very dilemma is remembered in *The Winter's Tale* by Leontes who complains that he cannot both remember his departed wife's virtues and forget his own blemishes in them (V, i, 5-8). Of course, in the romances the allegory of purgation and retribution is closer to the surface. Leontes had just been told: "Do as the heavens do, forget your evil!" (1.5). In the "problem plays," *All's Well That Ends Well, Troilus and Cressida* and *Measure for Measure,* in which theodicy is more conceptually articulated, one could even work out a sine curve representing the number of affirmative references to remembering (predominant in *All's Well That Ends Well,* the most positive/comic of the problem plays) and negative references to forgetting (predominant in *Troilus and Cressida,* the most tragic of the plays) and their balance (predominant in *Measure for Measure,* the most doctrinal of the plays). In short, patterns of remembering and forgetting permeate the entire fabric of Shakespeare's oeuvre.

At the risk of considerable oversimplification, a tentative sketch of the thematic spectrum in Shakespeare is possible. As I said, the problem plays are the most theoretical and structurally balanced in their articulation of memory and amnesia, and, in a longer essay, their analysis would better serve than my theoretical introduction here. In the comedies there is an active assertion of the will in regard to remembering and forgetting—a balancing of marital and filial demands which leads to marriage. The histories tend to evolve theodical memory and amnesia in terms of a balance between devination and retrospection, involving father and son in a prodigal myth in which the royal father, after a retrospective meditation, acts to forgive his son in anticipation. (Just as the comedies involve us in discussions of free will, predestination is one of the issues in the histories.) The tragedies evolve a theodicy in which the painful memory of guilt purges the hero—who is both agent and recipient—of his guilt. An initial resistance to memory—Hamlet's desire to forget ("Must I remember?") at the Ghost's injunction ("Remember me") and Lear's heart-breaking attempts to hold off his tumescent memory of Cordelia ("I did her wrong")—this resistance moves toward a full acknowledgment which accepts the evil endemic to self and the world: Hamlet enjoins Horatio for the time to forget felicity in order "to tell my story" and Lear envisages himself and Cordelia happily caged and able to reduce the polarities of historical and political struggle to the "ebb and flow" and the "in" and "out" of narrative. And, finally, in the romances we seem to see remembering and forgetting from a more-than-human perspective: a powerful but flawed father casts much of his world into oblivion and with the aid of time recalls it ameliorated from its excesses.

Of course, a simple illustration of the manifold Shakespearean references to remembering and forgetting and the generic configurations they achieve, is only the beginning. What is interesting is how they always respond to an Augustinian sense of the exercise of human will in the choice between aspects of good and evil. Most important is the way they deepen our understanding of the other major themes of the plays, and the way Shakespeare molds, adapts and transforms a central concept of Western humanism to suit a character, a situation, a particular slant of language. In many ways the comedies' treatment of the theme is the most radically displaced. And, therefore, I choose to end this book with a brief synopsis of what a theodical reading of a Shakespearean comedy might be like.

The role of memory and amnesia—of remembering and forgetting—in Shakespeare's middle comedies is centered on their concern with the transition from a backward-looking and filial, adolescent identity toward a forward-looking and mature, marital identity. The twinned pairs in the comedies—whether the two in one litany in *A Midsummer Night's Dream* describing Helena and Hermia, "two seeming bodies, but one heart" (III, ii, 192–219), or Celia's description of herself and Rosalind "like Juno's swans,/ Still we went coupled and inseparable" (I, iii, 73–74)—these pairs are all headed toward separation from their adolescent coupling and toward a new heterosexual union in marriage. The pairing externalizes and dramatizes the internal rupture with past and self that must take place before a new heterosexual identity can be achieved in marriage. The play of remembering and forgetting in this process does not remain static. In each play, there is an active assertion of the will in regard to remembering and forgetting—which moves the action forward toward a multiple marriage. In *As You Like It,* for example, Rosalind is able to resolve her remembering and forgetting dichotomy by thinking of Orlando as the future father of her child! When Celia asks Rosalind if her melancholy is for her father, Rosalind responds:

No some of it is for my child's father.   (I, iii, 11)

Obviously, Rosalind, one of Shakespeare's strongest characters, has willed her own and Orlando's future—as well as the trajectory of the play. Now she has only to put it into effect. This mirrored past and future, a simultaneously forgotten and remembered father figure and the pain and pleasure thus resolved through a willed—through an imagined—identification, achieves a perfect Augustinian theodicy. In this Shakespearean comic mood, evil is considerably displaced as a past which will not see the future or a future which will not remember the past.

Twelfth Night perfects the presentation in Shakespeare's comedies of the transition from adolescent narcissism to marital sexual identity with the symbolic potential of heterosexual twins and the internalization of blocking parental figures as remembered but absent or deceased brothers and fathers. The dramatic conflicts are internalized as individual exercises of the will. (It is no wonder Shakespeare abandoned this mode of comedy after *Twelfth Night*—its symbolism is so finely tuned.) The theme is first sounded in reference to Olivia, who is shrouded in:

> A brother's dead love, which she would keep fresh
> And lasting, in her sad remembrance. (I, i, 31-32)

(In the Captain's later Act I, Scene ii narration, the death of Olivia's brother is described as almost a proxy of the immediately preceding death of her father.) It is only the muted sexuality of Cesario/Viola, like a "eunuch" and "semblative a woman's part," which breaks through the mask of obsessive memory. Even though Viola herself becomes enamored of Orsino, she conceals her passion and remains throughout most of the play pretty much locked into the memory of her brother's identity:

> She never told her love,
> But let concealment like a worm i'th'bud,
> Feed on her damask cheek. (II, iv, 111-113)

It is certainly not difficult to see concealment and revelation—an important *Old Testament* mode of theodicy—as aspects of amnesia and memory in the play. Indeed, their varied, distanced forms—"negligence" (I, iv, 5 and III, iv, 261), disguise (Viola, Feste, etc.), leave-taking (Viola and Sebastian from each other and their captains, Sebastian and Viola from Antonio, Cesario from Orsino, etc.), Sebastian's being "recovered" (II, i, 37), the "forgotten matter" of identity lost in similar handwriting (II, iii, 161) or mirrored behavior (Olivia's and Orsino's passion [III, iv, 208-91])—these varied forms are typical of Shakespearean organic imagery for a unified theme.

While Viola's mature sexuality remains concealed, Sebastian effects a breakthrough for both. (It is as if heterosexual twins facilitated the ambiguity of character in Shakespeare's comedic plots by conventionally assigning the aggressive assertion of will to the male twin.) However, at first Sebastian, too, seems locked into an adolescent unisexual if not homoerotic confinement. When Antonio commends him to a rendezvous at the Elephant Inn, Sebastian closes the scene—which had begun with an attempt to break his tie to Antonio—with:

> I do remember! (III, iii, 48)

It seems to me difficult to take Sebastian's action and word ("remember") here simply literally or too casually, especially since the scene is echoed later when Viola—in a certain mirroring sense Sebastian's heterosexual identity—does reject Antonio: Act III, Scene iv, 11. 318-319 is one of the most dramatic scenes in the play, in which Terrentian's mistaken identity is turned into something terribly poignant. The scene can also be read as a dramatization—in rather more serious terms—of Celia's and Rosalind's "remember"/"forget" banter in *As You Like It*. Although Sebastian attempts a break with Antonio in the earlier scene, at that point his heterosexual identity is, as he tells us, "drowned" in his sister's "rememberance" (I, i, 31). But as soon as he encounters Olivia's advances, he becomes unafraid of the "madness" inherent in giving up part of himself to forgetfulness:

> Let fancy still my sense in Lethe steep:
> If it be thus to dream, still let me sleep!   (IV, i, 62-63)

The important foil here is Malvolio who—never forgetful of self—evades the "madness" of lovers and poets by a rigid adherence to identity. It is no accident that he intones—that he monotones—the word "remember" more frequently than anyone in the play when he is "smiling" and donning his "cross gartered . . . yellow stockings":

> 'Remember who commended thy yellow stockings.'   (III, iv, 46)

The self-love of which Malvolio is justly accused has a beneficent effect in saving him from the madness others attempt to thrust upon him. There are not too many characters in or out of Shakespeare who could survive his treatment by Sir Toby Belch and company. But ultimately such a sense of self is seen in *Twelfth Night* as—quite literally—confining. Even the structure of the play seems to present Malvolio as a foil in this regard. In one of Shakespeare's most felicitous scene pairings, Malvolio's rigid "I am not mad" scene with Feste in the darkness (IV, ii) is directly followed by Sebastian in the "glorious sun" (IV, iii, 1-21), who also wrestles with his senses and his reason but surrenders to an important "yet" and finally embraces "wonder." Olivia's final—and casual—"remembrance" (V, i, 280) of Malvolio adds to his liberation an overtone of the freedom which the plays' central characters (excluding Malvolio himself, of course) enjoy from narcissistic obsession. Indeed, Malvolio's final threat—"I'll be revenged on the whole pack of you!" (V, 376)—which has disturbed so many critics and seems misplaced in the coda of a Shakespearean comedy—is more easily assimilated if revenge is understood as a radical form of obsessive and unbalanced memory. Malvolio is well paired with Feste in the dungeon scene: Feste is the voice of ambiguity throughout the play whether in instructing Olivia as to the beneficence of her brother's death (I, v, 64-70) or in erasing the boundaries between friends and enemies with proverbial banter (V, i, 11-22).

It is Olivia's reckless initiative toward sexual otherness which finds an even stronger sense of brinkmanship in Sebastian and which, in turn, effects Viola's displaced rejection of Antonio. In fact, Olivia and Orsino—no less than Viola and Sebastian—are also required at the play's conclusion to bury and resurrect an old passion: Cesario for Sebastian and Olivia for Viola. This ability to simultaneously forget and remember old and new identities—even at the risk of madness—is what leads to *Twelfth Night*'s comedic pairings at the end.

While this balance between forgetting and remembering plays itself out in dramatic time, *Twelfth Night* also affords spatial metaphors: Malvolio's confinement in a dark cell is a perfect symbol for the narcissistic self in oblivion. And Viola's "willow cabin" (I, v, 272-280) projects an isolated memory. Their synthesis can be found in the misty and repeated recollections of unity in the play—addressed at large and as if half forgotten (which is to say half remembered) in a tone of prayer or in what I have come to think of as a voice of memory. This voice is almost the play's radical metaphor: whether Viola's sense of herself as "all the daughters of [her] father's house,/ and all the brothers too" (II, iv, 121-123) or her vow:

I have one heart, one bosom, and one truth.   (III,i, 160)

And, most poignantly, the Duke's own voice of memory:

One face, one voice, one habit, and two persons!
A natural perspective, that is, and is not!   (V, i, 214-215)

Many critics have gravitated to these lines as if they contain a mystical vision of the play. Their vision is not simply the dual identity of finally discovered heterosexual twins. It is also the comedy's marital identity which can be achieved only with the fearless displacement—a madness which is not madness—that the freedom to forget and to remember old and new commitments allows. To forget an old identity—whether narcissistic or unisexual, or incestuous—is to say no to a static "melancholy" which has a "dying fall" (I, i, 4) and to reject as well the fear of the new and the unknown as "mad" (IV, i, 60). This forgetting has clearly taken place for the twins by the last scene, and it allows its counterpart in that touching but narratively unnecessary (which is to say psychologically free) ritual of remembering: Viola's litany of Messaline, her father's mole, her thirteenth birthday and her father's death. The path is now cleared for a passionately affirmative embrace of the new which in its very otherness seems to remember an immemorial completion and wholeness—the "wonder," the "accident and flood of fortune" that exceeds "all instance, all discourse" (Sebastian, IV, iii, 1-21).

NOTES

Headnote

In general, although I do acknowledge several similarities to and differences from other critical interpretations in my notes, I have purposely
attempted to leave the body of my three essays as free from references to
other critical interpretations as possible. I wanted to be unencumbered
because my reading in terms of a theodical baroque myth is, as far as I am
aware, original, and my involved and segmented arguments depend on as
much unity and fluidity as possible.

While Tasso has received considerable attention as a baroque author,
none of this criticism considers the theme of illusion and beneficent evil.
Heinrich Wölfflin was the first to contrast Ariosto and Tasso in *Renaissance und Barock* (Munich, 1888). Wölfflin's argument bears some relation to my own in that his analysis of a certain grandiosity and unity of
imagery in *Gerusalemme liberata,* as opposed to *Orlando Furioso,* is not
unlike my discussion of the ultimate reference of the various dualities,
ambiguities and paradoxes of the poem to the same *mysterium.* Theophil
Spoerri's application of Wölfflin's linear-painterly categories to Ariosto
and Tasso has the same marginal relationship to my book (*Renaissance
und Barock bei Ariost und Tasso: Versuch einer Anwendung Wölfflin'scher Kunstbetrachtung* [*Bern, 1922*]).
   From the more conservative Tasso criticism I have learned a great deal,
although it has very little reference to my own reading. Eugenio Donadoni's book, *Torquato Tasso* (Florence, 1936), was, for me, the most suggestive. I disagree with some of his psychological interpretations of the
characters in *Gerusalemme liberata,* but his analysis of the emotive and
expressive nature of Tasso's language led me to some of my own analyses
of those stylistic effects. In this respect the stylistic analyses of Mario
Fubini ("Osservazioni sul lessico e sulla metrica del Tasso" and "La
poesia del Tasso," *Studi sulla letteratura del Rinascimento* [Florence,
1947]) and C. P. Brand ("Stylistic trends in the *Gerusalemme conquis-
tata,*" *Italian Studies* [Cambridge, 1962], pp. 136–153, and *Torquato
Tasso* [Cambridge, 1965]) were even more suggestive, as was Giovanni

Getto's study, *Interpretazione del Tasso* (Naples, 1957), with its interest in poetry of anxiety and poetry of solitude.

Tasso has been particularly well served by criticism in recent years. I have occasion to mention the historical study of Baldassari and the anthropological study of Braghieri in my notes. In addition, Carlo Ballerini, in *Il blocco della querra e il suo dissolversi nella "Gerusalemme liberata"* (Bologna, 1979), deepens the psychological insights of some of his predecessors in that mode of criticism. There has also been much Tasso criticism which compliments some of my structural and prosodic analyses. One could cite Francesco Iovine's *La "licenza del fingere": Note per una lettura della "Liberata"* (Rome, 1980), which correlates some of the binary couples in the poem. But no study is as rewarding or—in some respects—as close to my own as Ezio Raimondi's *Poesia come retorica* (Florence, 1980). In discussing the rhetorical or dramatic dialectic of Tasso's epic, Raimondi points out the many antitheses in structure, imagery and prosody, which he sees as the thrust of the poem's dramatic energy. Some of his analogies of the structural, imagistic and prosodic polarities of the poem are close enough to my own (especially his conception of a *"prospettiva etico-spaziale"*), that I am glad the original version of my study antedates his own. Nonetheless, informed as my book is by the history of theodical thinking, the dichotomies which interest me all press toward a unity which seems to belie the dramatic dialectic of Raimondi's work.

Beginning with Arthur O. Lovejoy's "Milton and the Paradox of the Fortunate Fall" (*ELH*, IV [1937], 161-179), criticism has been very acutely aware of beneficent evil in Milton's poetry. And since the romantic poets and Blake's statement that Milton was "of the Devil's party without knowing it" (*The Marriage of Heaven and Hell* [1793]) there has been no dearth of insights into the ambiguity of Milton's attitude toward evil. In regard to this latter theme, A. J. A. Waldcock's essay on "Satan and the Technique of Degradation" (in *Paradise Lost and Its Critics* [Cambridge, 1947]), and Empson's essay on "Milton and Bentley" (in *Some Versions of Pastoral* [London, 1935]) and his book, *Milton's God* (New York, 1961), have been most suggestive to me. In "A Defense of Dalila," William Empson argues convincingly that Dalila is sincere in wanting to help Samson (*SR*, LXVII, 240-255). But in discussing the fortunate aspects of Samson's fall, Empson is not interested—as I am—in a conscious embrace of evil, and he is mostly concerned with discussing the effect of the fall of the Commonwealth on Milton's attitudes. In general, earlier criticism of *Samson Agonistes*—even the most complete and revealing study by Arnold Stein in *Heroic Knowledge* (Minneapolis,

1957)—has not considered the drama's identification of antithetical worlds and Samson's final acceptance and use of deception. Both Wylie Sypher, in *Four Stages of Renaissance Style* (New York, 1956), and Roy Daniells, in *Milton, Mannerism and Baroque* (Toronto, 1963), consider Milton as a baroque poet. Their suggestive arguments touch my own analysis in that they both see greater classical resolution and symmetry in *Samson Agonistes* than earlier works by Milton which might be considered manneristic. I, too, find greater symmetry in Milton's treatment of the themes and patterns which Tasso treats with less polished resolution.

Anthony Low's *The Blaze of Noon* (New York, 1974) is an even more complete study of the resolution of ironies in *Samson Agonistes* than my own, but he does not focus on good and evil. The narrower range of my perspective is necessary in order to elucidate the monadic theme of theodicy. The most recent Milton scholarship has had two especially brilliant contributions to the study of Milton's theology. In *Milton's Good God*, Dennis R. Danielson presents a point-by-point comparison of Milton's own theodicy with his *Paradise Lost* and *Paradise Regained*. He does not consider *Samson Agonistes* which is not specifically doctrinal. While Danielson may well have reversed our understanding of "the Fortunate Fall" in Milton's epics, one wonders if theodicy is fully subject to his precise analytical approach when it is enmeshed in a literary matrix. Mary Ann Radzinowicz's encyclopaedic and brilliant analysis of theological themes in *Toward "Samson Agonistes": The Growth of Milton's Mind* (Princeton, 1978) would seem to disprove the impossibility of definitive analysis, but one of the most satisfying elements of her analysis is the ambiguity created when she joins poetic theory to theological doctrine. In any case, Radzinowicz does not analyze *Samson Agonistes* in terms of the specific elements of Augustinian and Irenaean theodicy which interest me. And both Danielson's and Radzinowicz's conception of Milton's "contingent" predestination is consonant with my description of the internalized will of the protagonists.

Since both my essay and notes on Calderón make several references to the critics to whom I am most indebted, it is less necessary than with Tasso and Milton to explain my relationship to previous criticism here. *Engaño* and *desengaño* have long interested critics of seventeenth-century Spanish literature, and they have explicated it at length. *La vida es sueño* and Calderón's *autos* have received much excellent critical attention. However, this is less true of the dramas based on mythological legends which I discuss. While Valbuena Prat's book on Calderón contains an excellent general chapter on the mythological dramas (*Calderón. Su personalidad, su arte dramática, su estilo y sus obras* [Barcelona, 1941]), the surprising excellence of these plays is just beginning to attract critical attention, and their obsession with the themes which I analyze has, I think, evaded most criticism. Even some of the metaphysical implications of the patterns Calderón develops with *engaño* and *desengaño, sueño* and *realidad,* in *La vida es sueño* have not as yet yielded their full richness to criticism.

The bulk of Calderón criticism has continued to develop the psychological insights which the plays invite, and in recent years it has grown considerably in depth and insight. In my notes I have occasion to refer to Gwynne Edwards' study of *The Prison and the Labyrinth: Studies in Calderonian Tragedy* (University of Wales, 1978). And it is a pleasure to see in recent work both Robert Ter Horst and Manuel Durán argue against the absurdity of earlier criticism in reading falangist ideology into Calderón. The most contemporary Calderón scholarship has benefitted immensely from the analytical and textual work of Charles V. Aubrun, Gwynne Edwards and Hans Flasche. The subject of Saint Augustine and Calderón has attracted various scholars—most recently Hans Flasche ("Ideas agustinianas en la obra de Calderón" in the *Bulletin of Hispanic Studies* [July, 1984]—but they have not addressed themselves to the problem of theodicy.

In my Prologue I mention the major ideological sources which have influenced me in writing about theodicy in baroque literature. But there are a few other writers whom I should perhaps mention here. In a brief but masterful and highly suggestive study, *Schein und Sein bei Shakespeare,* Wolfgang Clemen discusses the theme of illusion and reality in several of Shakespeare's plays—tragedies, comedies and romances (Munich, 1959). Illusion or appearance, as in the gold and silver caskets in the *Merchant of Venice* and Hamlet's hatred of "seeming," are associated with negative values, but it is precisely through illusion—Portia's later disguise and Hamlet's "antic-disposition"—that the positive goals of the heroes are achieved. This is true not only of the disguises which Kent and Edgar are forced to assume in *King Lear* but also of Viola's disguise in *Twelfth Night*:

> Aber so wie ein Schauspieler, der eine rolle spielt, in diese Rolle selber hineinwächst und sich eigener, ihm selbst bisher unbekannter Wesensmöglichkeiten bewusst wird, so ist auch in dem Spiel, das Viola bewusst gespielt hat, ein Stück ihres eigenen Wesens neuentdeckt und verwirklicht worden. Aus dem beabsichtigten Schein ist unbeabsichtigt Sein geworden, so wie bei anderen Personen neues Schisksal daraus entstanden ist. (p. 10)

Wolfgang Clemen's essay is brief and very comprehensive and, therefore, rather general in nature. He is not interested in some of the patterns, stylistic devices and imagery which I discuss and he does not mention theodicy, but one essential element—illusion and its beneficence—is similar to my interpretation.

A school of criticism which has obviously influenced me is archetypal criticism, as best represented by Northrop Frye's *Anatomy of Criticism* (Princeton, 1957), in both its mythological and formalistic aspects. On the one hand, my insistence on seeing the same archetypal myth of a fall into illusion and redemption from that fall through illusion itself in the use of disguises and dual identities in *Gerusalemme liberata,* in the Circe myth as well as the Narcissus myth in Tasso, Milton and Calderón, in Man's fall from Paradise, and in Calderón's elaborate patterns of *engaño-desengaño*—all of these readings are archetypal in Northrop Frye's sense of the world. On the other hand, my correlations between the tragic paradox in *Samson Agonistes* and *Gerusalemme liberata* with the *deus ex machina* and metamorphoses in Calderón's dramas and *autos* are obviously influenced, as my notes properly indicate, by some of Mr. Frye's formalistic principles. These formalistic principles are especially evident in my discussion of concentric and monadic symbols.

Well into the development of my ideas, I discovered Mircea Eliade's *Mephistopheles and the Androgyne* (New York, 1965). I had already noted the bisexuality involved in the disguises of Erminia and Clorinda in *Gerusalemme liberata* and Rosaura in *La vida as sueño* as well as the Narcissus imagery involving the heterosexual lovers in all the major works I discuss and Samson's concern with his femininity. I relate this imagery to the metaphysical resolution of the opposites of good and evil. Mircea Eliade's essay made me aware of all the anthropological and psychoanalytic literature which relates androgynous symbolism to the questions of *coindidentia oppositorum* and *mysterium coniunctionio:*

> All these examples are only particular and popular illustrations of the fundamental Indian doctrine, that good and evil have no meaning or function except in a world of appearances, in profane and unenlightened existence. From the transcendental viewpoint, good and evil are, on the contrary, as illusory and relative as all other pairs of opposites: hot-cold, agreeable-disagreeable, long-short, visible-invisible, etc. (p. 96)

> From a certain point of view one may say that many beliefs implying the *coincidentia oppositorum* reveal a nostalgia for a lost Paradise, a nostalgia for a paradoxical state in which the contraries exist side by side without conflict and the multiplications form aspects of a mysterious Unity. (p. 122)

This symbolism is not very far from the concerns of the renaissance Neoplatonists Ficino and Pico della Mirandola and the various renaissance mythographers, such as Conti and Giraldi. For example, in *Pagan Mysteries of the Renaissance,* Edgar Wind analyzes the iconography of renaissance painting according to these Neoplatonists and mythographers (New Haven, 1958). and his discussions of "Blind Love," "Virtue Reconciled with Pleasure" and "Amor as a God of Death" could easily be related to some of the themes which I analyze. But it seems to me that Tasso, Milton and Calderón create their own baroque myth which can be studied independently of possible analogies in Neoplatonism. In any case, the particular character of their myth must be fully understood before the analogies can be made.

PROLOGUE

1. The term "baroque" in reference to European literature between the Renaissance and neoclassicism has been increasingly accepted in the twentieth century by literary critics and scholars. It is not the purpose of this book to continue the debate as to its justification; something may be implied from my persistent use of the lower case. I merely suggest that theodicy in the thematic guise of illusion and beneficent evil in Tasso, Milton and Calderón may be considered a baroque theme since it is so predominantly present in authors who have been considered baroque by many critics and scholars. One of the most cogent and successful recent attempts to consider the use of the term is contained in the "Introduction" to *Baroque Lyric Poetry* by Lowry Nelson, Jr. (New Haven, 1961). The most important and complete discussion of the use of the word "baroque" in literary criticism is René Wellek's well-known essay, "The Concept of Baroque in Literary Scholarship," *JAAC*, V (1946), pp. 77–109, see note 5.

2. "In the former case [linear] the stress is laid on the limits of things; in the other [painterly] the work tends to look limitless. Seeing by volumes and outlines isolates; for the painterly eye, they merge." Heinrich Wölfflin, *Kunstgeschichtliche Grundbegriffe* (Munich, 1915); eng. trans. M. A. Hottinger, *Principles of Art History* (New York, 1932), p. 14.

3. New Haven, 1961, p. 23.

4. *La Littérature de l'âge baroque en France, Circé et le paon* (Paris, 1953).

5. This essay (op. cit., note [1], above) has been reprinted with a postscript in *Concepts of Criticism*, ed. Stephen G. Nichols, Jr. (New Haven, 1963), pp. 69–114. I use this latter edition: p. 108.

6. The most important of these is: F. Michael Krouse's *Milton's Samson and the Christian Tradition* (Princeton, 1949).

7. *El mayor encanto, Amor* (play) and *Los encantos de la culpa (auto)*.

8. I purposely shift the focus from the illusion and reality theme. The seminal essay on the latter is Helmut Hatzfeld's "El predominio del espíritu español en las literaturas del siglo XVII," *Revista de Filología Hispánica*, III (1914), pp. 9–23.

9. *Theodicy*, trans. E. M. Hubbard (London, 1951).

10. The best place to familiarize oneself with theodicy is the complete works of Saint Augustine (especially *The City of God* and *The Enchiridion*). But an

excellent introduction is to be found in John Hick's *Evil and the God of Love* (London, 1966). See also G. R. Evans, *Augustine on Evil* (London, 1982).

11. All my Saint Augustine quotations are from *The Enchiridion* in the following order: Chapters 23, 11, 14 and 18. I use *Basic Writings of Saint Augustine*, ed. W. J. Oates, trans. J. F. Shaw (New York, 1948) because of familiarity and convenience, with the exception of Chapter 23 where I have substituted a translation by A. C. Outler (Phil., 1954) because it is closer to the original, particularly in the use of the words "mutable" and "immutable," which are crucial to my discussion.

12. My two Irenaeas quotations are from *Against Heresies*: 4.39.2 and 5.29.1. I use *The Ante-Nicene Fathers*, eds. Robersts and Donaldson (Grand Rapids, 1975). This is an American reprint of the Edinburgh edition.

13. See Samuel E. Balentine, *The Hidden God: The Hiding of the Face of God in the Old Testament* (London, 1983).

14. See Wendy Doniger O'Flaherty, *The Origins of Evil in Hindu Mythology* (Los Angeles, 1979).

15. Trans. E. Buchanan (Boston, 1967).

16. London, 1955.

17. *Versions of Baroque: European Literature in the Seventeenth Century* (New Haven, 1972).

18. *Allegory: The Theory of a Symbolic Mode* (Ithaca, 1964).

19. Ibid., pp. 189-190.

20. "Horses of Wrath," *Hateful Contraries* (University of Kentucky Press, 1965), pp. 3-48.

21. Ibid., p. 21. See also Leo Spitzer, "Classical and Christian Ideas of World Harmony (Prolegomena to an Interpretation of the word *Stimmung*)," *Traditio*, II (1944), pp. 409-464 and III (1945), pp. 307-364; reprinted as a book (Baltimore, 1963).

22. Wimsatt, p. 47.

23. Princeton, 1966.

24. "Chiastic rhyme," the rhyming of words with antithetical meaning, is briefly discussed by W. K. Wimsatt, Jr., in "Rhyme and Reason," *The Verbal Icon* (New York, 1958) pp. 162-163. Its most sublime form as thesis, antithesis and synthesis in Dante's terza rima has not, to my knowledge, been adequately analyzed, and its relationship to the baroque prosody which I consider in this book is a problem which I hope to consider in the future.

25. See the entries in the *Oxford Companion to Spanish Literature* (New York, 1978).

26. Danielson (op. cit. in Headnote).

27. A good place to get a general idea of the renaissance mythographers—as well as an important source for Tasso which has still not been thoroughly studied—is those collected in Harrington's translation of Ariosto, ed. Robert McNulty (London, 1972).

28. For a brilliant discussion of the dual role of the baroque hero see the Introduction by H. Jenkins to the new Arden edition of *Hamlet* (London, 1982) pp. 143-147.

TASSO

1. In *Earthly Paradise and the Renaissance Epic* (Princeton, 1966), A. Bartlett Giamatti considers Armida's garden and its relation to illusion (pp. 184-210). But Mr. Giamatti's perspective on illusion in Tasso is different from my own; he does not consider its theodical aspects. My perspective allows me to see greater resolution of the poem's antitheses—whether they are seen as good and evil or Garden and City (the terms of Giamatti's analysis)—than he does. The degree to which Tasso uses illusion in a Christian context has also been studied recently by G. Baldassarri in *"Inferno" e "Cielo." Tipologia e funzione del "meraviglioso" nella "Liberta"* (Rome, 1977).

2. Most of my knowledge of the late sixteenth- and seventeenth-century debates concerning Tasso is secondhand: Bernard Weinberg's *A History of Literary Criticism in The Italian Renaissance,* 2 vols. (Chicago, 1962) and Claudio Varese's "Storia della critica tassesca" in *Pascoli politico, Tasso e altri saggi* (Milan, 1961), pp. 153-215.

3. See Marco Mincoff, "Baroque Literature in England," *Annuaire de L'Université de Sofia* (XLIII), 1946-1947, pp. 1 & ff. Mincoff's analysis of rigidly defined characters in renaissance literature as opposed to "the depiction of passions and ideas that lie outside the character" in baroque literature could be very easily compared to several literary qualities which I discuss in my three essays. The fact that I see a baroque myth behind so many episodes and characters is in itself related to Mincoff's thesis.

4. In *Torquato Tasso,* C. P. Brand (see Headnote) discusses briefly (pp. 87-89) Tasso's inventiveness with historical sources. Mr. Brand informs us that the Sofronia-Olindo episode "is invented on the basis of a report of the self-sacrifice of a Christian youth following the discovery of a dead dog in a Jerusalem mosque and threats of punishment of the Christians for profanation." It is clear from Tasso's re-creation of this episode—especially in the invention of two lovers—how specifically he intended to integrate it with the major themes of his epic. Also see the note for II, 5, in the Hoepli edition of *Gerusalemme liberata*—ed. Pio Spagnotti (Milan, 1898), p. 29.

5. I use emblematic in the simple sense of symbolic but also in the sense that Tasso's development of the Olindo-Sofronia episode almost seems to endow the final picture of the lovers bound at the stake with a motto which would be the theme of illusion and beneficent evil. I am also thinking of Fletcher's (op. cit., Prologue, note 18) definition of "the cosmic image" (Ch. 2, pp. 70-146). He speaks of its "part-whole relationship" (p. 84), its "visual aspect" (p. 97) and its "didactic function" (p. 120).

6. My Epilogue indicates the degree to which theodicy can be displaced in Shakespeare's comedies.

7. The prototype of this story is to be found in Heliodorus of Emesa *(Aethiopica)*. See the Hoepli edition (above, note 4) note for XII, 20 (p. 272). Again, as with the reinvention of the Olindo-Sofronia episode (above, note 4), Tasso's re-creation of the legend in terms of illusion, disguises and an ultimately beneficent purpose demonstrates his interest in the theme.

8. I am refering principally to Monteverdi's madrigal "Il combattimento di Tancredi e Clorinda" which has been a favorite score of choreographers since Monteverdi's time.

9. Unfortunately, the edition of *Gerusalemme liberata* which I used and to which I refer my readers does not include Tasso's *Allegoria*. Neither do many of the modern editions. It is, however, available in the critical edition by Angelo Solerti-Florence, 1895, Vol. II, pp. 22-23.

10. It is true that English and Italian in past times—and Italian still to some degree—were more permissive and casual in this regard. Still, the specific effect in Tasso is clear. I am reminded of Empson's discussion of the ambiguity of "logical or grammatical disorder" in *Seven Types of Ambiguity* (New York), p. 57.

11. See Dámaso Alonso, "La simetría bilateral," *Estudios y ensayos gongorinos* (Madrid, 1955), pp. 117-173.

12. See Mario Fubini (op. cit. in Headnote) "L'enjambement nella *Gerusalemme liberata*," pp. 256-270.

13. In his chapter on "Le Donne," Donadoni (op. cit. in Headnote) is very convincing in his analysis of the psychological import of the Armida-Rinaldo episode. He contrasts the uncomplicated epicurean pleasure of Ruggiero and Alcina in *Orlando Furioso* with the torment involved in the knowledge which Tasso's lovers possess of the transiency of their love. See also Getto (op. cit. in Headnote).

14. Paolo Braghieri, *Il testo come soluzione rituale* (Bologna, 1978).

15. See the passage from Fletcher which I quote at length in my Prologue. The passage is on pages 189-190 of Fletcher.

16. See Thomas M. Greene's eloquent discussion of this moment in *Gerusalemme liberata* in his *The Descent From Heaven* (New Haven, 1963), pp. 217-219.

17. I am here thinking of Frye's (op. cit. in Headnote) definition of a "monad" symbol: "A symbol in its aspect as a center of one's total literary experience; related to Hopkins' term 'inscape' and to Joyce's term 'epiphany'" (p. 366). Also see "Anagogic Phase: Symbol as Monad" (pp. 115-128) in Frye.

18. Op. cit. in Headnote, "'Ignoto,' 'Infinito,' 'Antico' ecc. nella poesia del Tasso," pp. 237-255.

MILTON

1. A. S. P. Woodhouse, "Tragic Effect in *Samson Agonistes*," *UTQ*, XXVIII (1958-1959), pp. 205-222; reprinted in *Milton: Modern Essays in Criticism*, ed. Arthur E. Barker (New York, 1965), pp. 447-466.

2. Una Ellis-Fermor, *The Frontiers of Drama* (New York, 1946), p. 17.

3. Radzinowicz, op. cit. in Headnote.

4. This is the perspective of not only Woodhouse, Ellis-Fermor and Radzinowicz but also William G. Madsen in *From Shadowy Types to Truth* (New Haven, 1968), Arnold Stein in *Heroic Knowledge* (Minneapolis, 1957) and Joseph H. Summers in "The Movements of the Drama," *The Lyric and Dramatic Milton* (New York, 1965).

5. Woodhouse uses this division (more or less) as does William Riley Parker in *Milton's Debt to Greek Tragedy in Samson Agonistes* (Baltimore, 1937).

6. B. K. Lewalski demonstrates Milton's use of this simile in "The Ship-Tempest Imagery in *Samson Agonistes*" (*N & Q*, VI, pp. 372–373). Lewalski also discusses possible sources for this simile, but she does not analyze the significance of its various appearances in the drama.

7. Parker discusses possible Greek models for this and other Choruses in *Samson Agonistes*. Like many other critics, I find Milton's tragedy more "positive" or religious than Parker's interpretation of the Choruses would allow.

8. Stein reads these lines as suggesting the internal drama to come, but he is not interested in the dichotomy they indicate ("choice of Sun or shade"). The lines are indeed a paradigm for the entire drama.

9. Stein sees the same prefiguration in the passage, although he reads it somewhat less ironically than I do.

10. Daniel C. Boughner, "Milton's Harapha and Renaissance Comedy," *ELH*, XI (1944), pp. 297–306.

11. Parker has a very good discussion of "tragic" or "Sophoclean" irony— "when the speaker, blind to a calamity which is about to fall upon himself, uses words which to the audience have an ominous suggestiveness"—in *Samson Agonistes*. I am more interested in a type of almost sarcastic irony which is related to the paradoxes of the drama.

12. "Putting the matter another way, for allegorical heroes life has a segmented character, and as each event occurs a new discrete characteristic of the hero is revealed, almost as if it had no connection with prior events or with other tied-in characteristics. The allegorical hero is not so much a real person as he is a generator of other secondary personalities, which are partial aspects of himself" (Fletcher, *Allegory*, op. cit., Prologue, note 18), p. 35.

13. Summers, p. 159.

14. Both Summers and Anthony Low (op. cit. in Headnote) discuss this "sort of doubleness" as Summers calls it (p. 157).

15. Krouse (op. cit., Prologue, note 6), pp. 124–132.

16. "Revolt in the Desert," *The Return of Eden: Five Essays on Milton's Epics* (Toronto, 1965), p. 142.

17. Madsen, op. cit.

18. Frye, "Revolt in the Desert," p. 134.

19. Danielson (op. cit. in Headnote) argues brilliantly that "the Fortunate Fall" was not a part of Milton's conception in *Christian Doctrine*; and he applies this reading to the epics. Nonetheless, it seems to me that a myth of beneficent evil is present in at least *Samson Agonistes*.

20. The note in the Hughes text (p. 428) acknowledges the ambiguity. Douglas Bush's (*The Complete Poetical Work of John Milton*, Cambridge, 1965) note (p. 420) reads: "unchangeable, referring to both Eve's being on her knees and her unhappiness." But this reading seems to diminish the passage.

21. Ralph Nash, "Chivalric Themes in *Samson Agonistes*," *Studies in Honor of John Wilcox*, eds. A. D. Wallace and W. D. Ross (Wayne State University Press, 1958), pp. 23–38; George R. Waggoner, "The Challenge to Single Combat in *Samson Agonistes*," *PQ*, XXXIX (1960), pp. 82–92. Nash, in fact, compares

Samson Agonistes and *Gerusalemme liberata*. His comparison is brief and rather vague in terms of chivalric heroism and what he calls being a prisoner of love.

22. Summers and Low analyze some of the double meaning of these lines very well.

23. My reference here is, of course, to Frye's (*Anatomy*) "symbol as monad," which I referred to more obliquely in my Tasso essay because Tasso's own development of *Un sol punto* is so clearly defined. The clearest definition of this type of symbol is to be found in neither Frye nor any other literary criticism but in Calderón's *autos*.

CALDERÓN

1. This is especially true of the *autos*. An important study of this aspect of Calderón is Eugenio Frutos' *La filosofía de Calderón en su Autos Sacramentales* (Zaragosa, 1952).

2. For the prevalence of similar "cave" images in Calderón see "Cavemen in Calderón" by J. E. Varey in *Approaches to the Theatre of Calderón*, ed. M. D. Mc Gaha (Washington, D.C., 1982) pp. 231-247, and Gwynne Edwards' *The Prison and the Labyrinth: Studies in Calderonian Tragedy* (See Headnote). Varey discusses the cave "discovery space" in terms of the limits of human knowledge, the enslavement of man's will, Plato's cave, the womb and the tomb.

3. This last line is italicized in the text. It is a part of a refrain which would read:

Solo el silencio testigo
ha de ser de mi tormento
Aun no cabe lo que siento
en todo lo que no digo.

4. Marcelino Menéndez y Pelayo, *Calderón y su teatro* (Madrid, 1910). Originally published in 1881.

5. E. M. Wilson, *"La vida es sueño,"* *Revista de la Universidad de Bueno Aires*, Tercera época, Año, IV, núms, 3 & 4 (1946), pp. 61-78; revised and reprinted as "On *La vida es sueño*" in *Critical Essays on the Theatre of Calderón*, ed. Bruce W. Wardropper (New York, 1965), pp. 63-89. I use this latter version and edition.

6. Wilson, pp. 70-71.

7. Wilson, p. 78.

8. Wilson, pp. 87-88.

9. A. E. Sloman, "The Structure of Calderón's *La vida es sueño*," *MLR*, XLVII (1953), pp. 293-300; reprinted in Wardropper (pp. 90-100). I use this latter edition.

10. Michele Federico Sciacca, "Verdad y sueño de *La vida es sueño*, de Calderón de la Barca," *Clavileño*, Año I, núm. 2 (marzo-abril, 1950), pp. 1-9.

11. "Rosaura's Role in the Structure of *La vida es sueño*," *HR*, XXVIII (1960); reprinted in Wardropper (pp. 101-113).

12. Calderón based his *autos* on mythology, history, his own plays, the Old Testament, etc. Angel Valbuena Prat studies these categories in his introductions

to the Aguilar and *Clásicos Castellanos*, 69 and 74 (Vol. I, Madrid, 1957 and Vol. II, Madrid, 1958) editions of the *Autos Sacramentales*. There are two *autos* based on *La vida es sueño*. My discussion refers to the more familiar second version, dated 1673.

13. Angel Valbuena Prat, "El orden barroco en *La vida es sueño*." *Escorial*, VI (1942), pp. 167-192.

14. Dámaso Alonso, *Versos plurimembres y poemas correlativos: capítulo para la estilística del Siglo de Oro* (Madrid, 1944).

15. It also has echoes in other seventeenth-century Spanish literature, cf. Góngora, *Polifemo*, "Pisando la dudosa luz del día." It is an image which can easily be associated with some of the particular obsessions of baroque literature.

16. "'Porque no sepas que sé,'" *Realidad y ensueño* (Madrid, 1963), pp. 20-41.

17. Sciacca, p. 4. Whitby is to some extent corrective of this view.

18. Augusto Cortina in the Prologue to his *Clásicos Castellanos* edition of the play—Madrid, 1955, p. xxx.

19. See Maynard Mack's eloquent discussion of this, as he calls it, "mirroring," in "The Jacobean Shakespeare"—*Jacobean Theatre*, Stratford-Upon-Avon Studies, 1 (New York, 1960). Several of my analyses of the allegorical projection of the central heroes on the world around them, such as the relationship between Solimano's death and Rinaldo's self-conquest and Samson's identification with the Philistines, are related to this concept of "mirroring."

20. Blanca de los Ríos Nostench de Lampérez, *La vida es sueño y los diez Segismundos de Calderón* (Madrid, 1926). Blanca de los Ríos mentions the heroes of the following plays: *El monstruo de los jardines, La hija del aire, Las cadenas del demonio, Apolo y Climene*, the two *autos* based on *La vida es sueño*, *Eco y Narciso, En esta vida todo es verdad y todo mentira* (Heraclis and Leónida), *Hado y divisa de Leónido y Marfisa*. To these we may add the analogous heroes mentioned by Arturo Farinelli (*La vita è un sogno*, Torino, 1916): Rosardo in *Los tres afectos de amor* and the heroes of *La estatua de Prometeo, La Fierra, el Rayo y la Piedra* and *La gran Cenobia*. In citing these sources, Valbuena Prat (op. cit., above, note 13) observes that almost all of the *autos* which represent man's predestined fall and redemption could be added.

21. In his introduction to the play in the *Dramas* volume of the *Obras Completas*, Angel Valbuena Briones quotes at length not only from the *Philosophia secreta* of Perez de Moya (one of the two most important Spanish renaissance mythographers—the other is Baltassar de Vitoria, who wrote *Teatro de los dioses de la gentilidad*) but also from Ovid's *Metamorphoses* and Boccaccio's *Genealogy*. Perez de Moya's *Philosophia* has been reprinted recently in *Los clásicos olvidados*, VI (Madrid, 1928). The best study of renaissance mythography is still Jean Seznec's *The Survival of the Pagan Gods*, trans. Barbara F. Sessions (New York, 1953). His study contains a very complete bibliography. For Calderón's particular use of the mythographers also see: Rudolph Schevill, *Ovid and the Renaissance in Spain* (Berkeley, 1913) and Pierre Paris, "La Mythologie De Calderón," *Homenaje a Menéndez Pidal*, I (Madrid, 1925), 557-570.

22. Robert Graves, *The Greek Myths*, Vol. I (Baltimore, 1957), 286; *The Greek Myths* was first published in 1955.

23. In two essays by Everett Hesse—"Estructura e interpretación de una comedia de Calderón: *Eco y Narciso*," *BBMP*, XXXIX (1963), pp. 57-72, "The Terri-

ble Mother' Image in Calderón's *Eco y Narciso*," *RomN*, I (1960), pp. 133–136—the cave is given a Jungian interpretation as the womb of a dominant mother who violates the laws of nature in thwarting her son's natural development. Although in "Estructura e interpretación" Mr. Hesse does discuss the "doble enfoque" involved in the debate between Silvius and Phebus on the nature of love (p. 67), he does not discuss the ambiguity and paradox involved in Narcissus' need (and failure) to embrace a malefic fate. Nor does he extend his discussion of the Silvius and Phebus debate on love to the central question of *engaño-desengaño*.

24. One of the most elaborate developments of the theme is to be found in *El mágico prodigioso* in which Lisandro conceals but then reveals Justina's origin and she fully embraces the revelation that she is Christian despite the danger it places her in.

25. *A Natural Perspective* (New York, 1965), p. 25.

26. "La correlación en la estructura del teatro Calderoniano," *Seis calas en la expresión literaria española*, Dámaso Alonso and Carlos Bousoño (Madrid, 1951), pp. 115–186.

27. Both Angel Valbuena Prat, in his book on Calderón (Barcelona, 1941) and Angel Valbuena Briones in his individual introductions to the plays in the Aguilar edition of the *Dramas*, make this claim several times. Also see Hesse (above, note 23).

28. Erich Neumann, *Amor and Psyche*, trans. Ralph Manheim (New York, 1965).

29. See passage from Fletcher (op. cit., Prologue, note 18) quoted in my Prologue.

30. Alexander Augustine Parker, *The Allegorical Drama of Calderón* (London, 1943), pp. 72–94.

31. Op. cit. (Prologue, note 20), p. 47.

32. Ibid., p. 32.

33. "La correlación," op. cit. (above, note 26), p. 116.

34. Ibid., p. 151.